THE COMPLETE

DOG BOOK

THE COMPLETE
DOG
BOOK

*A comprehensive, practical
care and training manual,
and a definitive encyclopedia
of world breeds*

DR PETER LARKIN
MIKE STOCKMAN
PHOTOGRAPHY BY JOHN DANIELS

southwater

This edition is published by Southwater, an imprint of Anness Publishing Ltd,
108 Great Russell Street, London WC1B 3NA; info@anness.com

www.southwaterbooks.com; www.annesspublishing.com

If you like the images in this book and would like to investigate using them for publishing,
promotions or advertising, please visit our website www.practicalpictures.com for more information.

A CIP catalogue record for this book is available from the British Library.

Publisher: Joanna Lorenz
Project editor: Fiona Eaton
Designer: Michael Morey
Photographer: John Daniels
Additional photography: Jane Burton p7 BL, BR; p11 TL; p20 T, B; p21 T, M; p22 T, M; p23 T; p32 B;
p40 B; p41; p55; p65 R; p95 B; p252; p253; p256.

PUBLISHER'S NOTE

Although the advice and information in this book are believed to be accurate and true at the time
of going to press, neither the authors nor the publisher can accept any legal responsibility or liability
for any errors or omissions that may have been made nor for any inaccuracies nor for any loss,
harm or injury that comes about from following instructions or advice in this book.

Contents

INTRODUCTION

The dog is humanity's oldest companion. Human and dog came together thousands of years ago for mutual comfort and slowly developed the interdependence seen today – human's caring for the dog in return for continuing companionship and a great variety of working functions.

The gradual recognition of the many different ways in which the dog could contribute to the association has led to the development of an enormous variety of dog types. All varieties of dog are members of a single species; it is the most varied of any species known, ranging from the tiny Chihuahua to the massive Irish Wolfhound.

So close has the association of dog and human become that there are now probably only two breeds of truly wild dogs left, the Cape Hunting Dog and the Australian Dingo. Many countries,

✦ RIGHT
The Golden Retriever is one of the most popular companion breeds and has an impeccable working background as a gundog.

of course, have roaming packs of wild dogs that lead an independent existence, but these are invariably domestic dogs that have "gone wild" for one of any number of reasons.

To a remarkable extent, a dog of any breed can mate with another of any other breed and produce fertile offspring. This fact in itself has led to even more varieties developing over the centuries, as new functions and

fashions were thought up. There are something like four hundred known breeds in existence today. The precise figure is impossible to determine as previously unrecognized breeds continue to emerge, and types of the same breed are recognized as distinct; or conversely, varieties previously

✦ BELOW
This German Shepherd is a true companion and guard, always keen to please his owner.

✦ ABOVE
Dogs are inveterate game-players, always learning from their play.

✦ RIGHT
Dogs may learn to carry out all kinds of helpful tasks, including collecting and delivering items around the house.

+ LEFT
The Great Dane is likely to weigh more than 54 kg (119 lb) when mature.

+ LEFT
A dog will roll on to its back as a sign of submission to its owner or to another dog.

considered as separate are combined as one breed.

As part of this continuing evolutionary process, breeds have also died out; several have disappeared even in the last one hundred years, possibly due to reduced fertility or the particular type ceasing to be fashionable. Loss of the traditional function of a breed may be another reason, but more often the breed has changed in conformation to such an extent as to be almost unrecognizable as the original breed. The war dogs of old, for instance, have developed into the civilized mastiff types.

Although every breed of dog, in the western world at least, is expected to be domesticated, certain type characteristics tend to persist through many generations, and these are not just characteristics of conformation. Everyone realizes that if you buy a Great Dane puppy, for instance, small though it may be at eight weeks old, it will grow into a very large dog. If you buy a terrier of whatever breed,

it will have terrier behaviour characteristics, inherited from its working ancestors.

If you have decided to buy a dog, look into all the breed characteristics, and consider them carefully before you decide which type of dog you want to live with. A dog may live for between ten and twenty years – it is yours to care for over a good part of your life.

+ LEFT
The young of every breed are appealing, but an owner's responsibility may last for over fifteen years.

+ RIGHT
Children and dogs are good for each other. Both have much to learn from their mutual love.

Choosing a
Suitable Dog

Many households are just not suitable for a dog. If you work long periods away from home, or even just very long hours, and if there is no-one else at home while you are away, you need to consider very carefully whether the comforts of coming home to a dog are not outweighed by the lack of company that the dog will have to endure, with all the potential behaviour problems that this may cause. Consider not just how the dog would fit into your own way of life, but how your lifestyle would affect the dog.

◆ FACING PAGE
Before getting a dog,
it is important to
ensure that you can
provide it with the
environment it needs.

WHAT TYPE OF DOG?

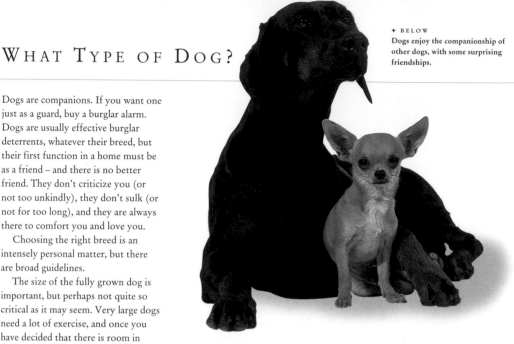

✦ BELOW
Dogs enjoy the companionship of other dogs, with some surprising friendships.

Dogs are companions. If you want one just as a guard, buy a burglar alarm. Dogs are usually effective burglar deterrents, whatever their breed, but their first function in a home must be as a friend – and there is no better friend. They don't criticize you (or not too unkindly), they don't sulk (or not for too long), and they are always there to comfort you and love you.

Choosing the right breed is an intensely personal matter, but there are broad guidelines.

The size of the fully grown dog is important, but perhaps not quite so critical as it may seem. Very large dogs need a lot of exercise, and once you have decided that there is room in your house for a large dog, exercise is the most important consideration. Most people, however, want a dog that fits reasonably into the home environment. A couple of Wolfhounds may be your ideal, but their bulk may make a small flat uninhabitable.

The Labrador Retriever, a dog which, if not overweight, will weigh when mature about 30 kg (66 lb), is the most popular dog in the United States and the United Kingdom, with 132,000 in the US and 32,000 in the UK. Second in the US is the Rottweiler, with almost 94,000 registered, and

✦ FACING
A common problem with insecure dogs is barking when they are left alone. Once established it may be very difficult to overcome.

✦ LEFT
Complete family integration with people and dogs all joining in as many activities as possible will usually prevent behaviour problems.

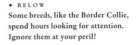

+ LEFT
Most dogs love
jumping for toys. It
can be a helpful
supplement to their
exercise when walks
are restricted.

+ BELOW
Some breeds, like the Border Collie,
spend hours looking for attention.
Ignore them at your peril!

third the German Shepherd with 79,000 registered. In Britain the German Shepherd is second (24,000) and the Golden Retriever third (16,000). These are all large dogs. By no means do all of them live in large houses.

Breed or type behaviour is probably more important in choosing a dog than any other characteristic. It pays to ask not just dedicated owners but knowledgeable people outside the breed – your veterinary surgeon sees a wide variety of dogs every day.

Typically, the terrier types are lively, not easy to train, but very responsive dogs. They are good with children if properly trained.

Toy dogs are usually better companions for owners who do not have young children. The dogs may be upset by what they perceive as large noisy humans rushing around. Their fear may make them snappy, with unhappy results. All toy dogs will be happy with as much exercise as you can give them, but they may be equally happy with only a moderate amount.

Hounds need as much exercise as possible. With this condition they make very good house dogs who love their comfort. Breeds in the other groups vary, but, in general, the working breeds are all better with an occupation that keeps them out of mischief.

The gundog (sporting) breeds are generally easy to train, and settle into the human environment without difficulty. They need exercise, and lack of exercise shows!

Certain of the herding breeds, typified by the Border Collie, are, or should be regarded as, specialist working dogs. They demand more attention than other breeds if they are not to become neurotic pets. Outside their traditional working function they have become the outstanding type in obedience work of all sorts. Provided you are able to give sufficient attention to them to keep their very active minds occupied, they are among the most rewarding of pets. But if you don't, they will find something to occupy themselves, and it will be trouble.

With so many breeds to choose from, as well as crossbreds and mongrels, there really isn't a typical household pet these days.

+ RIGHT
This charming
Bernese puppy will
make a beautiful
house pet, but he
will grow to 70 cm
(27½ in) at the
shoulder when
mature.

THE COST OF KEEPING A DOG

Can you afford it? Buying a dog is the start. Very few puppies can be acquired for nothing. Almost everyone will want to sell the litter they have reared, even if only to try to recoup the cost of feeding the puppies to weaning.

The cost of good pedigree puppies varies from country to country. In the United Kingdom, depending on breed, a puppy may cost from around £300, although probably the average price asked for a well-bred puppy of most breeds is between £400 and £600. In the United States asking prices are usually somewhat higher, from about $1,000 upwards. Australian prices are similar to those in the United Kingdom. Imported puppies in any country may cost a great deal more.

The initial examination by the veterinary surgeon, and the puppy's primary inoculations will be around another £30, perhaps $60 in the United States, and you can spend as much as you wish on toys and other equipment.

A substantial part of the cost of keeping a dog may be the cost of veterinary treatment. Veterinary surgeons are these days capable of sophisticated treatments of illness or injury, but they have no subsidy for the costs. If your dog ever needs complicated or prolonged veterinary treatment the cost may be high.

There are several pet insurance companies catering for veterinary treatments; each has its own approach, and dog owners would be well advised to study what each company offers before deciding which policy to buy.

◆ LEFT
A fair return for the cost of keeping a dog may be the exercise it encourages its owner to take.

◆ BELOW LEFT
The superb grooming of this dog may be achieved either by a professional at considerable cost or through hours of work by its owner.

◆ BELOW RIGHT
The cost of keeping a toy dog is probably very little less than for a larger animal. Veterinary attention is much the same and fussy eaters need special food.

✦ BELOW
Diet and exercise may both be critical to the
well-being of the older dog. Overweight dogs
are often reluctant to walk far; a few pounds off
works wonders.

The premium grade policies offer
sums for the death of your dog, and
for rewards to be offered if the dog is
lost. They may include kennelling fees
in case of your own illness, even
holiday cancellation costs. The level
of veterinary fees covered is variable
on most schemes, and it may be
worth discussing this with your
veterinary surgeon. All additions
cost money.

Some companies will offer a basic
veterinary fee insurance as an
alternative to the premium schemes.
It will be up to you to decide which
of the various forms of insurance best
fits your own needs.

Most insurers offer a puppy
scheme, sometimes with an incentive
to transfer to the adult scheme when it
expires. Many breeders will offer
puppy insurance to buyers, either as
part of or as an extra cost to the
purchase price of the puppy.

Feeding costs vary greatly. In
theory, the smaller the dog, the
less expensive to feed, but this is
frequently offset by choosing more
specialized, and therefore expensive,
foods for the very small pet. It is
possible to feed a 14 kg (31 lb)
dog very adequately for about
£3.50 ($6.00) a week.

✦ ABOVE
Running with a
companion dog is
terrific exercise, but
be sure you are in
control

✦ LEFT
Diets to rear healthy
puppies need careful
consideration. The
breeder will usually
offer sound advice,
but be wary of
bizarre feeding
regimes.

13

PEDIGREE OR NON-PEDIGREE

✦ LEFT
If you choose a pedigree dog, you must still look for a strain in that breed that fits your lifestyle. Gundogs (sporting) can come from a "working" or a "show" strain.

Crossbred dogs, the most identifiable of which is the Lurcher, are usually not expensive to buy, which is an obvious advantage. They have their own "mutt" charm, and their apparent type may be just what you are looking for. But remember the tiny puppy may become an enormous adult. The best way to judge is to see both parents, but in the nature of things the father is likely to be "away on business" when the puppies are ready to leave.

It is not necessarily true that crossbred dogs are healthier than purebreds, as many people believe. Every veterinary surgeon can tell you of crossbreds or mongrels suffering from recognizable, inherited diseases.

The advantage of picking a purebred dog is that you know what you are getting. From a reputable

breeder a Cocker Spaniel puppy will grow up into a Cocker Spaniel dog, of a size and weight that is within the breed norm, and with potential behaviour characteristics typical of the breed. There is, or should be, advice

available to deal with whatever problems may arise as a particular feature of the breed.

There is no doubt that many breeds have inherited problems associated with that breed, although these have often been exaggerated in the press. It is up to the potential owner to enquire about these problems, and to take independent advice on their significance. It is worth bearing in mind that no species of animal, including human beings, is free from inheritable disease. Dogs may be less afflicted than most.

✦ LEFT
A lovable mongrel. Did his owners know how he was going to turn out? And have they the time and inclination to give that coat the attention it demands?

✦ RIGHT
Crossbred dogs are often the basis for new working types. A cross between two recognized breeds is likely to have characteristics somewhere between the two.

DOG OR BITCH

Choosing whether to have a male or female – a dog or a bitch – is one of the early decisions.

Dogs tend to have a more "macho" outlook on life than bitches, and if that attracts you, the male of the species will be your choice. Dogs are

✦ LEFT
Labradors, dogs and bitches, are notorious for the ease with which they put on weight.

✦ RIGHT
The King Charles Spaniel is regarded by many as the ideal family pet.

possibly more outgoing, certainly on average a little harder to train, but often more responsive once trained.

They do not, of course, come into season twice a year, with the attendant bother of oestrous discharges, and the attraction of all the dogs in the neighbourhood. But don't forget that

it is the male dogs that are attracted, and if you have a male it could be yours that has to be dragged home each night from his wanderings.

On balance, if there is such a thing in this particular choice, the female is likely to make a better family pet. She is less likely to be aggressive, although dominance is as much a breed characteristic as it is related to the sex of the dog. Bitches are much less likely to try to wander for most of the year, and they are inclined to be more loving to their human family.

✦ BELOW
The Boston Terrier needs the minimum of grooming but likes its exercise.

✦ LEFT
The Rough Collie is a working dog; not for the lazy owner.

✦ FAR LEFT
The Airedale is a real terrier in every respect.

✦ BELOW
The Dachshund is a well-loved breed.

Buying a Puppy

◆ BELOW
The breeder may be unhappy to let you handle
very young pups for health reasons – she
doesn't know where you've been!

Let us assume that you know more or less the type of dog you feel you can best live with. Even though you may have no intention of ever showing your dog, dog shows are good places to visit while you are finally making up your mind. Talk to the people showing, find out what their views are about their breed – you may find that many of the exhibitors are remarkably frank about the drawbacks as well as the virtues of their breed. In the long run it pays them to be so.

The next step is to look for the right breeder, not necessarily the top one in the breed, who would, quite fairly, expect a premium price for puppies of show standard. Top breeders, however, will often be the most genuinely encouraging to the potential new owner.

Many dogs are still sold through so-called "puppy farms" and pet shops. Neither is a suitable place to find a puppy. Young dogs cannot be treated as commodities to be traded at the convenience of their breeder, and serious health problems regularly arise from this form of mistreatment of young animals.

Take your time, and be prepared to wait to get the dog you really want. Above all, visit the kennels and make sure you see the dam with the puppies in the litter (and other litters), and, if possible, the sire. Make your own mind up about the conditions in which the puppies have been reared.

There is some argument about the right age to buy a puppy, although the general consensus seems to be that about eight weeks is right. Much before that may be too early to remove the puppy from the nest; leaving it later can give rise to socialization problems, with the time between six and eight weeks regarded by behaviourists as a critical period in the puppy's development. Certainly, if the puppy is much older than eight weeks, you need to be satisfied that it

+ RIGHT
It is safe to let
prospective owners
handle the puppies if
they haven't been
handling other dogs.

+ BELOW RIGHT
Retrievers tend to
have very large
litters, often ten or
more. Weaning can
start as early as three
weeks with suitable
supplements.

You may be expected to sign a
contract setting out the limitations of
the breeder's liability in the event of
the puppy later developing an
inheritable condition. We live in a
litigious society. Recent court cases
have made it plain that if a breeder fails
to warn a purchaser of conditions that
are recognized in the breed, and the
puppy later develops such a condition,
the breeder may be held liable, even
though he or she is unaware of the
existence of the problem in that puppy,
and has taken reasonable precautions
to avoid the condition.

The contract you may be asked to
sign must be reasonable, and it is likely
to consist of a statement drawing your
attention to the known inheritable
diseases of the breed and an
expectation that you will have
discussed the significance of the
condition with your veterinary
surgeon. Your veterinary surgeon may
be advised to make his comments in a
written statement.

has been exposed to a sensible social
environment and not simply left in its
rearing kennel to make its own way.

Be honest with the breeder. If you
are looking for a dog that you may
later want to show, don't pretend that
you are only looking for a pet puppy,
in the hope that the price might be
lower. Explain truthfully and carefully
the life that the puppy will lead,
especially its home environment. At
worst, the breeder will explain why
that may not be suitable for rearing a
puppy; at best, you may get much
good advice.

Never expect a guarantee that your
puppy will be a show winner. Even
though it comes from the very best
show stock, with a pedigree as long as
your arm, no-one, including the most
experienced breeders, can pick a "cert"
at eight weeks.

The breeder should provide you
with the puppy's pedigree, and a

receipt for its purchase. If the breeder
has already taken the puppies for their
first inoculation, this may be included
in the quoted price or regarded as an
extra. You should ask.

✦ BELOW LEFT
The best way to decide on the suitability of
a particular kennel is to see as many of their
dogs as possible, both at home and at work
or in the show-ring.

✦ BELOW RIGHT
Ex-racing greyhounds make wonderful pets, but
occasionally have problems socializing after
years in a racing kennel.

The breeder should always provide you with a feeding chart for the next stage of rearing your puppy. It is worthwhile taking this to discuss with the veterinary surgeon when you take the puppy for its first visit. Many breeders give the new owner some sample feed to start the puppy off in its new home.

You should expect a healthy puppy, which has been wormed adequately, probably twice, and is free from skin parasites such as fleas or lice.

Pet insurance companies have short-term cover schemes, available to breeders for issue to new owners. Ask the breeder if he or she has such cover. If not, arrange your own as soon as you have bought the puppy. Puppies are at their most vulnerable during the first few weeks in their new homes.

✦ LEFT
The age to leave
home is a
compromise.
A critical
socializing time
is about six
weeks, when
ideally the puppy
should meet its
new family, but
other factors
usually dictate
that eight weeks
is probably the
best practical age
at which to buy
your puppy.

CHOOSING A PUPPY

Never be fobbed off with excuses about the condition a puppy is in or its behaviour; and never buy a puppy because it's the last one left and you feel sorry for it.

It is often said that puppies choose their new owners, rather than the other way around, and there is much truth to this claim. An overly shy puppy may have socialization problems later, and the puppy that comes forward from the nest, asking to be chosen, is probably the right one.

The puppy must be alert and have bright, clean eyes. Its nose must be clean (but forgive a little crust of food), its ears must be free of wax, and its coat must be clean and pleasant to handle and smell. There must be no sign of sores or grittiness on the skin and coat. Black "coal dust" is usually flea dirt – fleas themselves are more difficult to spot. Examine all the puppies briefly to ensure that they have been well cared for.

Make sure there is no discharge from the eyes. Forgive a scratch or two on the face – puppies in the nest don't always agree.

The membranes of the nose must be clear and free of discharge. There must be no sign of a runny nose.

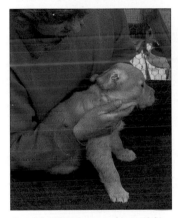

The inside of the ears must look pink and shiny, without inflammation or dark-coloured wax. It should not look sore.

Soreness or inflammation of the rims of the eyes, or eyes that are not completely clear, may be serious signs of present or potential disease.

The puppy's coat and skin should feel loose and soft. The skin should be free of sores.

Sturdy, strong limbs are a must for any breed, although if you fancy an Italian Greyhound don't expect him to be this sturdy.

Puppies should have a clean bottom. Signs of diarrhoea are obvious from a quick examination behind. The whole litter should be examined.

SETTLING IN

Bringing home a new puppy or even an older dog is an important family occasion. Everyone wants to touch, hold and stroke the new member of the family, especially the children. But do take things slowly.

In the case of a puppy, this will be the first time away from the only environment the puppy has known, and away from his mother and litter mates. The world is huge and frightening. For an older dog, there is still a lot of adjusting for him to do.

Bring him home when there are not too many people around, and introduce him to his new environment in as relaxed a manner as possible. Let him look and sniff around, offer him a little something to eat, which he probably won't accept, and allow him to have a run around the garden. Bring your family and friends to meet the dog one or two at a time, and give him time to make friends before introducing anyone else.

◆ **LEFT**
Puppies' curiosity about new toys helps to overcome their awe of strange surroundings.

At some stage you have to cause a little more trauma by taking the dog to the veterinary surgeon for a health check. If at all possible, take him to the vet on the way home from the breeder or kennels. If there should be a problem that necessitates returning the dog to the seller (fortunately, a very rare occurrence), it is going to be much easier if the family haven't met and already fallen in love with him.

Once the settling in process has begun, interrupt the dog's established routine as little as possible. For a puppy, follow the breeder's feeding regime, giving the same number of feeds at the same time each day. To start with, give the food the dog is used to – the seller might have provided a "starter pack" – even if you have decided eventually to use a different type of food. Make any dietary changes gradually.

Clean water should always be available; show the dog where it is. Make sure that not only is the water bowl always full, but that it is washed regularly – dogs are messy drinkers, and the bowl soon gets dirty. Most dogs, some breeds more than others,

◆ **RIGHT**
Puppies hate to be left alone until they are confident that you will quickly return.

SAFETY GUIDELINES ON TOYS FOR DOGS

The jaws and teeth of nearly all dogs are much stronger than you think, so toys should be very tough.

Fluffy dolls will be torn to pieces without fail, so if you must provide them, make sure that they do not have parts that can be detached and swallowed.

Balls are popular toys for dogs because the owners can throw them and join in the game. Fine, but make sure the ball is large enough not even to be half-swallowed by the dog. A dog being rushed to the veterinary surgeon choking on a tennis ball that is stuck in its throat is a common emergency.

The use of a bone as a toy is controversial. Most veterinary surgeons advise against it, unless the bone is so big that the dog cannot break pieces off and swallow them. There is no doubt that a good chew at a bone is a dog's delight.

◆ **ABOVE**
Toys should be solid enough not to risk pieces being chewed off and swallowed.

are also very splashy drinkers, spilling more water around the bowl than they swallow. So choose your water-bowl site carefully.

The ideal water bowl may be made of ceramic or non-rust metal, but it must be non-spill, and preferably too heavy for the dog to pick up and carry around. If you start with a heavy bowl, the puppy will soon get the idea that this is not a toy to be picked up and carted around, and he will look for something else to play with.

Feed bowls may be much the same as water bowls, with the same idea: the dog should not regard the bowl as a toy. Apart from anything else, if the bowl gets carried around, you can never find it when you want to feed the dog!

The new dog's bed is very important – the bed is the dog's own special place. It is important to introduce the dog to his bed as soon as he arrives, and to insist that the bed is where he sleeps. This may be difficult, but if you give in and let him sleep on your

+ LEFT
Hygiene is important for feed bowls. Never add another meal without first thoroughly cleaning the bowl.

+ BELOW
Rawhide chews are usually an excellent substitute for bones.

+ BELOW
Puppies take great comfort from a hot-water bottle, but beware leaks from chewing. An alarm clock seems to soothe them at night.

bed "just until he settles in", you have lost the battle – and probably the war!

To make sure the dog uses his bed, the best way is to shut him into a "bedroom" on the first night with nothing else to choose for a comfortable sleep but the bed. Make sure it is sited away from any draughts. Young puppies will miss their litter mates and perhaps their dam. A useful tip, if the puppy doesn't settle – that's if he is crying pitifully just as you are getting to sleep – is to provide him with

comforters. Traditionally, these are a hot-water bottle and a ticking alarm clock; and like many traditions, they often work well.

Toys are important, whatever the age of the dog, but particularly for a young puppy. There is an enormous range on sale, from fluffy dolls that amuse the owner but soon become unrecognizable once the puppy has had a chance to tear them apart, to specifically designed training aids.

Some dogs are obsessive about a particular toy – this occurs more in the terrier breeds than in other types – but mostly dogs have a rather short attention span, dropping one object for another after a short spell of play. There is no certain winner. Each dog has a different fancy, but do provide choice for a puppy, bearing in mind safety guidelines.

BEDS AND BEDDING

The dog must have a bed of his own. From the owner's point of view, washability is the priority. Plastic beds made for this purpose are not expensive and easily cleaned, but they must have soft bedding for comfort.

Providing a mobile cage as a bed and a private place for your puppy has several advantages, not least of which is that there is somewhere to put the puppy when non-doggy friends, who may not appreciate dog hairs all over their clothes, arrive.

Cages may be the completely collapsible type, useful for folding and taking with you when you are travelling with the dog, or, probably better in the long run, the "sky kennel" type which is fastened by nuts and bolts around the middle. This enables the cage to be divided in half for travelling but provides a more permanent kennel for the dog to use at home.

There are plenty of choices of bedding. The most satisfactory from the hygiene point of view, as well as for comfort and warmth, is veterinary bedding, sold under a number of brand names, made of synthetic fur backed by a strong woven base. These veterinary beds may be machine washed, they stay dry as moisture goes straight through them, they are long-lasting, and they are resistant (but not if the dog is really determined!) to being chewed up. They can be bought or cut to any size, and using the principle of "one on, one in the wash", you can easily keep the bed clean and free from doggy odours.

♦ LEFT
Flexible dog beds seem to pass the comfort test. They are usually insulated against cold floors and are easily cleaned. They may be expensive and destructible by determined dogs.

♦ ABOVE, LEFT TO RIGHT
An old blanket is best in a bed rather than just on the floor; synthetic veterinary bedding is probably more hygienic than any other soft bedding; the bean bag is supremely comfortable and warmly insulating; a plastic basket is easily cleaned, but it does need a comfortable lining to be given the dog's personal accolade.

♦ LEFT
Dogs all appreciate a warm covering to lie on, wherever they choose to sleep.

✦ TOP
The collapsible travelling cage has many uses at
home as well as away.

✦ ABOVE
An outside kennel must be dry, warm and of an
adequate size for the dog's comfort.

✦ RIGHT
An outside kennel and run must always be kept
clean (with wood this may not be easy). The run
is no substitute for proper exercise.

Cushions filled with polystyrene
granules are possibly the most
comfortable of all for the dog, but
they are less easy to wash than
veterinary bedding. Some dogs enjoy
chewing their bed and this results in a
myriad little polystyrene balls rolling
around the floor, which are almost
impossible to sweep up.

Still probably more used than
anything else is a square of old
blanket or a blanket off-cut. Nothing
wrong with them, provided you have
enough so that you can wash them
regularly, bearing in mind that they
leave a fluffy deposit which needs to
be removed from the washing machine
and they take forever to dry.

WHERE TO SLEEP?
The kitchen or a warm utility room are
the best places for the dog to sleep.
The kitchen floor often has non-
absorbent flooring, useful for a puppy

before he's able to avoid accidents.
Once he has become accustomed to
the kitchen, if it remains convenient to
you, it is possibly the best place for
him to stay. The kitchen tends to be
one of the warm places in the house,
and dogs like warmth.

Most dogs are not kennelled out of
doors. There is no particular reason
why they should not be, and if that is
your intention it must be instituted
from the start. Use plenty of warm
bedding and pay attention to draughts
and waterproofing. One problem with
outside kennels is that it becomes too
easy to ignore the dog. Few owners
would indulge in the outright cruelty
of neglecting to feed their dog, but if
the weather doesn't look too good,
plenty would put the walk off to
another day.

If a dog is to be confined in a
kennel, you must ask yourself if you
really want a dog. At worst, the kennel
must provide an adequate exercise
area, as well as the essentials
mentioned above.

HOME, GARDEN AND CAR SAFETY

◆ BELOW
The easiest way for a dog to get out of the garden is via the gate. The gate must be rigid and placed over a hard standing.

Of immediate interest to most new dog owners is the need to make the home and garden dog-proof. This may prove to be a difficult and very expensive undertaking.

You have a responsibility in law to keep your dog under control. This means that your garden must be fenced in such a way as to prevent the dog escaping. As the puppies of almost any breed other than the very smallest grow, so does their ability to jump over fences. There can be no hard and fast rule for the height needed to prevent this; even within the same breed, one will be a jumper and another never learn the skill. However, the minimum height for any dog-proof

fence for anything but toy breeds will be one metre (3 ft). Often, for dogs from the smaller terrier breeds, like Jack Russells, and the more agile larger breeds, this will not be sufficient. Plenty of dogs can scale a two-metre (6 ft 6 in) fence. A fence this high starts to make the garden look like Fort Knox, and the usual compromise is a fence of about 1.5 metres (5 ft). If it is a wire fence, it must be tightly strung. Many gardens are close fenced to this height, and close fencing has advantages as a dog fence. Being unable to see the world outside often removes the temptation to investigate it.

There are two ways through a fence, even if it is in good repair. One

way is over the top, and the other is underneath. Dogs enjoy digging. You need to be sure that there is no way under. Wire fencing is particularly vulnerable to the tunnelling dog, unless it is firmly attached to some sort of hard, impenetrable base.

Preventing the dog from escaping from the house is usually a matter of care rather than built-in precautions. The perfectly trained dog will not push past his owner when the front door is opened unless required to do so; plenty of others in real life try to. The family has to learn to keep the dog shut in the kitchen when they answer the door – one reason for not restraining the dog's barking when

+ LEFT
The same device can often be used for children and puppies.

+ RIGHT
The interior of a car with closed windows may easily reach 130°F (55°C) on a hot day. Install window grills.

+ BELOW
Electric flexes are dangerous if they are chewed.

someone knocks at the front door; at least the dog is reminding you to shut him away. Downstairs windows, and occasionally upstairs windows, may attract the dog. It is a matter of vigilance unless you are prepared to barricade yourself in.

DOGS IN CARS

The idea of travelling with a dog in the car is very appealing. In the event, it sometimes becomes a nightmare. Part of the very earliest training for the puppy must be to learn to travel in a safe and socially acceptable way in the car. For the smaller breeds, a collapsible cage is ideal.

If your car is a hatchback, a dog guard is an obvious and sensible investment. It needs to be well fitting and strong enough to prevent a determined dog from climbing through it into the front of the car. There are dozens of dog guards

+ ABOVE AND RIGHT
Dogs may escape despite precautions. Identity discs for collars should have a contact telephone number rather than names and addresses.

designed specifically for each make and model of car. They are advertised in the dog magazines or available from most of the larger dog shows.

Unrestrained dogs in cars cause accidents. If you are not able to use a dog guard or cage, the puppy must be taught to sit on the back seat and never to climb into the front. He will soon learn if you gently and patiently restrain him, and scold him firmly if he comes forward. It is one piece of training where the immediate "no" can work, but not if you sometimes relent and let him sit on the front seat. Harnesses, designed to clip to the rear seat belt fastening, are another way to keep the dog on the back seat.

Some dogs become "barkers" when in the car. This is dangerous and distracting, and steps to remedy it must be taken before the behaviour becomes totally engrained. Specialist advice may be necessary, but the first step is to restrain the dog, with a short lead, below the window level of the car. It's no good shouting at him to shut him up – the dog's response will be to redouble his efforts to be heard above his owner's voice.

BEHAVIOUR TIP

Any response to unacceptable behaviour may be taken by the dog as encouragement. The only sensible response is not to take any obvious notice.

Nutrition and Feeding

The diets of yesteryear, of home-mixed meat and biscuits, have long gone.
Nowadays, professional nutritionists produce feeds of a variety and quality that
should satisfy any dog in forms convenient enough to suit any owner.
Nutrition is a complex subject and there is a simple question: do you know
more about the nutrition of the dog than the experts? Teams of nutritionists
form part of a multi-million pound industry involving science, marketing and,
most importantly, competition between feed companies.
For modern dogs, palatability is considered to be of great importance,
and the professional feed laboratories spend a great deal of time getting
the flavour just right.

◆ FACING PAGE
It is important to
provide your dog with
a nutritious diet.

TYPES OF FOOD

Dogs are carnivores. Their digestive system, from the mouth through their intestines, is designed to cope with a meat diet. The dog's teeth are adapted to tear food into swallowable-sized chunks rather than to grind the food, and their stomachs can digest food in this state.

Dogs have probably evolved from animals that lived on a diet of other animals. However, as with the fox in modern times, meat was not always available to them, and the dog is able also to digest and survive on a diet that is mostly vegetable; but a complete absence of meat is likely to lead to nutritional deficiencies.

Foods, whether for dogs or humans, have to supply energy, from which, as well as being the means of movement, the animal's body derives heat, materials for growth and repair, and substances that support these activities. For dogs, this involves a satisfactory mixture of the major nutrients – carbohydrates, fats and proteins – in proportions similar to those required for a healthy human diet; they must also have a sufficient intake of the minor nutrients – vitamins and minerals – in proportions that do differ significantly from the needs of humans.

Dog foods may be divided into several broad categories. For many years the so-called **moist diets** held the major part of the market. They are the tinned foods seen on every supermarket shelf.

Over the past few years other types of food have infiltrated the market. **Complete dry feeds** are becoming increasingly popular. They need minimal preparation – if so desired, they can simply be poured into a dog bowl and given to the dog. Only very slightly more demanding is to pour hot water on to moisten the feed.

Semi-moist diets are not intended to provide a balanced diet on their own. They hold a small but significant place in the market, largely, in all probability, because they involve some degree of preparation before feeding. It is still fairly minimal, involving the addition of carbohydrate supplements as a mixer, often some form of biscuit, to balance the nutritional quality of the food. This is a psychologically important exercise for the owner, who likes to think that he or she is doing something for the dog, as previous generations did when they mixed a bowl of table scraps with some meat and gravy. The one thing to remember is that too much mixing of modern foods can result in nutritional problems. What too often happens is that the concerned owner adds, not just a carbohydrate mixer, but high-protein feed as well, resulting in a diet that is unbalanced, with too much

✦ BELOW
If a dog is hungry and healthy, he will eat. If he is healthy but won't eat, he isn't hungry, so take the food away and let him miss a meal.

NUTRIENTS

The **major nutrients**, required in substantial quantities by every animal, include:

Carbohydrates, which provide the body with energy, and in surplus, will be converted into body fat.

Fats, which are the most concentrated form of energy, producing more than twice as much energy, weight for weight, than carbohydrates, and which will also convert to body fats if supplied in excess.

Proteins, which essentially provide the body-building elements in the diet.

The **minor nutrients** include the vitamins, minerals and trace elements, which, although critical to the animal's health, are required in comparatively small amounts. The vitamins are usually divided into two groups:

Fat soluble: vitamins A, D, E and K.

Water soluble: the B complex vitamins and vitamin C.

✦ BELOW
Each dog should have his own bowl, although the food is often more interesting on the other dog's plate.

✦ ABOVE
Heavy feed bowls make eating easier as they don't skid all over the floor.

protein. There is usually no harm; animals, like man, can deal with an astonishing variety of diet, but too high levels of protein can occasionally exacerbate an existing metabolic problem. There is an old adage: "When all else fails, follow the instructions." It is worth bearing in mind when feeding your dog.

One feature of all modern compound dog foods is that they will contain adequate minor nutrients, which did not always happen in the meat and biscuit days. The outcome is that there is rarely any need for the proprietary feed supplements that are still widely advertised. Calcium, for instance, may have been lacking in some traditional diets, and a bonemeal supplement often used to be recommended. Such a supplement may today do harm in certain circumstances, such as pregnancy in the bitch.

Special diets are a development of the last ten or fifteen years. They are of two types: those that target healthy dogs with special requirements – puppies, for instance, with special growth needs, especially active dogs, and older dogs – and those designed as supportive diets for various illnesses. There are kidney diets, for instance, which control the amount and type of protein the dog is given. These latter special diets are dispensed strictly under the control of a veterinary surgeon, many of whom are now trained specifically in the use of such diets.

✦ LEFT
Canned food must be used within twenty-four hours of opening and kept refrigerated. Cover open cans with plastic lids, and reserve an opener and fork just for dog food.

✦ LEFT
Dogs love bones but vets don't because of the risks of bowel stoppages or choking. Very large bones minimize such risk. Never give a dog a chop bone.

FOOD REQUIREMENTS

Dogs are adaptable creatures. They can, for instance, utilize protein foods, like meats, for energy if their intake of carbohydrates is deficient. They must, however, be provided with a minimum level of each of around thirty nutrients, including the vitamins and minerals, if they are to stay healthy. All the modern prepared foods, and the great majority of home-mixed diets, will provide an adequate supply of essential nutrients.

Some animal protein is essential to maintain a dog's health. A vegetarian diet for dogs can be devised but requires skill, although there is no doubt that dogs do not need the level of animal protein in their diet that is commonly provided.

Some fats are also vital in the diet, providing certain essential fatty acids, and acting as carriers for the fat-soluble vitamins.

Carbohydrates form the bulk of most diets, including normal dog foods, whether commercially compounded or home-mixed.

Provided your dog's diet has a reasonable balance of the major nutrients, and the foods are not themselves wildly out of the ordinary, the owner's concern need only be with the actual quantity given to the dog, and the total calorie provision.

Butcher's scraps, canned or fresh, is not a complete feed.

Canned chicken must be balanced with other foods.

Frozen chicken is an inexpensive way of providing meat protein for small dogs.

Commercial canned food may be a complete feed or mixed.

Rice is a source of carbohydrates for home mixing.

Dry complete feeds have become very popular.

Semi-moist feeds must be kept in sealed packets.

The traditional feed of biscuits with gravy.

Dog biscuits are not adequate as a dog's only food.

At first sight the figures in the table below suggest that the obvious, and cheapest, way to feed a dog is to give it biscuits alone. They offer the highest calorie content, weight for weight, of any food except pure fat, and dog biscuits are cheaper to buy than canned foods. But this is misleading because a diet that consisted solely of dog biscuits would be seriously deficient in protein, and it would be deficient in fats, vitamins and minerals.

AVERAGE CALORIE REQUIREMENTS FOR 24 HOURS

Growing puppies:	6 weeks	3 months	6 months
Terriers, mature weight 10 kg (22 lb)	330	530	700
German Shepherds, mature weight 30 kg (66 lb)	1200	1800	2600
Giant breeds, mature weight 50 kg (110 lb)	1950	2500	4000
Adult dogs:	maintenance:		
Terriers	400		
German Shepherds	1600		
Giant breeds	2400		

The table gives average amounts and should be regarded as a guide only. Take account of whether the mature dog on this level of food intake is gaining or losing weight. Puppies should gain weight steadily, without becoming too fat.

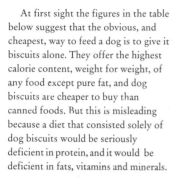
Meaty treats make excellent rewards.

Most dogs enjoy bone-shaped biscuits, and hard-baked (so safer) bones.

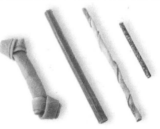
Chews made out of raw or processed hide are usually a safe substitute for bones.

Give only special formula dog drops (see panel below for warnings about human chocolate).

Some biscuits include a charcoal variety, intended to help digestive problems.

CALORIE CONTENT OF COMMON FOOD PER 100 G (3½ OZ)

Dog biscuits used as mixer feeds	300–360
Fresh meat	140
Soft, moist, complete feeds	320
Dry complete feeds	270

MANUFACTURER'S DECLARED CALORIE CONTENT PER 100 G (3½ OZ) IN THEIR RANGE OF CANNED FOODS (HILL'S SCIENCE DIET)

Canine Growth	136
Canine Maintenance	126
Canine Performance	140
Canine Maintenance Light	87
Canine Senior	117

Biscuit treats are produced in various flavours.

CHOCOLATE AND CANINES

Experts agree that certain chemicals in chocolate can be toxic to dogs, especially in large quantities. The chemical theobromine, found especially in dark (bittersweet) and baker's chocolate, can cause a toxic reaction, while caffeine may also lead to digestive problems. Reactions will vary according to dog weight and sensitivity, and although most owners report few or no ill effects where only small amounts have been consumed, it is safest to avoid giving your dog any chocolate.

◆ LEFT
Regular veterinary
examination of older
dogs will reveal the
possible existence of
nutritionally
controllable diseases.

SPECIAL DIETS

Quality of feed is particularly important during puppyhood, to provide nutrients for the rapidly growing animal. Similarly, an in-whelp bitch needs high-quality food if she is to produce healthy puppies without putting undue strain on her own bodily resources. Pregnant animals will deplete their own tissues to provide sufficient nutrients for their puppies both in the uterus and afterwards when they are suckling. A bitch with a litter of several puppies will almost inevitably lose some weight; her condition needs to be watched carefully. There is no point, however, in over-feeding the bitch while she is pregnant.

There may be specific demands for particularly active adult dogs, for the older dog, and for the overweight dog. Scientifically formulated diets are designed to provide for these various special requirements.

Several pet food manufacturers provide prescription diets that, used under veterinary supervision, aid in the management of a number of diseases. They are only obtainable through a veterinary surgeon.

The range is wide and includes products that may either contain greater proportions of certain nutrients than usual – one is a high-fibre diet, for instance, which may be of benefit in cases of diabetes, and in fibre responsive intestinal problems – or smaller elements of the normal diet. Low-protein diets assist in the control of chronic kidney disease, low-sodium diets are used in the management of congestive heart failure.

◆ ABOVE
If puppies share a bowl of food it is difficult to be sure they both get a fair share.

DAILY CALORIE REQUIREMENT FOR THE OVERWEIGHT DOG		
Target weight	*Scale 1*	*Scale 2*
2.5 kg (5½ lb)	120	90
5 kg (11 lb)	200	160
7 kg (15½ lb)	275	220
10 kg (22 lb)	350	270
12 kg (26½ lb)	400	320
15 kg (33 lb)	470	375
20 kg (44 lb)	600	470
25 kg (55 lb)	700	550
30 kg (66 lb)	800	650
40 kg (88 lb)	1000	800

OBESITY

One of the commonest afflictions in the dog is simple obesity. Owners will frequently not see it and, once acknowledged, it may still be extremely difficult for them to understand that reducing the dog's food intake is not cruel. The obesity diet has its part to play by enabling the owner to feed a low-calorie diet to the dog, which will satisfy the hunger pangs while reducing his intake of nutrients.

This table indicates a suitable intake of calories for an overweight dog with a target weight indicated in the first column. The diet needs to be balanced by sensible variations of other nutrients.

You can see from this just how few calories, and consequently how little food, a dog really needs if he is to lose weight at a satisfactory rate. Scale 1 will cause reduction in body weight at a fairly slow rate, and even with ordinary foodstuffs the dog should not be too drastically hungry. Scale 2 is necessary when a more rapid reduction in weight is called for. It is still not a drastic diet regime.

As an example, if you wished to reduce your dog's weight to 20 kg (44 lb), using the slower scale you would need to feed not more than 600 calories a day. Without resorting to a special diet, this could be achieved by a total daily feed of 115 g (about 4 oz) of meat and 130 g (4½ oz) of biscuit mixer. This is not a lot of food on a large dog's plate, and it explains why special reducing diets, which give bulk and fill the dog's stomach, are popular.

◆ RIGHT
Obesity is best controlled by careful attention to diet before the dog's weight gets out of hand.

Grooming

Grooming your dog performs two functions. The obvious one is to keep him looking, and smelling, acceptable to you and to other people. The second one is just as important. Grooming, of a very different sort, between dogs establishes and maintains the relative status of each dog. By daily grooming you are telling the dog, in the most gentle terms, that you are in charge. The whole ritual of insisting that your dog stands while you brush and comb him emphasizes that when push comes to shove, what you say goes. There is no more important lesson in dog training.

✦ FACING PAGE
Grooming should be
an enjoyable
interaction between
dog and owner.

EQUIPMENT &
HOME GROOMING

✦ BELOW
Wire-toothed grooming combs are essential for
some breeds, but use with care to avoid injury
to the dog's skin.

Many owners of long-coated breeds
positively enjoy grooming their dogs,
often achieving and maintaining near
professional results. It demands a
great deal of dedication, and time – the
show trim of a poodle, for instance, is
the result of several days hard work in
total, possibly spread over a week or
more. Owners of short-coated breeds
are likely to be less dedicated to such
perfection, although regular grooming
is still necessary to maintain the dog's
skin and coat in good condition.

Whatever the intention, you will
need the proper equipment. For
trimmed breeds, clippers are essential.
Electric clippers are probably the most
expensive item of actual grooming
equipment, although grooming stands
or tables can cost any price, depending
on their construction and how firmly
you feel it is necessary to restrain the

✦ BELOW
Professional grooming is a considerable skill
and demands a detailed knowledge of every
breed on which work is undertaken.

dog. Professional clippers do the best
job and last longest, but a compromise
on price and effectiveness can usually
be reached. Whatever the make or cost
of the clippers, they must be regularly
sharpened. This is a job for the expert,
and there are several companies in
every country that specialize in a
prompt and inexpensive service. Do
not be tempted to economize. The
dog won't like it, and you won't be
happy with the result.

Most breeders of long-coated dogs
do their own grooming. They will be
happy to advise on the equipment that
is suitable for your level of skill, and
they usually will help the novice to get
started. But don't expect show-
winning results immediately, even
with the best tools.

In addition to clippers, you will
need a suitable brush and comb. There
are many types. Again, take advice
from breeders. The hard brush that is
suitable for a mixture of massage and
loose hair removal for a Boxer, say,

may be death to the silky coat of an Afghan, and, conversely, a comb will do very little for the short coat of an untrimmed breed.

Many people give up on some of the long-coated breeds. They love the dog, but hate the regular chore of trimming and grooming and the coat-matting that is the inevitable result of failure to do both. Taking the scissors to such dogs is not an option. If you were tempted by a beautifully shaggy dog but find the reality all too overwhelming, there may be no alternative to taking most of the coat off. But please let a professional do it. Both you and the dog will feel less embarrassed at the result.

1 This Shih Tzu takes every bit as long to groom as an Afghan many times its size.

2 The first stage is to gently brush out the knots that always occur.

3 (right) Thoroughly brush the dog's entire coat, including the legs and tail.

4 A final grooming brings up the coat.

5 (right) The resplendent result – but for how long?

GROOMING FOR DIFFERENT COATS

Short-coated dogs may need less attention than other types and usually require no professional care at all. The downside to owning a short-coated dog is that they moult all the time, sometimes more than others. Dedicated owners of the short-coated breeds, especially breeds with white coats like Bull Terriers, will tell you that there is no colour or type of clothing that you can wear that does not get covered in dog hairs.

Daily grooming helps. A brush with stiff but not harsh bristles is all that is required, and it takes about ten minutes. Be careful to avoid the eyes, but otherwise brush the entire body.

Rough-coated dogs may need more attention. Some rough coats do not moult in the way that short coats do, but they "cast", which is a more substantial moult, every six months or so. When they cast, hair is lost in mats, especially if the dog has not been regularly groomed throughout the rest of the year.

Regular, daily brushing and combing will prevent the coat matting. Again, a stiff brush is the main piece of equipment, but a comb is also useful. It is essential to brush or comb right through the thickness of the coat. Just skimming over the top is of very little use.

Some rough-coated breeds need occasional attention from a professional groomer, particularly if you are intending to try your hand in the show-ring. All those artfully dishevelled creatures you see at major shows are the result of hours of attention by their dedicated owners.

The silky coated breeds – such as Cocker Spaniels and Irish Setters – need exactly the same attention as

SHORT COAT

1 A short-bristled brush is being used to clean the coat of this Brittany.

2 A wire-bristled glove makes easy work for short-haired breeds that need minimal attention.

ROUGH COAT

1 Rough-coated terriers need more attention to their coats than is realized.

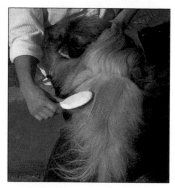

2 Regular, daily brushing out is essential. This dog looks about ready for a professional trim.

SILKY COAT

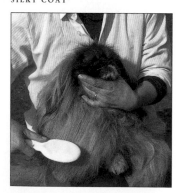

1 Dogs with long, silky coats demand much grooming. The coat should never be clipped.

2 Careful grooming right through the coat with a not-too-stiff brush must be a daily task.

✦ RIGHT
A Standard Poodle in perfect show trim, called
the lion trim.

✦ BELOW
No breed is more difficult to keep in perfect
trim than the Old English Sheepdog.

TRIMMING THE POODLE

The Poodle is generally thought of
as a trimmed dog, and the
prospective owner usually realizes
what is likely to be required. Daily
attention is still necessary, but the
monthly visit to the dog parlour
may become a welcome ritual.

The exaggerated trim, derived
from a working cut of long ago
(the Poodle was originally a
gundog), is not essential to these
breeds and a version of the puppy
trim can be carried on throughout
the dog's life. This is simply a
closer trim all over without the
topiary of the show dog. Many
owners feel it still keeps the
essential nature of the breed. It
takes less grooming than a show
trim, but nevertheless needs daily
attention. It also still needs regular
attention from the professional to
keep it in shape. The coats of
ungroomed Poodles quickly get
into an appalling state

family all cry, "That is the dog we
want." But none of them has the time
or the inclination to spend a long time
every day, brushing and combing and
cleaning up their new dog; and still
less when the novelty has worn off.

So if you must have a dog that
needs a lot of daily work, be sure you
are going to be happy to spend the
time on it. Before you make up your
mind, go and see the breeder to find
out just what is involved.

Expert owners and breeders will
usually trim their own dogs, but if you
are getting one of the trimmed breeds
as a family pet, it is sensible to contact

your local grooming parlour with your
puppy as soon as it is allowed out. The
groomer will give you advice on daily
care of the puppy's coat, and discuss
with you when to start trimming, and
what you can best do to keep the dog's
coat in good shape between
professional visits.

rough-coated dogs. Some tend to
grow rather heavy coats and need to
be trimmed regularly.

The breeds that demand really
skilled attention are, of course, the
long-coated ones – Poodles of all
sizes, Old English Sheepdogs, the
trimmed terriers.

Question one, therefore, is, "do
you want the expense and the trouble
of professional grooming for your dog
every four weeks?" This is the
question that many prospective dog
owners fail to ask themselves. Sadly,
the typical result is the Old English
Sheepdog that has its coat trimmed to
the skin to keep it socially acceptable.
A beautifully groomed dog is seen on
television advertisements and the

✦ BELOW
The coat of the Afghan is long and very fine-
textured. Gentle but thorough grooming is
necessary to maintain its condition.

BATHING A DOG

Dog owners in temperate climates are generally reluctant to bathe their dogs, remembering all sorts of old wives' tales regarding the adverse effects of doing so. These are probably the same arguments that people used in the Middle Ages about their own personal hygiene.

Some dogs may not need to be bathed, especially the short-coated breeds that tend to shrug off dirt; but the smell may remain.

There are, in fact, very few breeds of dog in which regular bathing causes any ill effects, although it is sometimes cited by breeders whose dogs' coats are less than ideal for the breed. "The new owner must have over-bathed or over-groomed the puppy" can be a convenient excuse. Some breeds should never, according to the

WHERE TO BATH THE DOG

1 Early training makes the task of bathing a dog easier, but few of them actually enjoy it.

2 A double-drainer sink is suitable for small breeds, while the family bath can be pressed into service for larger dogs.

✦ BELOW
Nail clipping is a regular necessity for many dogs. If you are not confident of your skill, ask a professional to do it – if you clip into the quick of the nail you will never be able to persuade the dog to submit to the task again.

breeders, be bathed. These are the dogs that veterinary surgeons can smell through the door when the dog is brought to the surgery!

In many tropical or sub-tropical countries dogs must be bathed weekly, without fail, if certain tick-borne diseases are to be avoided. There is no evidence of poor coats in show dogs in these countries.

There are three types of dog shampoo: the straightforward medicated shampoo, the anti-parasitic shampoo, and specialized, veterinary shampoos, which may be prescribed for particular skin conditions. If a dog is prone to allergies, any of these may precipitate one, but rarely. Shampoos from a reputable source will minimize such problems.

BATHING TIPS

1 A very small dog may fit into a basin, but wear waterproofs for the moment when it tips and spills everywhere.

2 Rubbing the dog semi-dry will prevent some of the water splashing all around the room when he shakes himself – which he will do shortly.

3 A good shake should be followed by some vigorous exercise to complete the drying out process.

4 Avoid getting water into the eyes during bathing, and wipe around them once the dog is out of the bath.

5 Grooming while the coat is still slightly damp, but not wet, will help make the job of removing tangles much easier.

6 *(right)* Clean and sweet smelling until some more horse manure to roll in is found.

Breeding

There are tens of thousands of four-legged reasons for not breeding from your dog. They occupy hundreds of welfare and rescue kennels. So consider very carefully indeed whether you are at risk of adding to the large number of unwanted dogs. If you decide to go ahead, it is a most rewarding experience. Never decide to breed in the expectation that you will make money. It is almost certainly not true – the appetites of eight unsold twelve-week-old puppies are devastating – and you would be breeding for all the wrong reasons.

◆ FACING PAGE
Breeding from your dog
can be very satisfying.
However, it does entail
a lot of hard work and
should not be entered
into lightly.

TO BREED OR
NOT TO BREED

The first thing to consider is that you cannot expect a crossbred dog or bitch to produce puppies in his or her own image. If you own a crossbred, and your reason for breeding is that friends have said that they want one "just like her", remember that the chances of a litter producing even one puppy that is just like its mother are small to very small.

Crossbred dogs, by reason of their own breeding, have a wider genetic pool than purebred animals. Any selection of the characteristics of either parent is a matter of chance, and the greater the variety of characteristics for nature to select from, the greater will be the differences between puppies in the litter, and the greater the difference between the puppies and their parents.

If you breed from parents of mixed ancestry, you will produce puppies that may not even remotely resemble the dog or bitch that your friends were looking for. Potential buyers may well melt away.

◆ LEFT
The standard Schnauzer, the middle size of the Schnauzer breeds, is not very common in English-speaking countries but is a delightful dog.

◆ BELOW LEFT
Looking after a litter of puppies is very demanding work for bitch and owner alike. For both it may easily involve many twenty-four hour days.

But it is not only with crossbred dogs that the phenomenon of the melting buyer exists. Many litters of purebred dogs are bred on the apparent promise that several friends are anxious to have a puppy of that breed, just like yours. From the time of your bitch coming into season there will be about two weeks before she is mated, nine weeks before the litter arrives, and another eight weeks before the puppies are ready to go to their new homes. That's nineteen weeks since the friends made their remarks – over four months for the enthusiasm to wane, for their circumstances to change, or for them to become really keen and buy a puppy from elsewhere. If you think this is a cynical attitude, try asking for a small deposit.

There are, however, good and sensible reasons for breeding.

The dog or bitch should be purebred. One or other should either be of a good working strain – and have shown itself to be a good working dog in the field – or be a sufficiently good show dog for the breeder or an expert to recommend that you should breed from it. The most straightforward way to determine the animal's show quality is to exhibit at shows with success.

The reason for restricting breeding to these two groups of animals is that

To many people the Airedale Terrier is an old-fashioned breed. It is less spoiled than most, but has the typical terrier temperament.

✦ BELOW
In every healthy litter the puppies are looking for mischief as soon as they are able to run around.

there is much less likelihood of your being left with puppies on your hands, or worse, running the risk of sending them to unsuitable homes. No reputable breeder would ever do this.

✦ LEFT
The pregnant bitch needs special care and feeding but should continue to exercise regularly until the day she whelps.

✦ BELOW
Cleanliness in the litter box is, as they say, "next to dogliness".

Remember that buyers of purebred puppies want the best, which means that both parents have shown their quality.

A litter of puppies is great fun. But after seven or eight weeks the fun may become an expensive and exhausting chore. Being left with six or more fourteen-week old crossbred puppies that are starting to show that they had Great Dane somewhere in their ancestry is not as amusing as it sounds.

The same applies whether you own the dog or bitch. There may not be the same imperatives if you own the dog and the bitch belongs to the lady down the road, but you both have the same responsibility for the outcome.

There is no truth in the commonly held belief that siring a litter will in any way settle a dog down. Neither is there any truth in the belief that a bitch needs to have a litter. There is no medical reason for either belief. The reverse may very well be true as far as the male is concerned.

CHOOSING MATING PARTNERS

THE STUD DOG

Stud dogs are always selected from the best. This may mean nothing more than being currently the most fashionable, but to be among the fashionable always means that the dog has sufficient merit, either as a working dog or as a show dog, to have attracted widespread attention.

It would be unusual for someone's pet dog to become a stud dog, but if a number of fellow enthusiasts ask if they can use your dog, take advice from someone you trust in the breed. Handling matings is a skilled job. If you want to learn, become an apprentice to an expert.

The better, or more fashionable, the stud dog, the higher will be the fee payable for his services. As a guide, the stud fee is likely to be somewhat lower than the price you might expect to get for a puppy. Special arrangements such as "pick of litter" are by no means

✦ LEFT
This outstanding Rough Collie may be the ideal stud dog.

uncommon. This means the stud dog owner has the right to pick whichever he or she regards as the best puppy from the litter, either in lieu of the fee, or as a consideration for a reduced fee.

However, it is not necessary or even desirable to go to the most fashionable stud dog for your bitch's mating. An experienced breeder will advise on which dog to choose, using the physical appearance and pedigree of your bitch and the available dogs as a guide. Some breeders take more notice of pedigree, others of conformation. Learn about the breed, and decide how close to your ideal each breeder's stock is.

PEDIGREES AND CHAMPIONS

The Kennel Club has sole responsibility for registration of pedigree dogs in Great Britain. National clubs have the same responsibility in their own countries throughout the world. The American Kennel Club, although not the only registration authority in the United States, reciprocates its registrations with the Kennel Club and the Federation Cynologique Internationale (FCI), to which the Australian Kennel Control is federated.

Most Kennel Clubs have reciprocal arrangements, and dogs registered in one country can be re-registered in another if the dog is imported. Official pedigrees are derived from the registration particulars of all purebred dogs that are themselves registered with the Kennel Club. Unless a dog is itself registered, its offspring cannot in turn be registered, except in certain special circumstances. Pedigree records are held for at least four generations, although some breeders will be able to show you much longer ones than that.

Different countries have different criteria for awarding the title of Champion. In the United Kingdom the title is awarded to show dogs and working dogs. Some aspire to, and some achieve, both titles.

To become a Champion in the United Kingdom a show dog must have been awarded three Challenge Certificates under different judges,

✦ BELOW
The Boxer is a very popular breed. There should be no difficulty in finding the dog to suit your bitch.

✦ LEFT
Careful noting of pedigree and breeding records
is essential if you are serious about your
breeding programme.

✦ BELOW
The Cairn Terrier,
another popular breed.

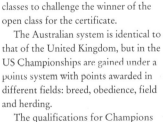

✦ RIGHT
All breeding
programmes start
from small
beginnings but may
end with a
Champion like this
Yorkshire Terrier.

with at least one of the certificates
being awarded after the dog has
reached the age of twelve months.
Challenge Certificates are awarded to
the best dog and bitch in each breed at
specified Championship Shows. The
term Challenge Certificate derives
from the fact that the judge may invite
any or all unbeaten dogs from earlier
classes to challenge the winner of the
open class for the certificate.

The Australian system is identical to
that of the United Kingdom, but in the
US Championships are gained under a
points system with points awarded in
different fields: breed, obedience, field
and herding.

The qualifications for Champions
in working dogs take account of the
dog's success in the working trials.

FINDING HOMES FOR THE PUPPIES

There is no point in breeding from a
bitch unless you can expect to sell the
puppies. Your best bet is to produce a
litter that will be acceptable to
enthusiasts, unless you have firm orders
that ensure the sale of your puppies.
The breeder of your bitch may be able
to help. In many breeds, good puppies
are at a premium. Reputable breeders
will be asked regularly when or where
there is a litter due. Your bitch's
breeder may be happy to pass on
applicants to you, and to explain to
them about the breeding of your bitch.

✦ ABOVE
At three weeks old all puppies are
delightful, but this pair are likely to get
into mischief next week.

✦ LEFT
A rough and
tumble is a vital
part of the
puppies'
learning
process.

MATING

THE BREEDING CYCLE

Male dogs become sexually mature at about six months of age. From that time their sexual behaviour is not cyclical, and they are capable of mating at any time and almost any place!

The bitch usually comes into season for the first time when she is aged about nine months, and fairly regularly every six months thereafter. It is not unusual, nor is it in any way abnormal, for the first season to be earlier, even as young as six months, or for it to be postponed until the bitch is over a year old. Neither is it unusual or abnormal for the interval between seasons to be longer than six months. If the interval between one season and another is very much less than six months, and particularly if it has become irregular in this respect, there may be some abnormality, and advice should be sought from your veterinary surgeon.

A bitch's season lasts for about three weeks. She will show some swelling of her vulva shortly before presenting a blood-stained discharge. The discharge is usually very bloody at the start of her season, becoming paler after about ten days.

Although no risks should be taken from the first signs of season, the bitch will normally not accept a dog until about halfway through the season, at which time she will become fertile (i.e. capable of conceiving). There is normally no odour detectable to a human from a bitch in season, but there is a very powerful one detectable by dogs a considerable distance away. Do not assume that because you live a mile from the nearest male dog, your bitch will not be mated.

Do not assume, either, that a dog that lives together with a bitch, though they may be brother and sister, will not be interested.

MATING AND CONCEPTION

True oestrus begins at about twelve days from the first signs of the bitch coming into season. From that time she will accept the male's attempts to

✦ BELOW
Mating takes place when the bitch has ovulated. Ejaculation occurs quickly, and the tie is not necessary for conception.

✦ BELOW
Although not essential, the tie has a physiological function in helping the sperm to move up the genital tract.

mate her, and will be fertile, for about five to seven days. Ovulation, the release of eggs into the uterus, takes place during this period. The timing is variable, and the dog and bitch are the best practical arbiters of the bitch's fertile period, although laboratory tests are available to help timing if the bitch fails to conceive.

The mating act may be prolonged. Once the dog has ejaculated, the bitch continues to grip his penis in her vagina, by means of a ring muscle, for up to about twenty minutes. The dog may climb off the bitch's back, and turn to face the other way, but both stand "tied". The tie is not actually essential for a successful mating, although all breeders prefer to see it.

Pregnancy lasts for about sixty-three days from mating. The normal variation is from about sixty days to as much as sixty-seven. Outside this range veterinary attention should be sought, although it does not necessarily indicate a problem and may simply be an extension of normal variation.

Bitches should not be bred from until they are physically mature. The ideal age for a first litter is about two years old.

✦ LEFT
Bitches should continue with normal exercise throughout pregnancy, although they are likely to become increasingly placid for its duration.

✦ BELOW
The bitch should be introduced to her whelping box at least a week before whelping is due in order to give her time to become comfortable with her surroundings.

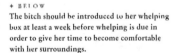

WHELPING

Whelping is a natural event. In nine cases out of ten there is no need for human interference; in ninety-nine cases out of a hundred, interference takes place before it is necessary.

Be prepared. Let your veterinary surgeon know well in advance. He or she may have confirmed that the bitch is in whelp, but ask the vet to note the expected date on the calendar.

Make sure that you have decided where the bitch is to whelp, and that

breeders will show you a suitable box with a rail around the edge to prevent the bitch lying on her puppies and squashing them. Some bitches are very clumsy. Bedding for the box needs to be disposable – whelpings are accompanied by a great deal of mess. Almost universally the basic bedding for a whelping box is newspaper in large quantities, so start saving them some weeks in advance. You can always do the crossword while you are

waiting for the puppies to arrive!

Most bitches give warning of imminent whelping by going off their food. If you have a thermometer you may use it at this stage. A dog's normal temperature is approximately 101.5°F (38.5°C). A drop in temperature of two or three degrees nearly always indicates that the bitch will start to whelp within twenty-four hours.

For several days before whelping many bitches will start to make a nest

1 Bitches do not normally need human assistance to produce their puppies, although whelping may be a prolonged business.

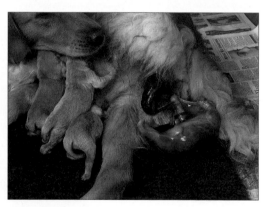

2 The bitch breaks the puppy out of the foetal membranes and often eats the membranes. It is not usually necessary to tie off the cord.

she has agreed with you. If it is to be in a special place, and in a special bed, introduce her to it a week or two in advance, and teach her that it is now her bed. The ideal place is a quiet corner without passing traffic, and away from where the children play. Bear in mind that you, or the vet, may have to attend to her at some stage. Under the stairs may not be perfect for this reason.

She should have a whelping box. It needs to be large to accommodate the bitch and a litter, which may number as many as twelve puppies. Most

3 The puppy needs plenty of stimulation by licking from the bitch or, if necessary, by rubbing in a towel, to be sure that it is breathing satisfactorily.

somewhere, usually somewhere inappropriate. Most bitches become very restless a few hours before they start to whelp.

Right up to the point of producing her first puppy, a family pet that in the nature of things is used to human company will probably want the comfort of human attention, but once she starts to strain for the first puppy, the great majority of bitches will become uninterested in the people around them and just get on with the job of producing a litter.

It may take several hours from the

✦ BELOW
New-born puppies spend virtually all their time
drinking or sleeping. If the litter is restless,
urgent attention should be sought.

✦ BELOW RIGHT
With a large litter it would be wise to make sure
all the puppies get their share.

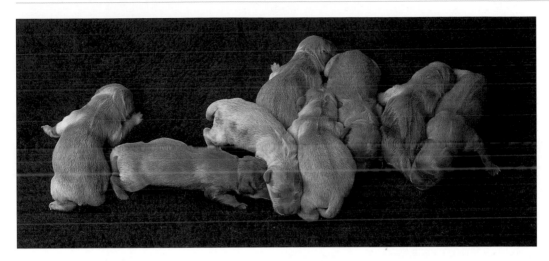

time the bitch starts to strain until the first puppy is delivered. Provided she is continuing to strain, there is no panic. If, after serious effort for an hour or more, she stops trying, ask your veterinary surgeon for advice.

The first sign that a puppy is due is the appearance of the water bag. This is an apt description for the foetal membranes; they look just like a small bag of water, which appears through the vagina. Do not attempt to remove it; it has the function of enlarging the birth canal to permit the following puppy to pass through.

The puppy may be born either head or tail first. Each is as common as the other, and the appearance of the tail first does not indicate a breach birth.

The first puppy may take some time to be born after you get first sight of it, and it may often seem to disappear back up the canal. The time for concern is when the puppy is obviously stuck fast with no movement up or down, despite continued straining, or when the bitch

appears to have given up straining and is lying exhausted. Veterinary attention is needed urgently.

CAESARIAN OPERATIONS
Veterinary assistance at a whelping is as likely to involve a caesarian operation as not. The bitch is too small to allow very much manipulation

if she has problems producing puppies. In earlier times assisted whelping involved the use of instruments inserted into her vagina, but this has largely been discontinued in favour of surgery. Caesarians are now more popular, partly for humane reasons, but mainly because of the existence of low-risk anaesthetics

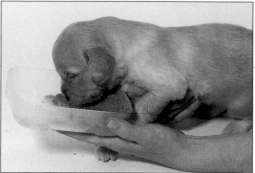

◆ LEFT
Puppies are able to
eat solid food from
about two weeks on.

◆ BELOW
Any puppies that do
not get their share
may be bottle fed
successfully with a
suitable bitch-milk
substitute.

coupled with surgical techniques that have improved so much over the years that a successful outcome of the operation can usually be anticipated.

To produce live puppies and a healthily recovering bitch, the operation must be carried out earlier rather than later. The subject should be discussed with the veterinary surgeon well before the whelping is due, so that both parties know the other's feeling about the operation. The veterinary surgeon must be called in before the bitch has become exhausted from straining unsuccessfully to produce her puppies.

Sadly, some breeds have such a poor reputation for natural whelping that caesarian operations are carried out routinely, without waiting for indications of failure by the bitch. Breeders in these breeds must reconsider their whole outlook on dog breeding if their breeds are to continue to be popular.

Other than in these special circumstances, caesarian operations are usually carried out as a matter of emergency. Most veterinary surgeons will ask you to bring the bitch to the surgery if there are whelping difficulties, rather than visit the house, so that operating facilities are at hand.

The otherwise healthy bitch and her puppies will thrive best back in her home environment, and the veterinary surgeon will release them as soon as possible. Once home she may need a little coaxing to accept and feed the puppies; as far as she is concerned, they just appeared while she was asleep. Careful introductions almost always work, but she may need some help initially to attach the puppies to the teats. Once they are sucking

normally, the bitch will realize what she is supposed to do.

After the first day or two, a bitch who has had a caesarian may be treated the same as a bitch who has produced the puppies naturally.

AFTER WHELPING

The puppies must be cleaned behind every time they feed. This stimulates the passage of urine and faeces; without the stimulation they will not pass excreta and may become fatally constipated. This is one of the bitch's jobs. If she has been under anaesthetic, she may not realize this. Holding the puppy tail first to her will quickly teach her the routine.

Normally, the bitch remains with her puppies constantly for at least the first couple of weeks. There may be difficulty in persuading her to leave them even for her own natural functions. If this is the case, don't worry. She will go eventually. Let her do it in her own time.

A healthy bitch with puppies quickly develops a large appetite. For the first few days it may be necessary to feed her in or very close to her bed, but make sure there is plenty of food available, and particularly plenty of fluids. She may prefer milk. Forget the once a day feeding routine, let her have food whenever she wants it. She has an enormous task.

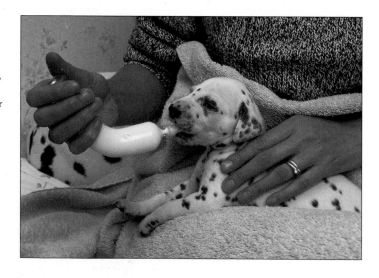

REARING PUPPIES

The first two weeks are the easiest. The puppies are relatively inert. They will wriggle around the bed a great deal but are incapable of recovering the nest if they accidentally fall out. Most whelping boxes have high fronts for this reason.

At this stage the puppies need no supplementary feeding, just their dam's milk, and should spend most of their time sleeping quietly. If they do not, seek help urgently.

Puppies open their eyes at about ten days old, though some breeds are notoriously lazy about this.

♦ RIGHT
Five-week-old puppies are active and alert and already learning lessons about the world.

By about three weeks old the puppies are moving around much more; they will mostly have fallen out of the box several times, indicating that it is time to add another layer to the barrier at the front. It may also be the time to start to supplement their diet. This is done by hand-feeding.

Although most people think of the puppies' first hand-feeding as an occasion for something delicate, milky perhaps, just try scraping a little raw beef from the joint on to your fingers. You will be lucky to have a finger left!

The main reason for starting to wean puppies at three weeks is to spare the

♦ ABOVE
At three days old the puppy's eyes are still closed, and its only active movement is likely to be towards its dam for feeding.

♦ ABOVE
By three weeks old the puppy will be trying to get out of the nest box.

♦ BELOW
By eight weeks it is time for the puppies to leave home, usually to the relief of their dam and often to the relief of their owner.

bitch. With a large litter there is a tremendous physical demand on her, and she will certainly lose a lot of weight during the course of rearing a litter. By starting to wean the puppies relatively early she will be spared some of this load. Puppies do, in any case, start to look for more solid food at this age if given the opportunity.

At three weeks of age the litter must have its first worming dose. Take advice on this. Modern wormers cause no side effects.

From three weeks to about five weeks a gradually increasing proportion of the puppies' diet should be supplied from sources other than their dam. By six weeks they should be completely weaned, although the dam may take some convincing of this, and may keep trying to feed the pups. The action of sucking by the puppies prolongs the production of milk by the dam, and after six weeks this should be discouraged.

At six weeks the puppies should be feeding on a puppy food of your choice. It is also time for a second worming dose to be given.

Training

Every dog is capable of learning a great deal more than is generally recognized. Although it may take a special type of dog and a special type of owner to create a canine film star, home helper or agility champion, there is no reason why every dog should not achieve the essential basics of obedience and well-socialized behaviour. A well-trained dog is less likely to develop unwanted behaviour patterns, partly because dogs often adopt bad habits when they are bored. Dogs enjoy the stimulation of training and most love to please their owners too.

◆ FACING PAGE
There are many ways that a trained dog is capable of helping its owner.

SOCIALIZING YOUR PUPPY

All puppies need to meet as many other dogs and as many people as possible. This is the essence of socialization, and when done effectively most of the behaviour problems that may occur later will be avoided.

From the day you acquire him, your new puppy should start to meet other people. The puppy must not be overwhelmed but, within reason, the more people he meets the better. The visitors should be asked to hold the puppy, handling and cuddling him gently, so that he learns that people are friends. However, until the puppy has had his vaccinations some caution is necessary to avoid second-hand contact with other owners' dogs. Ask dog owners to delay their visit until your puppy has had his second round of injections.

Apart from other dogs in the household, to which the puppy should be introduced at the earliest possible moment, meeting dogs must be delayed until the new puppy has had his two sets of injections and the "all clear" from the veterinary surgeon, at about twelve weeks old.

In the United Kingdom, one of the most useful, as well as entertaining, developments in puppy training in recent years has been the creation of puppy parties. These are exactly what they sound like. Once or twice a week a group of puppy owners with their puppies meet for an hour or so in the village hall or somewhere similar. Puppies from twelve weeks of age up to six or seven months, and of all sizes, are allowed to play with each other with only the minimum restraint from their owners. The smaller ones are rarely overwhelmed by the larger, and all learn that their fellow canines

can be approached without fear. It is an object lesson for their owners.

The puppy party has revolutionized dog training in the United Kingdom. Most puppy groups have experienced trainers in charge, and the transition from pure play into early obedience training can be seamless. Lead training is nearly always part of it, perhaps simply walking at heel without tugging, and the foundations to more advanced work may be laid.

Puppy playgroups introduce all shapes and sizes of dogs to each other and help to overcome alarm at strange animals.

Basic training classes are held in village halls, or similar places, all over the world. Attendance at a weekly class is usually sufficient.

EARLY LEARNING

◆ BELOW
Bribery is all important in encouraging a puppy
to come when called.

Teaching the dog good habits is best achieved by rewarding success, although it is nonsense to suggest that scolding is never necessary. From the earliest age, puppies learn to understand the word, or the action implying, "No". Their mother teaches them some discipline from a very early age, and their new mother – you – needs to carry that on.

Take the common game of chewing your shoelaces. A tap on the nose while saying "No" firmly, soon teaches a puppy that there are some things in life to avoid, and that "No" means just what it says.

Similarly, most puppies start the dominance game very early in life. Nipping whomever they see as being one down from them on the totem pole quickly develops into a bite to establish their rank. Immediate remedial action – another firm "No" – will save a great deal of trauma later.

◆ BELOW
Bribery is all important in encouraging a puppy to come when called.

In all training there is no substitute for persistence and patience.

HOUSE TRAINING
This is the number one priority. Many puppies will not have had any house training before they arrive at their new home. They will have lived in their kennel or box with their litter mates, but even there the sleeping area is usually taboo for toileting once the puppies are old enough to move

◆ RIGHT
By eight weeks puppies should be confident and have started their house training and lead training.

around. This can be used during the course of house training.

There are two methods of teaching a puppy to use an appropriate site for its toilet, and they can be used simultaneously.

The first method involves eternal vigilance. Puppies squat to urinate and use a slightly more humped squat to defecate. As soon as the puppy postures to do either you must scoop him up and put him on the designated spot. If you miss the signs, do not scold the puppy. He doesn't yet know what he's supposed to do; he hasn't done anything wrong.

The second method is to use newspaper to cover the entire floor area on which the puppy runs. He will learn that newspaper is a suitable medium for his natural functions, and a gradual reduction in the size of the available newspaper will result in the puppy using a smaller and smaller area of floor. The theory is that you can then move the paper outside, and the puppy will continue to use it, until he learns that only outside the house is

✦ LEFT
It is important to learn the signs and to encourage the puppy by putting him outside as soon as he wakes up, and after every meal.

appropriate. Both methods work, one will suit one puppy better than another. A combination of the two by using the paper at night and extreme vigilance during the day, will usually produce the best results. Not uncommonly, older puppies may

"unlearn" about toilet training. Some trigger will cause them to break their newly formed habit. Again, please don't punish them.

This is where a dog's instinct can be useful. A healthy dog will not soil its own bed. It can be extremely helpful, for all sorts of reasons, to teach a dog to use a cage as a bed, and this is one of them. If you make it comfortable, the dog will very quickly learn to regard it as his own place to retreat to when the world gets too complicated. If the puppy does "unlearn" his house training, let him sleep in the cage, and put him out into the garden in the required place immediately after you open the cage door.

The cage mustn't be a prison for the puppy, rather a refuge, but it is useful for him to learn that sometimes the door must be shut. Suitable treats, something extra tasty, will usually persuade him to accept it.

✦ LEFT
If you are using the newspaper system for house training, it may be necessary initially to cover the entire floor.

EARLY LEAD TRAINING

1 Soft collars are more easily tolerated than new stiff leather ones.

2 Once the dog is at the stage of having a lead attached, a treat will encourage him to associate the lead with pleasure.

COMING WHEN CALLED

Your puppy will normally have an instinct to come to you from the word go. Encourage this with treats. Call the puppy by his name and, when he responds, give him a treat. It takes a very short time indeed for the puppy to associate his name with a doggy treat. But if the puppy doesn't come immediately, do not get cross and scold him. It takes an even shorter time for the puppy to learn when to run away.

GETTING USED TO A LEAD

This really must be regarded as fun by the puppy.

Step one is to put a collar on. This will feel very strange, and his immediate reaction will be to try to scratch it off. But delicious treats will distract him and overcome the itchiness of the collar.

Step two, but not until the collar is tolerated happily, is to attach a light lead. Don't hold the lead at this stage – let the puppy become accustomed to it by dragging it around. Finally, hold the lead, and gradually wind it in loosely, calling the puppy for still more treats.

3 Bribery, yet again, will take the dog's mind off the new restraint.

TRAVEL SICKNESS

Overcoming travel sickness is, or should be, a matter of early learning.

Some puppies are never travel sick, but unlike some children, those that are can nearly always be taught to overcome the problem. You must act immediately when the problem arises, otherwise the puppy starts to associate cars with vomiting, and will salivate as a premonitory symptom as soon as you put him into the car. If travel sickness is allowed to persist, the puppy will learn to hate and fear car travel.

Simply taking the puppy on plenty of short journeys may be sufficient. If the puppy learns that he can go for a ride without being sick, especially if there is a walk or a game at the end of it, he may overcome his early nervous reaction.

If the short journey cure doesn't work, there is no substitute for travel sickness pills and a much longer trip. Bear in mind that travel sickness pills take some time to be absorbed and to work. They need to be given about an hour before the journey. To a considerable extent, the longer the journey, the more effective the treatment. Bear in mind also that most travel sickness treatments induce sleepiness, so giving the pills before going off for the family holidays can be doubly useful.

Most dogs will learn to overcome their travel sickness after a few training trips, but the longer the problem is allowed to persist before attempting a cure, the slower will be the response.

PUPPY BEHAVIOUR

Dogs are pack animals, which explains many behavioural characteristics. When you are having problems think "pack leader" and act accordingly.

One of the pack-behaviour features that all dogs bring to their relationships with human beings is hierarchy and, consequently, dominance. Puppies spend a great deal of their time trying instinctively to establish where their position is in the hierarchy, and they can only do this by attempting to establish their own dominance.

Some breeds are more dominant than others. The terriers, for instance, tend to be so; generally the gundogs do not try so hard. Being in the dominant role is not necessarily comfortable for a dog, particularly when the signals from their human companions are mixed and confusing. Most dogs settle happily in the submissive role once they are clearly placed there and learn that they do not have to attempt to keep everyone under control.

The dog's place must be established as soon as he arrives in his permanent home. He must learn that all the humans in his home are above him in the pecking order. This is not a matter of punishment for the dog. There are simple keys to make it plain.

FEEDING
The leader eats first. It is often convenient to feed the dog before you eat, but if the dog observes this, you are sending one of those confusing signals. If the family and the dog are going to eat at more or less the same time and in the same place, let the puppy wait. Puppy-feeding times are best arranged well away from your own meal times, which will avoid sending this signal.

From the start, it is useful to make

Early grooming is simply a progression from handling the dog.

Introduce the brush as soon as the puppy has become used to sitting quietly on the table.

the puppy come to you for his food and wait until you are ready, perhaps by teaching him to sit before you put the bowl down.

GROOMING
Touching and handling are potent signals to a dog. Daily grooming under proper control will indicate who is in charge. Some puppies will resent the handling involved – dominance again – they may react as though they are being hurt. Ignore it and insist. All puppies are capable of learning very quickly whether you really mean it.

NIPPING AND BITING
Most puppies will "mouth" things, including your fingers, when they are very young. This will progress to a nip. Mouthing is normal behaviour in the young as they learn with their mouth and nose. Nipping is the first step in learning dominance. It is not amusing; stop it immediately, by a sharp reaction – the "No" it has already learned – and a tap if necessary. Remember your pack leader role!

GAMES AND FIGHTING
All puppies like to play games; they are part of the puppy's education, and in the light of that you should think carefully about them.

Avoid contest games with your puppy. Tug-of-war is fun, but can easily develop into a contest of dominance, with the puppy either winning the tug, or growling or snarling while hanging on. If you must play tug-of-war keep it on the very lowest key and stop immediately if the puppy starts to become too excited. Simply to stop and go away after retrieving the tug is probably as good a lesson as any.

Running after a suitably large ball (not a stick, please, or a ball small enough for the puppy to choke on) can be fun for the dog. But teach your puppy to bring the toy back to you by not running after the dog to get the ball. Show indifference if the puppy runs away with the ball, and reward him with praise and pats if he brings it back to you. You have started obedience training, congratulations!

EARLY FEEDING

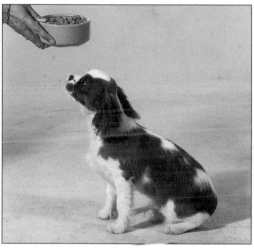

1 Show the puppy his food as a preliminary to persuading him to sit.

2 The puppy has sat down, so bring him his food bowl.

3 Make the puppy wait a moment or two before allowing him to put his head into the bowl.

4 Finally the puppy gets the reward.

BASIC OBEDIENCE TRAINING

The world is a crowded place. Every dog must be able to fit into the social system around it without causing problems. Dogs may have all sorts of functions and duties, but the first, and often the only, basic necessity is that they are sufficiently trained and biddable not to cause problems for their owners. To achieve this the dog must learn basic obedience to his owner's commands.

This does not mean that the dog should be beaten into submission by a dominant owner. Apart from the cruelty of such a regime, it doesn't achieve its objective: the dog will be cowed rather than obedient, he will run away rather than respond to his owner's commands.

Basic training and obedience should be a happy experience for dog and owner. Dogs are happy to work for rewards, from a titbit to a pat on the head in praise, but they must know what you are seeking from them. Rule one is **do not confuse your dog.**

Dogs react to the immediate, not to something that happened ten minutes ago. Several other things will have happened since. Let's take as an example recalling a dog that is running free. You call him. He doesn't come back. You get cross and call him again in an angry voice, and he still doesn't come back. So you chase after him, catch him and give him a slap, or even a beating with his lead.

What does the dog learn from this? If I hear my owner calling me, I run away because if he catches me he will beat me. If I see him with the lead, I also run away because if he has the lead in his hand he uses it to beat me.

The dog shows impeccable logic in his reactions, rather than the reasoning

WALKING TO HEEL

1 Standing by his owner with a loose lead, the puppy is smelling the chance of a reward.

2 Still with a loose lead, the puppy's interest is held by the owner.

3 Moving out, the puppy stays close to his owner still with hopes of a treat.

4 Finally, the puppy has learnt that the treats will come later if he keeps by his owner's side.

that you might wish him to use. Rule two is **think like a dog**, not like a sophisticated human being.

WALKING TO HEEL

In the early learning section we explained how to accustom your young puppy to a collar and lead.

The next stage, the first in obedience, is to teach your puppy to walk on the lead without pulling. From the sight of the average dog on its lead, this is a lesson that is commonly never learned.

First steps are best taught in your own back garden or somewhere equally quiet. The puppy is already aware that a lead is attached to his collar but not that this is intended to restrain him. Pick up the lead and walk the puppy round the garden, telling him to "heel". As soon as the puppy starts to pull, simply stop and encourage him to come to you – bribes work. Do not have a tugging battle. Start moving around again, with the promise of more bribes, donkey-and-carrot style. The puppy will soon overcome his fear of the restraint. Remember, you are thinking like a dog. Trading a little restriction on freedom of movement for a choc drop (dog treat) is fair exchange.

These first steps need to be repeated for as long as it takes, but in sessions of only a few minutes. You will get bored but the puppy will not think "training session", it will think "choc-drop time".

Professional trainers often declare that bribes like treats are not to be encouraged, because they teach the dog to expect a treat whenever it does the right thing. This is true, but remember that dogs of different

breeds vary in the ease with which they can be trained. A Border Collie may be so anxious to please that a pat on the head is sufficient reward for any obedience success. But a terrier is a very different matter. Pats are all very well, but they don't taste as good as choc drops.

Once the puppy has overcome his fear of the restraint of the lead, some discipline does have to be introduced. Every puppy will decide that being on a lead should be challenged, and he will try an experimental pull to see what happens. This seems to be where everything goes wrong. The owner merely pulls against the dog's pull, and the dog quickly learns that the normal thing is to lean into the lead and pull the owner around behind him. This is the stage that a high proportion of dogs on leads reach.

Do not allow the pull to become established. Call the dog back to you immediately and stop walking. Praise him, yes even bribe him, when he comes back. Start again and keep the puppy on a very short lead so that he is not moving out ahead of you. Remember also that the top dog walks

◆ ABOVE
The flexi lead is a useful training aid. All leads must be strong enough to restrain the dog in an emergency.

ahead. Who is top dog in your family?

There is something to be said for remedial training immediately if loose lead walking seems to elude you and your dog. The simplest device is the "Coke can". This is exactly what it sounds like – an empty soft drink can that has been filled with small pebbles to make a rattle. If the dog persists in pulling ahead, throw the pebble can just ahead of the dog. The surprise will often help to break the habit. Repeat as often as necessary to convince the dog that if he pulls on the lead a startling noise will occur, which has nothing to do with the ineffectual human hanging on to the lead.

A little more expensive, but a useful investment, is to buy an extending flexi lead. These are nylon leads that extend to a considerable length, unwinding from a spring-loaded handle. Many owners use them to give their dog plenty of room to roam around them on a walk, without losing control of the dog.

The lead can also be used to cure a pulling dog. Allow the dog to run out on the lead – do not pull against it – and when the dog feels that he is

1 Teaching a dog to sit starts with him standing, under control.

2 The dog has been encouraged to sit by light pressure on his haunches.

3 At a more advanced stage, hand signals may be used to instruct the dog to sit or go down.

running free, put the brake on the lead. It pulls the dog up suddenly. Use of the flexi lead with a normal buckled collar avoids the risk of injuring the dog. The sudden stopping action teaches the dog that his lead is there as a restraint rather than to pull against. The lesson is usually learned very quickly if accompanied by a suitable command that the dog will associate with the sudden stop to its run. Clever owners learn to use the clicking noise that the lock makes as the signal to their dog to stop in his tracks.

The choke chain has not been mentioned as a training aid for teaching walking to heel, mainly because it doesn't work until it is used so fiercely that there is danger of injury to the dog.

The choke chain and the slip lead are sometimes confused. They are two different things. The slip lead, which is usually a leather or nylon lead with a ring in one end threaded to form a noose, is a useful piece of equipment if there is a risk of the dog slipping its collar and lead. It is easily loosened, and does not have the harsh restraining action of the choke chain.

Once your dog walks to heel on a loose lead, and responds to your command to heel with reasonable alacrity, you are on your way to having an obedient dog.

SIT AND DOWN

Teaching the puppy to sit on command, and to "down", are the next practical steps for the dog owner.

As a matter of observation, if you restrain a dog in the standing position on a lead that is sufficiently short to prevent him from jumping to reach an offering, and move the offering from in front of the dog to just behind his head, the dog will sit and tip his head back to try to reach the offering. Give him the sweet, and you have taught him to sit! Repeat the exercise, telling him to sit as you do so, and keep doing it until the dog has learned that "sit" means "sit for a sweet".

The "down" is an extension of the same exercise. Once your dog has learned the sit, and while keeping him under the same restraint, offer the sweet on the floor between his front paws; push the dog down at the same time telling him to "down".

All other obedience training is based on exactly these same principles, with patience and praise as the twin essentials for a happy partnership.

OBEDIENCE CLASSES

Elementary obedience lessons do not need skilled assistance, but even these can contain pitfalls for the new owner. There is an obedience class in practically every town, and it is well worthwhile for anyone with a new puppy to enquire about them. Most local obedience classes are run by experienced dog people who are only too happy to pass on their knowledge to newcomers. These obedience groups all have classes for beginners, dogs and owners, and certainly do not expect you to turn into an enthusiast for competitive dog obedience competitions. A well-trained house pet is the objective. If you get the bug and decide to join in the more advanced work, you will have started on a demanding but fascinating hobby.

An offshoot of the conventional obedience class is the ring-training class. This has much the same basis, but is intended specifically to produce well-trained show dogs. The emphasis

DOWN

1 Teaching the dog to lie follows the sit. As before the dog is encouraged to lie down by the reward of a treat.

2 Once the dog has lowered his head, his front legs may be moved gently forward into the down position.

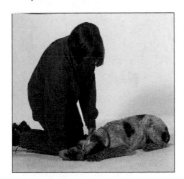

3 The dog is gently restrained in the down position and once again encouraged to remain there by bribery.

is on good behaviour on the lead in the presence of other dogs and a crowd of people, training the dog to allow strangers to examine it, and, one particular quirk, to stand while on the lead rather than to sit, which is the practice in obedience classes.

AGILITY AND FLYBALL COMPETITIONS

Two sports that have achieved great popularity in the United Kingdom derive directly from advanced obedience training: agility and flyball.

The **agility** competitors run an obstacle course that includes a seesaw, a tunnel, jumps, a stay on a table and weaving in-and-out obstacles. The dogs are timed, with points deducted for failure to negotiate each obstacle correctly. The requirements are strict; if the dog jumps off the seesaw before he reaches the bottom, for instance, he will lose points.

Flyball appeals to owners who want some excitement with their dogs, and if the noise coming from the flyball competition ring at Crufts dog show is anything to go by, they certainly get it. The flyball course is a short straight strip at the end of which is a box with a trap and foot lever. On a signal, the dog is released by his owner, races to the box and leaps on the foot lever, which causes a ball to fly into the air. The dog leaps to catch the ball and rushes back to his owner to give it to him or her. All is timed to the second. Flyball competitions are usually run as a relay, with four teams of six or so dogs each.

Both these activities engender great enthusiasm among their supporters and demand great dedication from the trainers and competitors.

FIELD TRIALS AND GUNDOG (SPORTING) WORKING TESTS

Field trials and gundog trials have received the status of competitions in their own right, and championships are awarded in both.

The essential difference between the two is that field trials are conducted as similarly as possible to an ordinary day's shooting of live game birds, whereas gundog trials assess the working ability of gundogs without game being shot.

Both types of trial vary in their content, depending on the breed of dog undergoing the trial. Retrievers are expected to pick up and retrieve game or the dummy; spaniels, whose job on the shooting field is to find and flush out game, are expected to quarter the ground and mark the same. Pointing is considered difficult to assess, and trials for that purpose alone are rarely held. The Springer Spaniel, which is considered the general workhorse of the shooting field, performs "hunt, point and retrieve" tests.

WORKING DOGS

◆ LEFT
The English Springer Spaniel is a traditional, hardworking gundog.

From the earliest days, humans have considered their dogs to be not just companions but working allies. The dog probably came into the camps of early humans for scraps of food, the comfort of association and warmth. But it soon became apparent to the dog's host that here was a guard, warning against strangers, and on occasion, actually attacking intruders with whom it was unfamiliar.

Dogs have worked ever since. Their trainability has led to them being used over the centuries in roles varying from the simple barking burglar alarm – a role that is today recognized by some insurance companies – to out-and-out attack dogs, epitomized by the mastiff breeds, which functioned as war dogs in the Middle Ages.

Roles have been refined over the centuries, and the most important function of the majority of dogs nowadays is that of household

The Springer Spaniel, a versatile gundog, has lately come into its own as a working dog in another field, that of "sniffer". The Customs department and many police forces maintain teams of sniffer dogs to ferret out drugs being smuggled into the country, and to perform various other tasks where a keen ability to scent a suspicious substance is required. Several breeds are used, but the Springer is unsurpassed for this work.

companion, a role that is not to be underestimated.

Modern guard dogs are expected to be highly trained and totally responsive to their handler's control. The police, the prison service and the armed forces all maintain teams of dogs whose function is to guard and, if necessary, to corner an intruder or attack and bring down an assailant. It is rare for such a dog to go out of control.

There is a regular demand for young dogs to train with the services. They are looking for dogs that are bold and, in civilian owners' hands, often difficult to train. The majority of these dogs are German Shepherds, dogs that are a delight in the right hands but that may be dangerous without proper control.

Two of the oldest roles for working dogs are as livestock guards and herders, a distinction that is often misunderstood.

The Collies and various British sheepdogs have historically had a herding role. Their function is to keep the sheep flock under control at the behest of the shepherd. They circle, help move the sheep and bring strays back into the flock. Their response is to the shepherd, not the sheep.

This type of herding work depends on a carefully controlled "attack" by the dog, which runs in almost to nip the heels of the sheep, pushing it away in the direction that the shepherd calls for. Despite the shepherd's handling, the dogs learn more from their parents than from any other source.

Many of the European sheepdogs have a completely different function, acting as guards to the flock against predators. Some of the working dogs of these breeds may actually be reared

Manwork should only ever be undertaken under carefully controlled, professional supervision.

This police dog has been carefully trained to show aggression on demand when his handler requires it.

+ LEFT
There are legal restraints to keeping guard dogs, intended to avoid risks to law-abiding citizens.

+ ABOVE RIGHT
The Siberian Husky, bred for the specific purpose of pulling sleds, makes a delightful house pet, given the right environment.

+ RIGHT
Police and Customs dogs are widely used for the detection of illicit drugs.

with the sheep from an early age, growing up as one of the flock, but better equipped to ward off intruders.

These dogs, when moved out of their own working environment and into the human's, become guards of property. As with almost any breed, however, when given the right upbringing, they can make wonderful house pets for their owners.

For many years, perhaps centuries, dogs have been used as guides for blind people. The work is highly organized, by the National Guide Dogs for the Blind Association in the United Kingdom and Guiding Eyes in the United States. Guide dogs are Golden or Labrador Retrievers, but less conventional breeds can also be trained. At least one standard Poodle has been trained to the necessary level and allocated to an applicant. The training is carried out at one of the organization's centres, and the individual dog tailored to the individual person, although sometimes applicants think it's the other way around after they have been on the introduction course!

The success of the scheme for guide dogs for the blind has encouraged enthusiasts to set up various other programmes for dogs to aid disabled people. Hearing Dogs for the Deaf is now well established in the United Kingdom, with dogs that have learnt to alert their deaf companions when, for instance, the front door bell rings.

One of the most successful schemes is Pat Dogs or Pet Partners. These are companion dogs whose owners take them to hospitals and hospices to visit the patients. Many people miss their own dog, or find comfort just from having a dog to talk to and stroke while they are in hospital. The therapeutic effect on the patients is demonstrable. Any breed is suitable, though not every dog; they must be dogs that enjoy human company but don't demonstrate their enjoyment too effusively.

The Harrier, one of the oldest breeds of hunting dog, has never been included in the Kennel Club registers.

Tracking, sometimes to search for criminals but often to seek out people or objects that may be lost, is another specialist duty of the ubiquitous German Shepherd.

BEHAVIOUR
PROBLEMS

Behaviour problems develop because the dog has received signals that the type of behaviour now regarded as a problem has been acceptable, up to now. This nearly always arises because we give conflicting signs to the dog.

Take sitting on the sofa. If you allow a sweet little puppy up on to your lap, how is he to know that when he gets bigger he can't do it? Until one

◆ ABOVE
Chewing of household objects may arise simply from boredom or separation anxiety.

◆ LEFT
Jumping up is probably the commonest objectionable behaviour by dogs. It is far better prevented than cured.

day you push him off, and there is a confrontation.

Curing behaviour problems is much more difficult than preventing them. Obedience training has a considerable role in overcoming potential behavioural problems, and many enthusiasts have developed their interest through the need to create a reasonably well-behaved pet.

DOMINANCE

The development of dominance is by far the most common cause of real problems. Dominant behaviour will lead to biting. Often enough, the dog will have learned that one or more of the family is in the pack leader's position, but that some, often the children, appear to be below the dog in the pecking order.

Dominance cannot always be cured, but it can usually be controlled, provided the whole family co-operates. The method is to re-establish the order of dominance in the pack.

Rule one is never to confront the dog unless you know you can win. A dominant dog becomes aggressive in order to protect his position. His bite is often worse than your bark.

Start by totally ignoring the dog, and that must include all the members of your family. Almost always the dog

♦ BELOW
Apparent over-sexed behaviour, often by small
dogs, is frequently an expression of frustrated
dominance.

♦ BELOW
If muzzles are to be used they must be effective
and humane, permitting the dog to wear them
comfortably and to breathe without difficulty.

reassert his own dominance – don't
allow him into your bedroom, for
instance. Keep him strictly off chairs
and that sofa. Physical height, achieved
by getting on to chairs, is a dominance
signal, and sitting on a chair may be
sufficient to indicate to your dog that
he has made himself tops.

You don't need to be in any hurry
to take the trailing lead away. This
gives you a lot of control without risk
to yourself. Games must be entirely in
your control. You start them and you
stop them, and above all avoid
confrontational games that the dog
can feel he has won. At the same time

will very soon approach you for
attention. Make sure he doesn't get it.
Put a long lead on as soon as you can
do so safely, and leave it to trail. Use
the lead to make the dog do what you
want him to.

If the problem has been that he
won't get off the sofa without
growling at you, pull him off from a
distance. You are beginning to reassert your authority.

Re-establish the feeding regime
make the dog wait, and then make him

approach you for his food rather than
taking the food to him. Then ignore
him again.

Stop greeting the dog. If he wants
attention, he must come to you, and
then be rebuffed until you have
decided that he has behaved well
enough to relax your attitude a little.
He must be given no opportunity to

♦ LEFT
All dogs enjoy
foraging in
dustbins. If you
don't want the
dog to get at the
dustbin, put it
out of reach.

Aggression needs professional attention. It may
have several causes.

AGGRESSION TOWARDS GUESTS

1 Aggression towards guests is often a defensive or fear reaction.

2 Letting the dog realize that guests are not intruders may often be accomplished with a suitable treat.

as you are asserting the new regime, it is essential that the rest of the family behave in exactly the same way.

Most dogs never exhibit dominance problems; if they did they wouldn't be such popular companions for humans, but when a dog does start to show signs of dominant behaviour he must be controlled totally, or it will lead to trouble, and trouble means biting, humans or other dogs.

If you do not seem to be able to control incipient dominance, or aggression, quickly by these simple rules, take professional advice before the problem becomes serious.

FEAR BITING

A high proportion of unacceptable behaviour involves the dog biting someone. Aggression that arises from dominance accounts for much of this, but fear biting occurs regularly in less dominant dogs. The only way a dog has of protecting himself is to bite his perceived attacker or to run away. Fear biting will occur if the dog cannot run away.

Fear of the unknown is usually the problem. If a dog does not meet many

3 Overcoming this type of aggression is easier with a well-trained dog that can be kept under restraint.

people as a puppy, he may, depending on his natural disposition, regard people as a whole as the unknown and react accordingly. Early training will nearly always prevent this reaction. If early contacts are insufficient and the

dog is nervous of people he does not know, there is no substitute for slow and careful broadening of the dog's circle of acquaintances, until he has met so many people that nobody seems to be a stranger. The same approach must

+ BELOW
A dog which doesn't come when called means back to square one.

be taken if a puppy takes fright at cars, for instance. Non-confrontational acquaintance with his particular fear object will cure the problem.

BARKING FOR ATTENTION
It is not unknown for a dog to use a fear reaction as an attention-getter. If a

contrariness in our dogs. Nobody's perfect, and it's part of their charm.

There are other, more bizarre, behavioural problems that usually do not involve actual risk to the owner. One of the commoner of these problems is the dog that tears the house to pieces when the owner goes

out. It doesn't help just to say that this is another anxiety manifestation. Sometimes the reasons are complex, and the cure always demands considerable commitment on the part of the owner. It should always be undertaken with the supervision of an expert animal behaviourist.

+ LEFT
It is natural for dogs to howl like their cousin the wolf. In domestic circumstances howling is usually a sign of distress.

+ BELOW
Decide early what is tolerable in the way of begging for titbits, and stick to it.

puppy learns that barking at an object, any object, will result in his owner giving him all sorts of comforting attention, he will very quickly realize that if he wants attention, he should bark, and preferably in an alarmed fashion for an instant response.

ODD PROBLEMS
You may think you cannot win, but we all tolerate a certain amount of

Health Care and First Aid

In order to recognize when a dog is ill, you must know the signs of good health. A healthy dog is alert and lively, and takes a great interest in its environment, although young puppies will be, quite normally, rushing about one minute and sound asleep the next. There should be no discharges from the eyes or nose. The nose is usually moist and shiny, but this will depend on what the dog has been doing – people are often concerned that their dog's nose is dry, when all that has happened is that he has been digging for his favourite bone! The ears should be clean and free of visible wax. The coat should be free of dandruff and, depending on the coat type, more or less shiny. The skin should be free from sores or spots. The dog should move soundly, that is to say without favouring one leg over another, and he should move freely. A healthy dog should have a healthy appetite. He should be ready for his food, and eat it with relish.

+ FACING PAGE
Vets' surgeries are usually relaxed places and visiting one should not cause your dog any stress.

INTRODUCING YOUR DOG TO THE VETERINARY SURGEON

Ideally, if you have not previously owned an animal, you should make the acquaintance of your local veterinary surgeon before you acquire the dog. How you choose a vet is a matter of personal preference. You may be guided by friends, or the convenience of the surgery, but there is no substitute for a personal interview to get an idea of how the practice runs, its surgery times and facilities, all of which the veterinary surgeon will be pleased to discuss with you.

Within twenty-four hours you and your family are going to have grown very attached to your puppy. That is just the way it happens. It is important

that, if the veterinary examination discovers anything that indicates the puppy should be returned to the seller, you should know immediately before this bonding has taken place. So you must arrange for the puppy's examination to take place on the day you collect him.

The veterinary surgeon will repeat the superficial health checks that you will already have carried out before buying the dog, but will go into greater detail, with a check on the puppy's heart and lungs, his ears and skin, his legs and feet and his genito-urinary system as far as possible.

This examination should not alarm the puppy. The veterinary surgeon will spend time getting to know your new dog with a little friendly fussing to give him confidence, before making the more detailed examination.

Almost certainly, unless he has already received his first inoculation, he will be given it now. Again, this should not alarm the puppy, and many don't even notice the injection. At worst there may be a squeak, followed by some more comforting. The whole event should be very low key.

The veterinary surgeon will also probably advise on worming and anti-flea regimes, and tell you how long it must be before the puppy meets other dogs in order to give the vaccine a chance to develop the dog's immunity to infections.

♦ ABOVE
Minimum restraint is important in encouraging your dog to relax at the surgery.

♦ LEFT
Most dogs, if handled with confidence, will not require heavy restraint during veterinary procedures.

THE INOCULATION REGIME

The dog's inoculations cover a core of four major diseases: distemper, which includes hardpad; leptospirosis, a liver and kidney infection; hepatitis, caused by a liver virus; and parvovirus. Kennel cough vaccine may also be included at a puppy's primary vaccination stage.

The first component of the vaccination course is usually given at seven to eight weeks old, although in circumstances where there has been a perceived risk in the breeder's kennels, much earlier protection may be given against certain diseases. Such very early vaccinations are usually disregarded for the purposes of routine protection.

The second injection is given at around twelve weeks of age. The interval between vaccinations is necessary to allow the puppy's immune system to react properly to the first dose of vaccine; the second dose then boosts the level of immunity to such an extent that the dog is protected for a prolonged period.

The vaccines are repeated annually, a process known as "boosters". Owners are inclined to be lax in their response to booster reminders as the dog gets older. Don't! Although some elements of the dog vaccination programme may confer a solid immunity for life, this cannot be relied upon, and other elements definitely need boosting annually.

LIFELONG IMMUNIZATION

Some infections in dogs are unlikely to strike the dog more than once in its lifetime. Vaccination against these diseases may confer a lifelong immunity. The virus hepatitis of the dog is one of these diseases.

BOOSTER INOCULATIONS

Unfortunately other infections, although again unlikely to affect the dog more than once, do not confer such a solid immunity for life, although the immunity that they do confer is excellent for as long as it lasts. Typical of this group is distemper and hardpad (which is caused by the same virus). Distemper vaccinations must be boosted about every second year to maintain a high level of immunity.

There is a third group of infections that may recur and to which the immunity offered by vaccination is relatively short-lived. It is still worthwhile to use the vaccine because of the dangerous nature of the illness. Such a disease is leptospirosis, transmitted usually by foxes or other dogs, but occasionally, in the case of one type of the disease, by rats.

Not all diseases to which dogs are susceptible can be avoided by vaccination, but the commonest killers certainly can.

KENNEL COUGH

A particular problem for which there is no total preventive control is kennel cough, an infectious inflammation of the larynx and trachea. Kennel cough may be an unfair description. The disease is transmitted by droplets coughed into the air by dogs actively suffering from the illness. Fairly close contact between dogs is necessary for its transmission, such as a nose-to-nose greeting through the wire by dogs in kennels. At least as common a cause is dogs meeting at shows, competitions or training classes.

Kennel cough is caused by a mixture of infectious agents. The most effective vaccine, although it still does not include every possible component of the infection, is given as a nasal spray. Most kennels advise owners to make sure their dogs have had a kennel cough vaccination shortly before going into kennels. Some insist before accepting the dog. The advice is sensible.

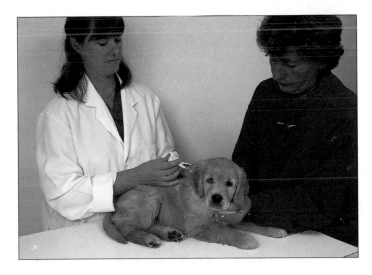

WORM CONTROL

Dogs are prone to both internal and external parasitic infestations. There are two common worms in dogs: the tapeworm and the roundworm.

TAPEWORMS

Tapeworms may affect dogs at any age, although they are less common in young puppies than in older dogs. The tapeworm has a life cycle that depends on two different host species, in the case of the most frequently seen worm, the dog and the dog's fleas, although in another species they are transmitted through sheep.

Tapeworms may be recognizable as "rice grains" in the faeces, but the dog may give you an indication by undue attention to its anal region.

Control of the tapeworm in the dog is simple; modern treatments are straightforward, requiring no fasting before dosing, and highly effective, with very little in the way of side-effects (occasional vomiting).

It is a good idea to treat your dog routinely against tapeworms every six months. However, prevention of re-infection depends on control of the flea population in your house.

ROUNDWORMS

Roundworms are practically universal in puppies. They may be transmitted directly from dog to dog by faecal contamination, which is almost impossible to avoid. A high proportion of puppies are actually born infected with roundworms, transmitted via the uterus of the mother. Worms that had lain dormant in the tissues of the dam are activated by the hormones produced during pregnancy, circulate in the mother's bloodstream and pass into the unborn

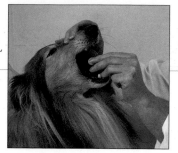

Any tablet needs to be given right to the back of the dog's mouth. Wrap it in something pleasant to distract him from spitting it out.

pups. There are control regimes that depend on using a safe anthelmintic early in pregnancy to destroy the maternal worm load, but this treatment is by no means universal.

A proper rearing regime will include dosing the litter when it is three or four weeks old, and perhaps again before leaving the kennels. Once in your home the puppy should be treated regularly, according to your veterinary surgeon's advice, every three to four weeks until it is six months old.

Adult dogs build up a level of immunity to the effects of roundworm infestations, and after six months do not need such regular treatment. Keep a constant look-out, although roundworms are not always easy to detect in a dog's faeces.

A dog will eat grass when his stomach is upset, but many dogs simply enjoy a little grazing.

WORM TREATMENTS

There are drug treatments that are effective against tapeworms and roundworms in one dose. One possibility is to give older dogs this type of treatment once every six months. The ascarid roundworm may be the cause of a very rare eye condition in children. If the dog is regularly wormed, the risk, already remote, is eliminated. With this exception, the worms of dogs and of humans are not transmissible.

Other species of worms, including the hookworm, may occur in dogs. Treatment is not difficult, but diagnosis may not be straightforward. Consult your veterinary surgeon. In the United States, heartworm is a common problem. A preventive medicine is given orally; treatment can be costly, and dangerous for the dog.

♦ RIGHT
All dogs will lick and clean their anal region, but frequent licking is a sign that veterinary attention is needed.

EXTERNAL PARASITES

✦ BELOW
Dogs will lick and occasionally chew their paws, but if your dog does this persistently, examine his feet. Grass seeds are a common irritant.

FLEAS

Start by assuming that your dog has fleas! They are by far the commonest external parasite of the dog. A high proportion of skin problems may be caused, directly or indirectly, by their presence.

Fleas thrive in the warm and cosy environment of a centrally heated house, and there is no longer a flea season in summer followed by a flea-free winter. Treatment should be continued all through the year.

Fleas are often difficult to diagnose. They are small, move rapidly and are able to hop considerable distances. They are not very easy to see on the dog, but they never live alone. If you see one flea it is safe to assume that there are plenty more. If you see none at all, they are probably still somewhere around.

A useful home test is to scrape hair detritus on to newspaper, and then to dampen the paper. If red smears appear it is a certain indication that the dog does have fleas. The detritus may look like coal dust, but it is flea excreta.

Once you have convinced yourself that even your dog may have fleas, treatment is straightforward, although control is anything but. There are several effective sprays and washes available that will kill fleas safely (but some for which care is necessary), and most have some residual effect. But re-infestation is very difficult to prevent. If protection is, say, for three months, in practice the effectiveness is likely to decline well within that time. So some fleas come back.

Recent advances have been made with non-toxic preparations to be given to the dog monthly in tablet form. These do not kill adult fleas but act by breaking the flea's breeding cycle. All flea treatments are demanding in that they must be given regularly if they are to work.

The important thing to remember is that fleas leave the host to reproduce, and that for every flea you find on the dog, there are literally thousands in your dog's bed, in the nooks and crannies in the floor, in the carpets, between the cushions on the sofa, all breeding away like mad.

✦ RIGHT
Scratching is normal, but persistent scratching demands attention. In nine out of ten cases it will be something as simple as fleas.

◆ BELOW
The Elizabethan collar is extremely useful to
prevent self-mutilation around the head. The
cause of the inflammation must be determined.

There are a number of preparations on the market that provide effective protection around the house. Thorough vacuuming of the carpets helps but will not overcome the problem. Flea eggs, laid in their thousands, are able to survive for long periods in a warm environment. Disturbance causes the eggs to hatch, in itself a reason for regular vacuum cleaning, as the eggs in their shells are resistant to insecticides.

TICKS

Ticks tend to be a country dog problem. Their usual host is the sheep. In the United States, Australia, South Africa and the tropics, ticks transmit certain rapidly fatal diseases to dogs, and the dogs are routinely dipped or sprayed against infestation, often on a weekly basis. This is not necessary in Europe, where tick-borne disease is uncommon in the dog.

Ticks engorge on the blood of their host; the engorged tick is sometimes mistaken for a wart on the dog's skin.

Dogs will occasionally pick up a solitary tick, but may sometimes be seen to have several. Adult female ticks lay groups of eggs, which hatch at more or less the same time to form a colony of young ticks attached to grass stems waiting to find a host. If a dog comes by, several of the "seed ticks" may attach themselves to him.

The ticks are usually removed individually. Do not try to pick them off. That's rarely successful, and there are various substances that will kill them. Ear drops that are intended to destroy parasites are useful as is methylated spirit, or even gin! The tick will not fall off immediately but it should have disappeared twelve hours

after application. Most anti-flea preparations will also kill them.

In the United States, Lyme disease is transmitted by ticks that live on deer and mice, and is a serious threat to dogs. Fortunately, a vaccine is available.

LICE

Fortunately lice are now uncommon parasites of the dog. Lice are detectable by the presence of just

visible groups of eggs attached to the hair, often of the ears or head of the dog. Lice are small and are not mobile. They tend to occur in large numbers, but do not seem to be as itchy to the dog as fleas.

Lice are transmitted directly from dog to dog by contact. They are not transmitted to humans or to other animals. They may be controlled by the use of insecticidal shampoos.

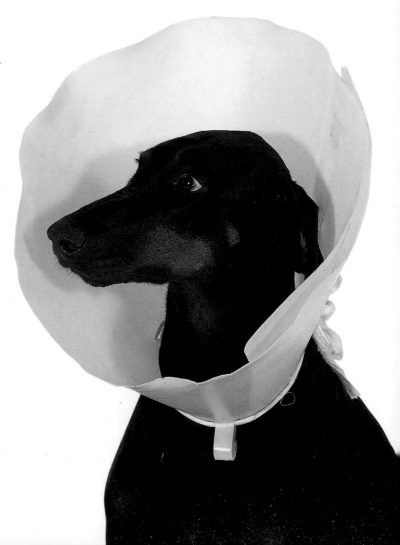

SIGNS OF ILLNESS

One of the first signs that a dog is ill is if he refuses his food. Most fussy dogs will at least smell the food on offer, but a sick dog may have no appetite and simply not approach his food.

The dog will tend to become duller than usual, although many sick dogs will still respond to their owner's enthusiasm for a game or a walk.

ACUTE ILLNESS

The term "acute" does not necessarily mean a serious illness. When your

The ear is an extremely sensitive organ. Any inflammation demands immediate attention from the veterinary surgeon.

Dogs on modern diets are inclined to acquire tartar on their teeth, which needs attention if it is not to lead on to more serious problems.

SIGNS OF ACUTE ILLNESS

Tense, swollen stomach. A drum-like swelling of the abdomen an hour or two after feeding, accompanied by obvious distress with panting and salivation, may indicate that the dog has bloat. This is an emergency.

Vomiting several times, particularly if it persists for more than twelve hours. Vomiting once or twice is common, and a normal reaction to eating something unsuitable. Some dogs eat grass, appearing to do it to make themselves sick. If this happens occasionally, there is probably nothing to worry about. Persistent vomiting after eating grass may suggest an acute problem.

Diarrhoea persisting for twenty-four hours or longer. Diarrhoea will often accompany vomiting. If the faeces are bloodstained, treatment may be needed urgently.

Difficulty breathing, gasping, choking.

Collapse, loss of consciousness, fits.

Each of these conditions needs immediate attention from your veterinary surgeon.

veterinary surgeon refers to an acute illness he simply means one that has come on rapidly, whereas a "chronic" illness is one that is long lasting and has appeared gradually.

Young puppies are occasionally subject to fits, from which they usually recover quickly. Observe the fit carefully so that you can describe it when you get to the vet's. Did the dog just collapse silently, did it squeal or howl, did it paddle its legs, did it urinate or defaecate during the fit? Once a dog has recovered from a fit it may be very difficult for the veterinary surgeon to be precise about the cause; there may be nothing for him to see.

Other signs of acute illness include serious bleeding, or bleeding from any orifice (see First Aid); obvious pain, indicated by noise (squealing, crying, yelping on movement), lameness, or tenderness to touch; straining to pass faeces, or inability to pass urine; any obvious severe injury, or swelling on the body; a closed eye, or inflammation with excessive tears; violent

scratching or rubbing, particularly around the ears or head.

CHRONIC ILLNESS

The signs of chronic illness appear gradually and are likely to be more subtle and difficult to recognize.

Loss of weight, persisting over a period of weeks, is a common indicator of chronic disease. This may be accompanied by a normal or reduced appetite.

Gradually developing swellings may indicate the growth of superficial tumours, often not cancerous but usually needing attention.

Other signs include hair loss, with or without sore skin or itching and scratching; slowly developing lameness; excessive drinking, with or without an unpleasant odour from the mouth or body. Occasional vomiting may indicate an internal problem, although many healthy dogs may also vomit. In the normal course of events, bitches may frequently regurgitate food for their puppies.

FIRST AID FOR YOUR DOG

+ BELOW
Sores and rashes may develop beneath a long coat for some time before they become obvious.

First-aid treatments may be divided into problems that you can deal with yourself, and treatments to carry out to keep the problem to a minimum before you take the dog to the veterinary surgeon.

SORES AND RASHES

A dog may get a sore place or a rash through chewing itself. Many dogs will chew their skin raw if there is an itch. The dog may get a rash from insect bites – typically flea bites, from skin contact with irritants such as nettles, or as an allergic response to an external or internal substance. It is often difficult to tell to what extent the sore area is caused by

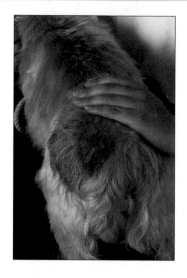

the irritant or is self-inflicted as a result of the irritation.

The object of treatment, whether your own first aid or your veterinary surgeon's, is to eliminate the cause before attempting to cure the effect.

If a dog has been scratching itself a little more than usual, the commonest cause is the presence of fleas. Fleas never come singly. If you see a flea, there will definitely be others. One or two may be sufficient to start the itch cycle off. The answer is to treat the fleas (see External Parasites), and the problem will usually disappear. If it doesn't, a soothing cream, such as rescue cream, will be sufficient.

FIRST-AID KIT

The most important item in your first-aid kit should be your veterinary surgeon's name and telephone number. Even though you may have it elsewhere, it doesn't harm to duplicate it.

Absorbent cotton wool

Adhesive and gauze bandages, 5 cm (2 in) and 10 cm (4 in)

Gauze swabs, sterile wraps

Cotton buds

Scissors, sharp-pointed

Thermometer

Forceps, medium-sized, blunt points

Plastic syringe, 20 ml (½ fl oz)

Eye drops

Cleansing ear drops

Antiseptic or antibiotic ointment

Antiseptic powder and wash

Rescue cream

Medicinal liquid paraffin

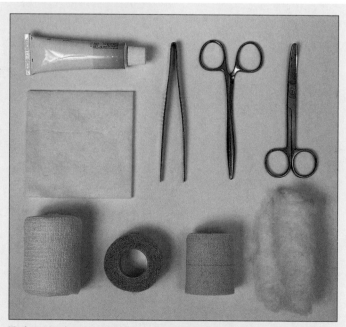

The forceps in a first-aid kit should never be used for probing around. You must always be able to see whatever it is you are attempting to remove.

TAKING TEMPERATURE

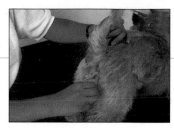

1 First, shake the thermometer so that the level of mercury is well below the expected temperature of the dog.

2 Slide the lubricated thermometer carefully into the dog's anus and press lightly against the side of the rectum.

3 The thermometer should be held in place for at least sixty seconds before reading.

BANDAGING A PAW

1 First, pad the leg with cotton-wool strips between the toes.

2 Place a generous amount of further padding over the end of the foot to cushion it before starting to bandage.

3 The bandage must always include the foot and be extended above the wound.

4 Bandage the leg firmly, but take care that the bandage is not so tight that circulation is restricted.

5 Tie the bandage off well above the site of the wound.

6 Cover the whole of the bandage in an adhesive dressing, firmly but not tightly, and secure it at the back of the dog's leg.

CUTS AND SCRATCHES

Treatment depends on how large and how deep the cut or scratch is. The dog's skin does not usually bleed profusely, and it is easy to miss even quite a large cut because there may be very little bleeding and the dog's fur covers the site.

If there is any sign of blood on the dog, look carefully and once you have located the cut, clip sufficient hair around it to expose the wound. If the cut looks deep, or longer than about a centimetre (½ in), it will need attention and, probably, a stitch or two at the veterinary surgery.

If you decide to take the dog to the vet, do nothing with the wound, unless it is bleeding profusely. The nurse is likely to take longer cleaning your dressing off the wound than the stitching itself will take.

A minor cut, or a scratch that does not penetrate the skin, will usually need very little treatment. Soothing cream will be sufficient, and even that may do more to prolong healing than to help, by bringing the attention of the dog to the wound.

Similarly, a small cut needs no particular attention once you have trimmed the hair away, other than to keep the wound clean with a mild antiseptic solution, and to keep an eye open for any swelling. Swelling may indicate that an infection has set in.

HEAT STROKE

1 First signs of heat stroke are obvious distress and incessant panting.

2 The dog should be cooled immediately by sponging or hosing down with cold water. Ensure that the head is drenched.

BITES

Dog bites will often become infected. This is particularly the case when the bite causes a puncture wound. Unless the wounds are multiple, or large enough obviously to require veterinary attention, there is no emergency, but the dog should be taken to the veterinary surgery within twenty-four hours to allow the vet to assess whether antibiotic injections are needed. Prior to that, the wound may be cleansed with antiseptic lotion.

BLEEDING

Treatment will depend on how heavily the wound is bleeding. Skin wounds may only need cleansing, followed by the application of a little antiseptic cream and a careful eye on the progress of the wound. It will probably stop bleeding in a short time.

Profuse bleeding is an emergency, usually indicating a wound that is sufficiently deep to need urgent veterinary attention. Steps to control the bleeding while on the way to the surgery are worthwhile, and may be life-saving. Tourniquets are no longer used, do not attempt to make one. Use a pressure bandage over the wound.

The rare need for a pressure bandage is one reason for the cotton wool and bandages in your first-aid kit. When needed, take a large wad of cotton wool, as large as is available in your kit. Place it directly over the wound, and bandage firmly. If the wound is on a limb, bandage right down to the foot and include the entire leg below the wound in your bandage. Make sure the site over the wound is firmly bandaged, and take the dog to the surgery.

HEAT EXHAUSTION

Some breeds of dog are more prone to heat exhaustion than others – Chow Chows and Bulldogs come to mind, but several other short-nosed breeds can also be affected.

The most common reason for heat exhaustion is human error. Dogs are too often left inside cars in summer without adequate ventilation. The owner is usually just thoughtless, or caught out by a change in the weather during a longer than expected shopping trip. The temperature inside a closed car in summer in even a temperate climate can kill a dog. Many have died in this way. The signs of heat stress are obvious distress, heavy

BANDAGING AN EAR

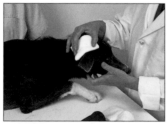

1 Ears are often damaged in dog fights and can bleed profusely. Clean the wound, then place an absorbent pad behind the dog's affected ear.

2 Carefully fold the ear back on to the pad.

BANDAGING A TAIL

1 Successful tail bandaging is fraught with difficulty. First enclose the tail lengthways in a bandage.

2 Lay strips of bandage along the length of the tail.

3 A wet towel, frequently changed, will help to cool the dog down and in a hot environment may help to prevent heat stroke.

panting, and an inability to breathe deeply enough indicated by a half strangled noise coming from the dog's throat. The dog's tongue looks swollen and blue.

Treat as an immediate emergency, and do not attempt to take the dog for veterinary treatment until you have started its resuscitation.

Plenty of cold water is the first-aid

treatment. Ideally, immerse the whole dog in a bath – use a cattle trough if there is one nearby. Bathe the dog all over with cold water, but especially drench its head; and keep doing it until the dog shows signs of easier breathing. Then take it to the veterinary surgeon. The vet will possibly put the dog on to an oxygen air flow, and will probably give it an injection to reduce the swelling in its throat, but unless the vet happens to be at hand, as he may be at a dog show, the life-saving treatment will have been given before the dog gets to the surgery.

3 Place the pad over the folded back ear.

4 Start bandaging around the neck from behind the ear and work forward, enclosing the affected ear, not too tightly.

5 The unaffected ear should not be included in the bandaging.

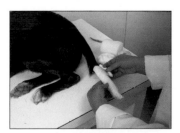

3 Bandage the tail around its length, whenever possible including some of the dog's tail hair within the turns of the bandage.

4 Cover the bandage with an adhesive dressing.

5 Take the adhesive dressing well above the end of the bandage and include strands of hair within each turn.

EXAMINING AND BRUSHING TEETH

1 Regular brushing will slow up the formation of plaque and tartar.

2 Some dogs will resent the use of a brush, but toothpaste on the end of a finger can be almost as effective.

3 Specially made dog toothbrushes are often well tolerated.

EXAMINING EYES

1 Take great care when administering eye drops or ointment. It is important to hold the dog's eyelids open so that the medication actually goes into the eyes.

2 After the drops have been put in, the eyelids must be gently massaged over the surface of the eye to encourage the spread of the medication.

Sick dogs must be kept warm, dry and comfortable. They may be encouraged to eat but never force fed. The dog should always have easy access to water.

SNAKE BITES, AND STINGS FROM OTHER VENOMOUS CREATURES

These are often difficult to recognize unless the bite is witnessed. The degree of urgency depends on the type of venomous creature, where on its body the dog was bitten, and the age of the dog. Small puppies are obviously more at risk than older, larger animals.

The only venomous British snake is the adder. The risk is greater in areas with certain types of soil – sandy downs seem to harbour more adders than most other areas. In the United States, Australia and Africa the most common snake bites in dogs are from the viperine snakes. Poisonous North American snakes include rattlesnakes and coral snakes.

Snakes are often more likely to bite when they come out to sun themselves on a warm spring day, and the dog goes to investigate. So the dog is most likely to be bitten on the face, head or neck.

If the dog's face starts to swell up while you are out on a walk, the chance of a snake bite must be considered. Unless the swelling starts to cause obvious breathing distress, treatment is urgent, but this is not a life-threatening emergency. You can afford to walk back to the car, no need to run, but make sure the dog walks quietly – exercise should be minimal. Carry a small dog. Take the dog straight to the

◆ RIGHT
Disturb an injured dog as little as possible, although be prepared to lift it carefully and take it to a veterinary surgeon immediately.

surgery. Very few dogs in Britain die from the effects of adder venom, but many each year have distressing abscesses caused by a combination of the venom and infection.

Bites from non-venomous snakes should be thoroughly cleaned as the snake's teeth may be carrying bacteria, which could cause infection.

The only reason to include snake bites in the first aid section is that there is a belief that the venom of a snake should be "sucked out" of the wound. Do not attempt to do so.

Bee and wasp stings carry a similar risk of death to snake bites – generally, they are only likely to be lethal if the swelling from the bite blocks the dog's airway. The exception to this is the case of multiple stings, the shock of which can cause the death of the dog. Such events are rare.

Venomous spiders are unknown in the United Kingdom and uncommon in the United States, although they do occur there. The Australian funnel spider, however, is an extremely venomous arachnid.

A single swelling from a bee or wasp sting does not usually require veterinary treatment, but home attention with a soothing cream will speed the dog's recovery, and possibly stop the "sore scratch" cycle.

CHOKING

Some dogs are inveterate pickers up of sticks and stones, or ball chasers. All carry the risk of getting an object stuck in the mouth or throat. A half swallowed ball may be an emergency by reason of a blocked airway. First aid may be a two-handed job. You could get bitten. If the dog seems to be choking, look in his mouth with

care. A block of wood to prevent him closing his teeth over your fingers can help, with one person holding the dog's head while the other looks into his mouth. If there is a ball in the dog's throat, try to lever it out with a fine rod rather than with your hand.

A frequent occurrence is that a piece of wood becomes wedged across the teeth, or between the back teeth. Treat removal with similar caution, using some sort of lever to remove it. This type of incident not infrequently requires a trip to the vet and sedation to remove the object.

WHAT TO DO IN A ROAD ACCIDENT INVOLVING A DOG

It is virtually certain that a dog involved in a road accident will not be under control. The first step, even before looking to see what may be wrong, is to leash the dog with whatever comes to hand. But you must do it without risk to yourself.

A noose needs to be made and slipped over the dog's head without actually touching the dog. The noose may be easily made from your own

dog's lead or any other line or even a piece of string.

The next step, unless the dog is obviously unconscious, is to muzzle the dog. Any dog that has been involved in a road accident is likely to be in shock, and even the most friendly can bite whoever is

Many road accidents and injuries to dogs may be avoided if the owner exercises the dog sensibly by restraining it with a lead.

♦ RIGHT
Large injured dogs may be carried with one arm at the front of their chest, under the neck, and the other looped through to allow the back legs to hang. A muzzle may be necessary.

moving an injured person, you are better to take the dog straightaway to the veterinary surgery than to wait while someone phones around to find a vet who can leave the surgery to attend the accident. There is no organized emergency ambulance service for animals.

Once the dog's mouth is bound and it cannot bite, it is almost always safe to carry the dog. If possible, let the affected leg hang free – you will avoid further damage, and pain.

Dogs in road accidents will often run away, despite serious injury. If you see this happen warn the police, who will at least be able to inform anyone who enquires about their missing dog.

Sometimes the police will accept immediate responsibility for the care of dogs involved in road accidents. If they are informed of an accident and are able to attend the scene, they will usually know the local veterinary surgeons and be able to advise on the vet's phone numbers.

attending it, through pain or through fear.

You are unlikely to be carrying a proper muzzle with you. Once again, a cord, or a dog lead, or a bandage can be used. Only once the dog is secure, and you are unlikely to be bitten, should you try to examine the dog.

If the dog is not conscious, do not try to resuscitate it – get it to the veterinary surgery as quickly as possible. If other people are there, ask someone to phone ahead to the surgery

to warn them that you are coming.

A coat or blankets may be used as a makeshift stretcher, but only a dog that is so badly injured that it is unaware of its surroundings is likely to tolerate being carried in this way.

If the dog is bleeding heavily, use whatever is available to make a pressure pad; bind the wound and take the dog to the surgery immediately.

If the dog is carrying a leg, or is limping, there may be a fracture. Despite the first-aid warning about not

MUZZLING AN INJURED DOG

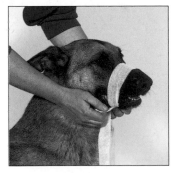

1 An improvised muzzle may be made with a bandage or almost any material. Make a loop, pass it over the dog's muzzle and under its chin.

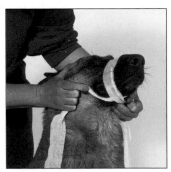

2 Take the ends of the material behind the dog's ears.

3 Tie the muzzle firmly behind the dog's head. An improvised muzzle must be tied tightly. It will not choke the dog.

✦ BELOW
If poisoning is suspected, take the container
and, if possible, some of its contents to the
veterinary surgeon with the dog.

✦ BELOW
Cigarettes are toxic to dogs and may cause
nicotine poisoning. Fortunately, few dogs will
eat cigarettes.

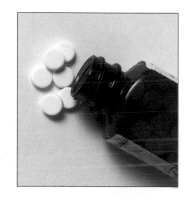

POISONING AND COMMON POISONS

The poisons likely to be encountered by a dog are almost always those found around the house and garden. They include tablets and medicines intended for human consumption, or not for internal use at all, household chemicals such as bleach or detergents, and garden chemicals.

Puppies will try anything. You must keep all potentially dangerous materials out of their reach, preferably in a locked cupboard.

If an accident does occur, and you think your dog has eaten something that could be poisonous, there are two things to do.

1 Make the dog sick. If this is to be of any help, it must be done before the poisonous substance has had a chance to be absorbed from the stomach, so do it before contacting your veterinary surgeon. But if you know your vet is immediately available for advice, and you are certain what it is the dog has eaten, do not make the dog sick until you have spoken.

The most effective substance to use to make the dog sick is washing soda. Put two small crystals on to the back of the dog's tongue, and make him swallow them by holding his mouth shut and stroking his throat. Vomiting will take place within minutes so be prepared with old newspapers at hand.

2 Contact your veterinary surgeon. Retain some of the poisonous substance, or at least its wrapping, to show him or her. There may be no ill effect, or immediate further treatment may be necessary.

Do not make the dog vomit if the toxic substance is already being absorbed, which occurs within thirty or so minutes of ingestion.

SOME COMMON POISONS

Rat poisons – all rat poisons are coloured to indicate the active substance. They are of low toxicity to dogs when used properly, but dogs may get hold of bulk quantities.
Blue: Anticoagulants
Brown: Calciferol
Green: Alphachloralose
Pink or Grey: Gamma-HCH (Lindane)
If rat poisoning is suspected, the package or some of the suspect material must be retained for examination by the veterinary surgeon.

Barbiturates – human sleeping pills.

Sodium Chlorate – weed killer.

Detergents – usually safe, but if concentrated may cause external lesions, or vomiting if swallowed.

Antifreeze – Ethylene glycol.

Lead – old paint chewed by dogs.

Slug bait – metaldehyde, attractive to dogs, now has anti-dog component.

Cigar and cigarette ends – nicotine

Organochlorine, Organophosphorus compounds – flea and lice killers.

Paraquat – herbicide.

Aspirin – taken in large quantity.

Strychnine – vermin killer, dogs may get at carcasses.

Toad – from mouthing the toad. Exotic toads are more venomous.

Tranquillisers.

INHERITED DISEASES

An inherited disease is one that may be passed from generation to generation through affected genes of the sire or the dam, or sometimes through a combination of both. Genetics, the study of inheritance, is a highly complicated science, becoming increasingly so the more we learn of the subject.

There are two main problems in the control of inherited diseases in dogs. Some diseases are partly inherited, and partly occur as a result of some environmental influence, often difficult to determine precisely. The inherited element may depend on several inherited factors rather than a single gene.

Typical of this type of disease is hip dysplasia, probably the most widely known of all inherited diseases of the dog. It is a hind-leg lameness, caused by severe erosion and damage to the hip joint.

It is generally considered that inheritance accounts for about fifty

◆ BELOW
This Irish Setter is free from the distressing condition of Progressive Retinal Atrophy (PRA), which responsible breeders are doing a great deal to eliminate in the breed.

◆ LEFT
Dalmatians may be tested scientifically for deafness before they are six weeks old.

per cent of the clinical signs of hip dysplasia, and that the remainder is caused by some environmental circumstance – the dog's weight, exercise, diet, perhaps – but precisely what is not known. In these circumstances, attempts at control are slow at best, depending on diagnosis of the disease and the avoidance of affected dogs in breeding. This may sound simple but is not.

The condition affects many breeds, mostly the larger ones, including the German Shepherd. Largely due to the efforts of German Shepherd breeders, control schemes have been operating in several countries for many years now. Progress has been real but is slow, and sometimes heartbreaking for breeders, who may have used a dog and a bitch that both have excellent "hip scores", only to find that the offspring are seriously affected.

The second problem is that the disease may not show itself until the affected animal is mature. The dog or bitch may well have been used in a breeding programme before any signs that it has the condition are seen. To some extent this may be overcome by control schemes that do not give certificates of freedom from the disease until the dogs in the scheme are old enough for the particular disease to have shown itself. Hip dysplasia is again an example: hip scoring is by an expert panel who examine X-rays of submitted dogs. These X-rays may not be taken until the dog is twelve months old.

There are several diseases that are known to be inherited in a straightforward way and are present at birth. These diseases can be controlled, depending for the success of the control scheme on the co-operation of the breeders, and their recognition that animals that show signs of the disease are actually afflicted, rather than the subject of

◆ BELOW
Until a specific gene test becomes practicable, it
is important that not only this pregnant bitch,
but the sire, have been certified healthy.

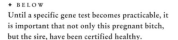

sale, not only for total deafness, but
for partial deafness in one or both
ears. There is evidence that partially
deaf dogs can pass on partial or
complete deafness to their offspring,
and the numbers of dogs being tested
are increasing rapidly in several
countries. The test for dogs originated
in the United States, which is probably
leading the world in this area.

Almost certainly, present studies of
the "genome", the genetic make-up, of
all species will result in a revolution in
the study and control of genetic
diseases. Once the precise positions of
inherited diseases on the DNA
molecule are known, specific action
may be taken to eliminate the
problem. This approach is no longer
pie in the sky. Within a very few years
DNA testing will become routine.

mysterious accidents that merely
mimic the condition.

The outstanding example of breeder
co-operation in control of inherited
disease must be the experience of
Progressive Retinal Atrophy, night
blindness, in Irish Setters. By the
involvement of nearly all the breeders,
and with recognition that the disease
had a straightforward inheritance
pattern, the condition has been
virtually eliminated from the breed.

Up-and-coming schemes include
one to control deafness in Dalmatians.
For many years, a proportion of
Dalmatian puppies have been born
deaf or partially deaf; but breeders
were generally only able to recognize
stone-deaf puppies, which were put to
sleep soon after birth.

Scientific testing, developed for use
in people, has now enabled breeders to
have their puppies examined before

◆ BELOW
The breeder carries a heavy burden
of responsibility to produce a
healthy, keen-to-please dog such as
this German Shepherd.

NEUTERING

The advantages of neutering both male and female dogs far outweigh the possible disadvantages, and overcome the specific problems associated with either sex. Neutered males do not wander, and neutered females do not come into season.

Fewer owners in Britain neuter their dogs than in America, where the operation is as routine as neutering cats in Britain. It is noticeable also that fewer male dogs than females are neutered. Females, of course, are at risk of having a litter.

Both dogs and bitches may be neutered at the age of about six months, and it is not necessary to wait until a bitch has had a first season before having her spayed. To a considerable extent, the earlier the dog is neutered, the less complicated the operation. Early neutering does not result in failure of the dog to mature

mentally; all the dogs bred by the Guide Dogs For The Blind Association are neutered before they reach the age of six months. There are several disadvantages to neutering. After dogs of some breeds have been neutered their coats become heavier and fluffy. This happens to breeds such as the Irish Setter and the Cocker Spaniel, both of whom have naturally silky coats. The extent of the problem varies. In some dogs it may be necessary to trim the coat.

A problem that may be associated with spaying the bitch is the development of urinary incontinence

in later life. This problem is easily cured by hormone replacement therapy, but it would still be sensible to discuss this possible problem with your veterinary surgeon before the operation. A research project currently underway may provide an answer. The problem does not occur after castration of the male.

Dogs and bitches often put on weight after being neutered. This need not happen. Dietary investigations suggest that neutered dogs have a lower nutritional requirement than entire (un-neutered) animals, possibly by as much as fifteen per cent. To avoid a dog putting on weight after it has been neutered, simply reduce its daily food ration. As with any weight-control regime, it is much easier to prevent the weight going on than to take it off once it's there. Weigh the dog regularly for a time after the neutering operation, until you have established that its weight is steady.

If you intend to keep more than one dog in your house, the situation is somewhat different. Two animals of opposite sexes will tend to live more easily together than two of the same, other than when the bitch comes into season. Two dogs kept together will tend to sort out their dominance once and for all, but two entire bitches are quite likely never to sort out their arguments, with problems tending to arise whenever one of them is coming into season.

Once you start to keep larger numbers you are likely to come across dominance problems that will have to be sorted out. Neutering has some effect on the control of dominance problems but should not be looked upon as the complete answer.

◆ RIGHT
One of the few genuine disadvantages of neutering is that it could cause the beautiful glossy coat of this Cocker Spaniel to become coarse and fluffy.

ALTERNATIVE MEDICINE

Modern conventional veterinary medicine is science based. It depends on research that produces repeatable results in the hands of competent scientific investigators, and it is subject to a considerable measure of official control with respect to safety and efficacy. The science-based approach to illness is essentially that of treating the root cause of the disease itself. Critics of this approach worry that too little attention is given to possible side-effects of potent medicines.

Holistic medical practitioners, typified by homoeopathic doctors and veterinary surgeons, regard the symptoms as essentially the reaction of the animal's body to the disease. They aim to treat the whole animal, rather than the symptoms of the disease alone.

Some alternative therapies are difficult to assess scientifically. For

◆ LEFT
Osteopathy may produce more satisfactory long-term results in musculo-skeletal problems in dogs than the continuous use of corticosteroids, with their risk of side effects.

HOMOEOPATHIC REMEDIES

Arnica – bruising, shock and after injury

Belladonna – aggressive behaviour, ear problems and acne

Cantharis – cystitis and kidney problems

Cocculus – travel sickness

Gelsemium – nervousness and timidity

Nux Vom – digestive upsets

Pulsatilla – irregular seasons

Rhus Tox – arthritis and rheumatism

Scutellaria – nervousness, apprehension and excitability

Sulphur – skin conditions

instance, the holistic approach may require an animal, with apparently the same set of symptoms as another, to be treated differently because it is perceived by the practitioner to have a different basic temperament.

HOMOEOPATHY

Homoeopathy is based on an ancient medical practice of treating "like with like". There are three basic principles:
1 A medicine that in large doses produces the symptoms of a disease will in small doses cure that disease.
2 By extreme dilution the medicine's curative properties are enhanced, and all the poisonous side effects are lost.

3 Homoeopathic medicines are prescribed by the study of the whole individual and according to basic temperament.

Conventional veterinary surgeons acknowledge that all side-effects are removed in extreme dilutions, and to that extent, homoeopathic medicines are safe. Many argue that to be safe, if ineffective, by reason of the absence of any therapeutic substance is a spurious safety. Despite reservations about homoeopathy, it is almost certainly the most widely applied form of alternative therapy.

Homoeopathic remedies are invariably given by mouth, including the homoeopathic equivalent of vaccines, known as "nosodes". The medicines are either in tablet or powder form, with no unpleasant taste.

A few veterinary surgeons use homoeopathy exclusively, while a number use it regularly as part of their armoury of treatment. They tend to select cases that they consider likely to respond better to homoeopathy than to conventional medicine, often the more chronic conditions in which conventional treatments can only suppress the symptoms, sometimes with undesirable side-effects.

Veterinary surgeons using homoeopathic medicine are usually known to their colleagues locally, who will happily refer patients to the appropriate practice on request.

ACUPUNCTURE

Acupuncture is another form of treatment with roots going back thousands of years. The practice originated in China.

Treatment involves the insertion of fine needles into the skin of the patient along what are known as "meridians", which bear no relationship to recognized nerve tracks. Application of the needles reduces pain considerably, sometimes to the extent that surgery can be carried out without the patient experiencing discomfort.

Although for many years it was assumed by western doctors that the effect was purely psychological, acupuncture appears to have definite analgesic properties in animals, rather giving the lie to the "purely psychological" claim.

Many dogs seem remarkably tolerant of the application of acupuncture needles, and there is a considerable body of empirical

evidence that it can have a beneficial effect on musculo-skeletal problems in dogs, as well as a less documented effect on other chronic diseases.

Acupuncture is a whole system of medicine in Chinese tradition, but in western veterinary medicine it's used as an auxiliary to other more conventional treatments.

There are few associations of veterinary acupuncturists, and practitioners of this skill in veterinary medicine are relatively uncommon. There are, however, sufficient vets with an interest in acupuncture to make it worthwhile asking your own veterinary surgeon for help if the occasion arises.

HERBALISM

Herbalism has probably the longest tradition of any system of medicine known to man. Plants have been used for their medicinal properties since time immemorial, and they have provided the basis of the modern pharmaceutical industry's research programmes since its foundation. Many modern drugs are derived from plant products.

It is inevitable that with a practice as steeped in antiquity as herbalism, different traditions have grown up in different parts of the world. For instance, there is a Chinese tradition, and Islamic influences in western herbalism are clearly marked.

Herbalists differ from conventional therapists in their use of the whole plant, or unrefined extracts of parts of the plant, rather than specific chemical entities isolated from the plant.

The best-known illustration of this difference in approach is the use of the foxglove plant. The foxglove (*Digitalis*

Liquorice root has mild laxative properties.

purpurea) was discovered to have a beneficial effect on some of the symptoms of heart disease many hundreds of years ago. An extract of the plant has been in use since the eighteenth century, but it has always been recognized as being dangerous in

COMMON HERBAL REMEDIES

Buchu – diuretic and urinary antiseptic

Cascara – laxative, bitter tonic

Cayenne – circulatory stimulant

Dandelion – liver problems

Elderberry – rheumatism, anaemia

Eucalyptus – bronchitis

Garlic – infections, worm infestations

Liquorice – anti-inflammatory, mild laxative

Peppermint – colic, travel sickness

Raspberry – reproductive problems

Rhubarb – constipation and diarrhoea

Skullcap – hysteria, anxiety

Valerian – colic, travel sickness, behavioural problems

overdosage. Pharmaceutical chemists were able to isolate active elements in foxglove extracts, which enabled them more accurately to prescribe the drugs for control of heart disease. But Digitalis, the original extract of foxglove, still has its adherents in medical practice, who prefer it to the more refined alternatives, suspecting that the process of refinement has removed some part of the efficacy of the original.

Compared with conventional medicine, herbalists have, once again, a more holistic approach, preferring to treat the whole animal rather than a specific disease.

Despite the holistic approach of the veterinary herbalists, some of their preparations have become so well established that they are regarded almost as conventional medicines. One remedy, available in Europe, with remarkable powers is rescue cream. This is a general salve that soothes and

Skullcap is a calming herbal remedy.

restores damaged skin. Its efficacy is at least comparable with many restricted, prescription-only skin preparations.

There are very few veterinary herbalists, but some countries have an official institute of medical herbalists, which could put you in touch with a practitioner.

AROMATHERAPY

Aromatherapy could be regarded as an offshoot of herbalism, in that the system uses extracts from plants, prepared as the essential oils of those plants, as a form of therapy. The oils are used either for massage or simply inhaled by a diffusion into the air, and are considered to be useful for a wide range of ailments. Aromatherapy is rarely used by veterinary surgeons, although some owners are sufficiently knowledgeable to be able to use the therapy as an adjunct to conventional medicine.

OSTEOPATHY

Veterinary osteopathy is now well established as a supportive therapy in veterinary medicine.

Osteopathy, as originally understood, held that most or all diseases are caused by displacement of bones and are curable by manipulation. It is doubtful if any practising osteopaths now adhere totally to this doctrine, but there is no doubt that manipulation can effect considerable improvement in a number of chronic-disease conditions. Musculo-skeletal problems in the dog seem to be particularly responsive to osteopathic manipulation. As with the insertion of acupuncture needles, dogs seem to tolerate osteopathy remarkably well, although some naturally unruly dogs may need sedation before treatment.

PHYSIOTHERAPY

Physiotherapists have long had an association with conventional medicine. Their approach is more scientifically based than traditional osteopaths, and their training and work is medically supervised. Physiotherapy treats illness by physical measures. It includes massage and manipulation, in which respect it is like osteopathy, but also uses heat, electricity, and passive or active exercise. It aims to restore the functions of joints and muscles.

Many physiotherapists are involved in veterinary medicine, but there is no specific association. Veterinary surgeons will usually know of a local physiotherapist with an interest in veterinary work, and will invariably be happy to refer a patient. Fractured legs on the mend often respond well to physiotherapy, which stimulates muscles and tendons that have tended to waste or lose their strength during the period of bone healing. Physiotherapy may be used in any circumstances where gentle manipulation is likely to improve mobility.

The leaves of the peppermint plant are mainly used for their effect on the digestive tract.

DOGS AND HUMAN HEALTH

✦ BELOW LEFT
The many advantages of association between children and dogs far outweigh the risk of cross-transmission of diseases. Sensible hygiene will almost always overcome the risks.

There are some diseases that may affect both dogs and humans. The technical term for such a disease is "zoonosis".

The most feared of these diseases is undoubtedly **rabies**, the reason for long-standing quarantine laws between the United Kingdom and all other countries, which have only recently been changed. The laws throughout the EU countries have now been dramatically relaxed for many domestic pets. It is now possible to acquire a "pet passport", which allows owners to bring their pet into Britain without them spending six months in quarantine kennels, as the old laws used to require.

The passport requirements are very stringent and include a full healthcheck by a vet, which includes up-to-date immunizations against rabies and many other diseases. Animals must also have an identification chip inserted, a photo, current certificates and pet insurance.

When travelling in an area that is not rabies-free, consult a doctor immediately if you are bitten by a dog or any other animal.

Fleas, common on dogs – most frequently actually the cat flea – will bite humans. It is unlikely that dog or cat fleas can survive on humans, so a few intensely itchy bites are the only likely problem. The presence of flea bites on you or your children is a timely reminder that flea control on your dog has, perhaps, not been as effective as you thought.

Rabbit mites frequently cause a skin rash in dogs. They are capable of biting humans, and may cause an itchy rash on the forearms from contact with the affected dog. The rash is unlikely to spread.

Ringworm is not a common disease in dogs but, when it does occur, precautions should be taken to avoid its spread to human members of the family. It is a true zoonosis and can establish itself on the human skin. Affected areas are again likely to be those of contact – the hands and forearms.

Toxocara, the most frequently encountered roundworm in puppies, and indeed almost universal in very young puppies, has been implicated in a rare specific type of eye disease in children. Roundworms that are ingested by a species other than their normal host may encyst and settle in almost any part of the body, but are known to invade the eye. These cysts have been known to cause blindness. Such an accident is extremely rare but,

✦ LEFT
Dogs should never be permitted to run freely where children may play because of the risk that they may deposit faeces.

✦ BELOW LEFT
Owners must always collect faeces deposited by their dogs.

✦ BELOW RIGHT
Many local authorities now provide dog litter bins. They are to be encouraged.

of course, a tragedy for the child and his or her parents if it happens.

Good hygiene and vigilance should prevent any child from coming in contact with dog faeces. Puppies must be wormed regularly, every three weeks until they are six months old. Their faeces must be collected, at home as well as on the street, and the puppy should be taught to defecate in a prescribed spot in the garden, not in a public place. If an accident does happen while you are out exercising your dog, scoop it up. Always go prepared. Legislation now covers fouling by dogs in public places, and "poop scoop" laws are in force in many areas.

Simple hygiene for children must be practised: they should wash their hands after playing with the dog. But children should not be discouraged – there is so much to be gained from a happy association between child and dog that, provided risks are minimized by adopting sensible precautions, their close companionship should be encouraged. Remember, the dog is our oldest friend.

✦ BELOW LEFT
Dogs should be discouraged from playing with the baby's toys.

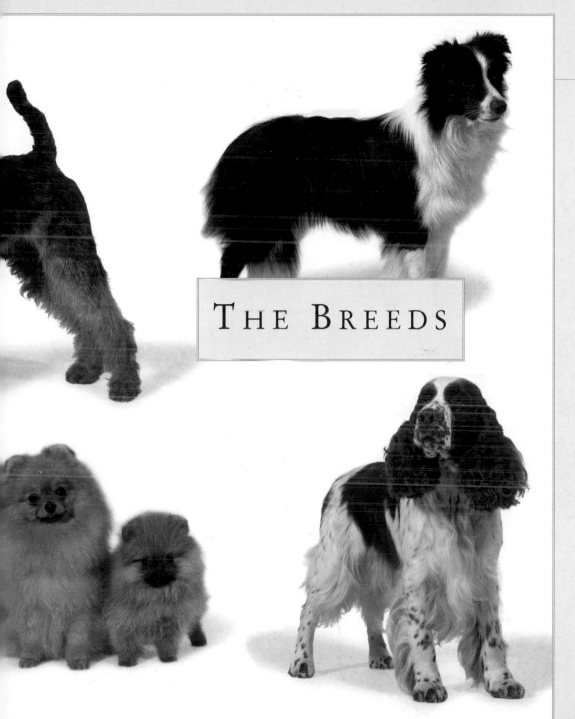

THE BREEDS

THE PEDIGREE DOG

The enormous number of different pedigree dogs recognized today are all derived from a creature that first associated with human beings many thousands of years ago. When humans found out how to light fires, the precursor of the dog must have been keen to share their warmth, and to also scavenge for left-over food. Humans soon realized that the dogs could be put to good use as assistant hunters, guards and companions. They would also soon have realized that some dogs were better at one job than another, so for breeding they selected the best for each task, and this, in a nutshell, describes everything that has happened since.

The classic prick-eared hunting hound seen for hundreds of years in the Mediterranean area, from Egypt and Malta to Ibiza and Tenerife, is still with us, virtually unchanged, in two breeds, the Ibizan Hound and the Pharaoh Hound. Most breeds trace their ancestry by much vaguer routes. The mastiffs of the world, for instance, possibly originated in Tibet and, over the centuries, moved with traders and seafarers through Asia and Europe, but the records of such movements are not clear. What can be stated at best is that most of the breeds that form pedigree dogdom in Britain, Europe and the USA today are of relatively recent origin – 200-550 years old. Some of them can only be traced back to the nineteenth century.

A pedigree is the written record of a dog's genealogy for at least three generations.

The barkless Basenji.

The German Wire-haired Pointer.

The Lakeland Terrier.

A purebred is a dog whose parents belong to the same breed and who share unmixed descent since the recognition of the breed.

THE GROUPS

Dogs are divided into six groups in Britain – Hounds, Gundogs, Terriers, Utility, Working and Toy. In the United States and some other countries dogs are divided into seven groups – Sporting, Hounds, Working, Terriers, Toy, Non-Sporting and Herding. Allocating breeds to a group is not always easy, and there are variations between kennel clubs in different countries. Such variations to the groupings used here are noted in brackets.

HOUNDS

As the name suggests, these are the hunting dogs. The so-called sight-hounds (Greyhound, Afghan Hound, Borzoi, Irish Wolfhound, Saluki, Whippet, Deerhound) do their chasing by direct sight, whereas the scent-hounds (Beagles, Bloodhounds, Bassets) use their noses on the ground to follow their target. The Finnish Spitz is unusual in that its purpose is to find birds, specifically the capercaillie, and to indicate to the hunter the bird's presence up a tree by standing by it and barking.

As a general characteristic, hounds tend to concentrate on the chase and not to listen to the entreaties of their owners to come back to base. They do not regularly figure in the placings in advanced obedience tests. They also have loud voices, which they are not averse to using.

GUNDOGS (SPORTING)

These dogs assist in finding and catching feathered and furry game. The group includes the setters and pointers, which indicate where birds are; the retrievers, which fetch shot birds, hare and rabbits; spaniels, which do both jobs; and a large number of breeds, most of them from the European mainland, which are collectively known as the Hunt, Point and Retrieve (HPR) breeds.

Gundogs tend to be kindly, gentle creatures, tractable and not noisy. They are not all suited to living in towns rather than rural areas, but they are capable of adapting to family life.

might be the "Companion Group". In the Utility group you will find the Bulldog, the Dalmatian, the Poodles, the Japanese Akita (Working), the Schnauzer, the Chow Chow and the Shih Tzu (Toy).

As a generalization, the term "companion" does indeed cover them all, but there are varying degrees of companionability, and these are discussed under the individual breeds.

TOYS

This is a group of small dogs, but they are not to be regarded as ladies' pets. The group includes such characters as the Chihuahuas, the King Charles Spaniel, the Yorkshire Terrier and the Japanese Chin. They are normally kept as pets, but they are clever and can be trained to perform in obedience tests; the Papillon is a good example. They are brave, as shown by the Pug and the

The French Bulldog.

The German Shepherd Dog.

The Belgian Griffon.

TERRIERS

This crowd are the rodent-operators of the canine world. They vary in size from the Airedale, the tallest, down through the Fox Terrier and the Lakeland Terrier, medium, to the West Highland White and Norwich Terrier, the shorter-legged varieties.

They are generally smart dogs, sharp in appearance and character; they are all vocal to a degree; and they make excellent pets as they adapt extremely well to castle or cottage.

UTILITY (NON-SPORTING)

This cosmopolitan bunch seems to include all the breeds that did not fit comfortably into any of the other groups. A more acceptable name

WORKING (WORKING, HERDING)

Working covers a multitude of breeds. There are guard dogs such as Boxers, Rottweilers and Bullmastiffs; herding breeds, such as Border Collies and Shetland Sheepdogs, which in the US form the Herding Group; and all-purpose breeds such as the German Shepherd Dog. Sizes range from the Great Dane to the Pembroke Corgi.

Temperament and trainability vary tremendously; the ranks of the Working Group include many breeds that make excellent household pets and obedience competitors. As a group it has expanded enormously in terms of the number of breeds since the middle of the twentieth century.

Pekingese; and they make wonderful companions, the Cavalier King Charles Spaniel being a favourite.

These groups include almost two hundred different breeds. The pedigree dog has its critics who tell us that mongrels are more intelligent, tractable and healthy, and that they outshine the purebred canines, but the great advantage of the pedigree animal is that it is much more predictable. If you mate two Golden Retrievers you will get Golden Retriever puppies.

In the following descriptions the height is always measured at the withers (shoulders). Heights and weights are given either as a range or an average.

The Hound Group

The temperament of any breed should be as important to prospective owners as size or appearance, although it is one factor that cannot be exactly described or standardized. Official Kennel Club breed standards do contain clauses under the heading "Temperament", but these describe the ideal. Included here are observed traits that may not always conform to the ideal.

What is accepted by most dog-minded folk is that hounds are basically hunters and have been bred to work over all kinds of terrain searching out different quarries. To take on any hound as a companion or family animal and expect it not to behave as a hunter is misguided. Some hound breeds can more readily be taught new tricks than others but it is never easy.

Some breeds in the Hound Group, such as the Beagle and the Whippet, are extremely popular, while others are virtually unknown and unobtainable outside their country of origin.

✦ FACING PAGE Deerhound

AFGHAN HOUND

+ LEFT
The Afghan is an ancient breed. It was discovered by the western world in the nineteenth century.

The Afghan, one of the most glamorous breeds, has a superbly elegant silky coat on an athletic frame, as befits a hunting creature originating in the mountains of Afghanistan.

The Afghan's expression is one of dignity and superiority, but he can have moments of hectic eccentricity, racing across garden or field.

Not inclined to heed the wishes of an exasperated owner unless handled with firmness as he grows up, this is a dog that is not for the uncommitted. Treating one casually will not lead to a happy relationship in the household.

More than capable of acting as a watchdog, the Afghan may use his powerful teeth on intruders if his warnings are not heeded.

In spite of standing over 70 cm (27½ in) at the withers, he is not a greedy feeder; in fact he may be a little finicky if allowed to have his own way. He is an athlete and needs a lot of exercise to cope with his restless energy.

BREED BOX

Size	medium-large
	dog: 70–74 cm
	(27½–29 in), 27 kg
	(60 lb)
	bitch: 63–69 cm
	(25–27 in), 22.5 kg
	(50 lb)
Grooming	frequent and
	thorough
Exercise	essential
Feeding	medium
Temperament	wary of strangers

The Afghan's silky coat will not look its best without constant care. It needs regular and thorough grooming, and any knots must be removed every day. The breeder from whom he is purchased will show the new owner how this is best done.

The Afghan is a dog for the true enthusiast who has the time and the patience to get the best out of a canine glamour star.

+ ABOVE
A shining silhouette that characterizes one of the most dignified of all the breeds.

+ ABOVE
The Afghan's eyes look straight through you, one of the truly glamorous expressions of dogdom; they seem to defy you to resist them.

BASENJI

The Basenji may originally have come from the Middle East, but is regarded as of Central African (Congo) derivation from some three hundred years ago. Certainly that is the area from which the breed was exported in the mid 1930s.

A neat dog of sharp outlines with stiffly upright ears, he has a square-frame standing around 43 cm (17 in) high, and ending with a tightly curled tail. He attracts a small but enthusiastic following with his gentle, friendly attitude. He has a questioning

+ LEFT
Sharp outlines on a neat dog, the Basenji is renowned for his cleanliness and for being odour-free.

BREED BOX

Size	small–medium
	dog: 43 cm (17 in),
	11 kg (24 lb)
	bitch: 40 cm (16 in),
	9.5 kg (21 lb)
Grooming	minimal
Exercise	reasonable
Feeding	undemanding
Temperament	intelligent,
	affectionate

look on his wedge-shaped face and a wrinkled brow; his curiosity is a real feature of his temperament.

He is known for the unusual fact that he does not give voice by way of a bark but has a yodel-type cry.

The Basenji's short, close-fitting coat is sleek and very easy to groom; he comes in variations of black and white, and red and white, with an

occasional tricolour, and he has a tendency to carry out his own grooming in the manner of a cat.

The Basenji's movement is clipped in style and suggests that he is quite tireless, although he does not require an excessive amount of exercise. He will not cost much to feed. All in all, he is a dog that will suit most households because he is thoroughly companionable.

+ LEFT
Poised to spring even from a lying position, the Basenji gives the impression of constant restlessness. He will hunt any form of vermin.

+ ABOVE
The Basenji is always alert, with a permanent frowning, quizzical expression.

BASSET FAUVE DE BRETAGNE

All the Bassets originated in France. They vary greatly in size, colour, shape and coat type. The Fauve is one of the shortest, standing around 35 cm (14 in) at the withers, but he is neater and has a more terrier-like appearance than his cousins.

Almost always a reddish fawn colour, he possesses a harsh and tough-textured coat. Strangely enough, he does need a bath more often than one might expect, because he is an expert at picking up the odd odour of the countryside!

The Fauve is a true hunter with a surprising turn of speed, especially if his sights are fixed on a retreating rabbit; like so many hounds, once into the chase, he may not heed his owner's call to return to base in a hurry.

A dog that really enjoys life and people, his small size makes him a natural for the growing family; he can be picked up by children. He is not a greedy dog but at the same time he is not choosy about the contents of his food-bowl.

◆ RIGHT
A harsh, tight coat on the Fauve makes him easy to groom wherever he hunts.

BREED BOX

Size	small 32–38 cm (12½–15 in), 16–18 kg (35–39½lb)
Grooming	relatively easy
Exercise	moderate
Feeding	undemanding
Temperament	busy and cheerful

GRAND BASSET GRIFFON VENDEEN

The Grand Basset Griffon Vendeen is another of the Basset family, and even in his native France is not numerous, which is a pity as he is a kindly, intelligent dog.

He stands up to 45 cm (18 in) at the withers on his tiptoes, and he is not a hefty hound. He is nimble and purposeful in his style of going and gives the impression of enjoying life to the full as long as he is given things to do. He will put his mind to all sorts of exercise that appeal to his sense of fun.

Like most of his type he enjoys his food, but he does not seem to object to being rationed to keep him trimly athletic. He has a rough coat that is basically white with lemon, orange, tricolour or grizzle markings; underneath the top-coat he sports a thick undercoat, so he is fairly weatherproof and easy to keep clean.

A breed that deserves popularity as long as it is not inbred any more than is inevitable with a small pool of breeding stock.

◆ BELOW
The GBGV has a merry disposition and takes to any sort of canine activity with enthusiasm.

BREED BOX

Size	small-medium maximum 45 cm (18 in), 18–20 kg (39½–44 lb)
Grooming	relatively easy
Exercise	essential
Feeding	undemanding
Temperament	friendly and humorous

BASSET HOUND

◆ BELOW
The Basset Hound is a cheerful character
even if his expression could be described as
lugubrious.

The Basset Hound is the best known of the Basset group, originating in France. His normal prey is the hare, which he follows in a persistent, lumbering fashion. He can break into a run, but his natural pace is steady over long distances.

In spite of the fact that he stands about 38 cm (15 in) at the withers, he weighs around 32 kg (70 lb), which makes him a big dog on short legs. If he has to be lifted into the car or on to the veterinary consulting-room table, he may present a problem to the slightly built owner.

He has a reasonably hearty appetite, which may lead him to put on an inordinate amount of weight, especially as he can be idle given the opportunity. As befits a hunting hound with a big chest, his voice is akin to the sound of a ship's foghorn. This can come as a distinct surprise to those in the immediate vicinity, but it should never give the impression that he is of an unfriendly disposition.

At first sight the Basset looks as if his skin was made for more dog than it contains, and there are a certain amount of wrinkles on his forehead. His most exaggerated feature is the length of his ears; this has been allowed to increase to the extent that he can tread on his ears with ease. As a result the flaps can be injured and their weight can cause problems by interfering with the circulation of air into the ear canal. The droop of his lower eyelids can also cause problems.

The Basset's forelegs tend to twist outwards below the wrist, and this may produce limb problems. His short smooth coat is easy to keep clean and wholesome even if he does rather enjoy rolling in various offensive-smelling farmyard and country substances.

The Basset Hound is for the enthusiast who wants to take on a canine companion of great character as a member of the family.

BREED BOX

Size	low-slung but heavy dog: 33–38 cm (13–15 in), 22.5 kg (50 lb) bitch: 33 cm (13 in), 19.5 kg (43 lb)
Grooming	relatively easy
Exercise	steady but necessary
Feeding	has a hearty appetite
Temperament	placid but loud

◆ RIGHT
The Basset Hound usually comes in black, white and tan, or in lemon and white. His coat is easily kept clean and tidy.

PETIT BASSET GRIFFON VENDEEN

The Petit Basset Griffon Vendeen, or PBGV as he is known to his multitude of admirers, has rapidly increased in popularity over the last 25 years, since he began to be exported from his native France. All French hounds are expected to be able to do their job, and this fellow is no exception. He is a bustler of a dog, seemingly never able to sit still. Hence he is for the active and tolerant only.

✦ LEFT AND BELOW
LEFT
Cheeky-faced PBGVs positively swarmed across the Channel between their native France and the UK in the mid-1970s, and it was not long before they migrated on to the United States.

BREED BOX

Size	small
	dog: 34–38 cm
	(13½–15 in), 19 kg
	(42 lb)
	bitch: 35.5 cm (14 in),
	18 kg (39½ lb)
Grooming	necessary
Exercise	essential
Feeding	reasonable
Temperament	happy and extroverted

The PBGV stands up to 38 cm (15 in) at the withers; his length is greater than his height, but not to an exaggerated degree – in other words, he does not suffer from problems with his intervertebral discs to any extent. On his sturdy, well-proportioned body he sports a rough, harsh top-coat with a thick undercoat, which together make him weatherproof. He is inclined to get muddy on his country rambles. He has lengthy eyebrows, so a curry comb is a good grooming tool. He needs good feeding to supply the energy that exudes from him at all times.

The PBGV is not a dog for a town-dwelling family that never visits the countryside.

✦ RIGHT
The Petit Basset Griffon Vendeen is a rough-and-ready breed, built to face all weather and ground conditions.

BEAGLE

As a breed, Beagles produce their puppies easily in reasonable numbers and seem to accept a life in kennels in philosophical fashion. As a result they have been bred extensively for use in medical/veterinary research laboratories, making them victims of their own super-friendly temperaments.

From the point of view of life as a member of a human household, they are similarly accommodating. They enjoy being part of a gang in much the same way as they make good team-members of a pack hunting hares. They are tidy creatures, although they are not always easy to housetrain. Their short waterproof coat makes them drip-dry in the foulest of weathers. Even after a day running across clay, a quick sponge-down soon makes them acceptable in the kitchen.

The Beagle is not greedy, though life in hunt kennels tends to make him swallow his daily ration fast. He is not prone to veterinary problems and lives to a reasonably ripe old age.

It is unusual to see a Beagle winning an obedience competition, as the breed has a tendency not to stay around for the recall once off the lead.

This is a breed that pleases families who lead active lives.

✦ RIGHT
Tough forelegs and tight feet make the Beagle able to last all day whatever the activity, in the field, the park or the garden, as long as there's human company.

✦ LEFT
Beagles are hunters with handsome muzzles designed to make a thorough job of sniffing out their quarry.

BREED BOX

Size	small 33–40 cm (13–16 in), 9 kg (20 lb)
Grooming	easy
Exercise	considerable
Feeding	reasonable
Temperament	genially stubborn

BLOODHOUND

The Bloodhound is a big dog with a mind of his own. As he stands some 66 cm (26 in) at the withers and can weigh up to 55 kg (121 lb), he is heavy. He is also clumsy, with a tendency to pursue his path regardless of obstacles such as ditches, walls and fences. Once on collar and lead, he may choose to take his handler on without great regard to physical or vocal opposition.

Most people will be familiar with the breed's appearance; the Bloodhound

+ ABOVE
The Bloodhound has a history as the number-one tracker of the canine world. His long ears are said to sweep scent from the trail up into his large nostrils.

+ RIGHT
His deep chest gives him good lung capacity.

BREED BOX

Size	massive dog: 63–69 cm (25–27 in), 41 kg (90 lb) bitch: 58–63 cm (23–25 in), 36 kg (79 lb)
Grooming	easy but extensive
Exercise	ponderous but considerable
Feeding	demanding
Temperament	requires understanding

has a super-abundant quantity of skin overhanging his eyes, and this is often accompanied by sagging lower eyelids. His ears hang low on his skull in pendulous folds, and these are said to sweep scents from the ground into his large nostrils and over his highly efficient olfactory mechanism.

His large body is supported by massive bones, but the bloodhound has suffered over the generations from

+ LEFT
The huge size of the dog requires solid bone. The Hound of the Baskervilles of Conan Doyle's book of the same name was supposed to be based on the breed.

hip-joints that cannot always take the strain of conveying him along head-down on the scent.

Bloodhounds eat massively and greedily. As with other breeds that have deep chests and wide bellies, the Bloodhound suffers from more than his fair share of a condition called bloat in which the gases in the stomach tend to be produced in great quantities. For various anatomical reasons these cannot be belched in the normal fashion and may lead to torsion of the stomach, which is rapidly fatal unless veterinary intervention is prompt.

The general advice is to feed small quantities several times a day and not to take a Bloodhound out for exercise on a full stomach. It is wise to ask a breeder offering puppies for sale about the incidence of bloat in the ancestry of sire and dam.

Bloodhounds, like most giant breeds, tend not to live to a ripe old age.

Most Bloodhounds are dignified and affectionate, but this is not a breed with which to take liberties as they can take exception to undue familiarity. Properly handled by those who are prepared to understand them, they are a fascinating breed to live with.

BORZOI

The Borzoi, as befits a hound from Russia that was dedicated to hunting wolves, is tall, aristocratic in bearing, and possesses a pair of impressive jaws. His height at the withers is a minimum of 74 cm (29 in), which makes him tall by anyone's standards.

+ BELOW
Borzois need these elegantly long and powerful jaws to snatch and hold wolves.

BREED BOX

Size	tall and elegant dog: 74 cm (29 in), 41 kg (90 lb) bitch: 68 cm (27 in), 34 kg (75 lb)
Grooming	regular and thorough
Exercise	moderate
Feeding	not excessive
Temperament	requires understanding

+ ABOVE
A gentle expression in the eyes belies the fact that the breed can have a slightly fierce temperament.

Added to his height is a lean head, shaped to give an impression of supercilious aristocracy, carried on an arched, longish neck that runs into well laid-back shoulders; all of which produces a superlative representative of the sight-hound group.

The silky coat varies in length over different areas of the body; it requires enthusiastic handling from an owner willing to learn from an expert.

These dogs are capable of running at tremendous speed but do not demand great amounts of exercise. A Borzoi does not have a large appetite, and is not particularly choosy. He is usually faithful to his owner and reasonably biddable.

The Borzoi gives the impression of being fond of people but it is wise not to take liberties with such a creature; he is capable, on occasion, of becoming dangerous if he is annoyed. Such behaviour is rare, but there is some suspicion that certain strains inherit a less than perfect temperament. It would be as well to look into this further before deciding to take on a Borzoi.

+ RIGHT
The immensely variable pattern of coat colours is one of the distinctive features of this noble Russian breed.

DACHSHUNDS

The Dachshund breed comes in six varieties. They vary in weight from under 5 kg (11 lb) in the case of the miniatures, to 9-12 kg (20-26½ lb) in the case of the standards. They also vary in coat-type being divided into Long-haired, Smooth-haired and Wire-haired versions.

✦ RIGHT
The Standard Smooth-haired – if any of the six varieties of Dachshund is to be considered the original, this is it. The body lines are neat and trim.

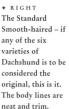

✦ LEFT
The depth of the chest between the front legs of this Standard Smooth-haired is very obvious.

✦ BELOW
The name Dachshund translates literally as badger dog and as such reveals its original use in following badgers to ground.

All six varieties are similar in body-shape, being low to the ground in order to be able to go to ground after their prey, which is generally considered to be the badger (although

✦ BELOW
The Standard Long-haired is the glamour dog of the sextet – same lines masked by silky hair.

BREED BOX

Size	small–medium Standard: 9–12 kg (20–26½ lb) Miniature: maximum 4.5 kg (10 lb)
Grooming	varies with variety
Exercise	reasonable
Feeding	undemanding
Temperament	independent

they will do an equally good job if required to go after a fox).

In the past all the varieties suffered from severe problems with their backs, basically because there was a tendency to breed for longer backs without due consideration being given to the musculature needed to cope with that structural build. Today there is a much better overall type, but it is wise to seek out breeders who can demonstrate a sound strain. Grooming of Smooth-haired and Wire-haired

✦ RIGHT
All versions should have a bold head carriage and an intelligent expression.

+ RIGHT AND FAR RIGHT
The head of all the varieties of
Dachshund tapers uniformly to the
tip of the nose.

varieties is straight-forward, but the
Long-haired has a soft, straight coat
that does need regular attention.

Exercise is accepted readily by all
six varieties, but they are not over-
demanding on the matter. From the
feeding viewpoint they are all also
undemanding good eaters.

Temperamentally they are sharp as
far as acting as sentinels around the
family premises and possessions is
concerned, and they will not hesitate to
use their teeth if pushed. They are loud
barkers, and the smaller sizes have a
tendency to yap, but they stop once the
intruder has been pointed out. They
make excellent companion animals and
deservedly attract a large following.

+ BELOW
The Wire-haired coat was developed to protect
these hunting dogs from thorn bushes and briar.

+ ABOVE
The Miniature
Dachshunds may
have been used to
follow smaller
animals to ground,
such as the rabbit,
the stoat and the
hare.

+ ABOVE LEFT
Breeding between
the different coat
types was banned
very early on in
Germany.

+ ABOVE
The Dachshund is an
affectionate and
companionable dog.

+ RIGHT
The Miniature Wire-
haired has a harsh
coat and a small
moustache.

DEERHOUND

✦ RIGHT
The Deerhound has been used to hunt
red deer for a thousand years.

The Deerhound (Scottish Deerhound) hails from Scotland and is in fact a Greyhound with a harsh and shaggy overcoat. It is said that he has hunted deer for a thousand years, and ancient depictions of him suggest that he has altered little over the centuries. He appears to capture the heart of all who fall under his spell, but in return he demands great loyalty.

He stands 76 cm (30 in) and weighs around 45 kg (100 lb), so he is not a lightweight, but he has a surprising ability to curl up in a corner and not get in the way, even in a small house. He is not a big eater and gives the impression that ordinary oatmeal would be welcome along with the venison.

Grooming should be regular but is not a chore as the harshness of his shaggy coat renders him relatively easy to keep tidy.

As far as his temperament is concerned he is a friendly, faithful creature with a dignified attitude to strangers. One of the most venerated among his breeders travels with a team of Deerhounds from the outer regions of mid-west Scotland to shows all over Britain and does so by train, which must say something about the breed's charm and adaptability.

BREED BOX	
Size	medium–large dog: 76 cm (30 in), 45.5 kg (100 lb) bitch: 71 cm (28 in), 36.5 kg (80½ lb)
Grooming	moderate
Exercise	moderate
Feeding	medium
Temperament	highly companionable

✦ ABOVE
The shaggy coat comes in mainly
pastel shades, from grey through
brindle to fawn.

✦ ABOVE
A narrowish front shows the depth of
chest displayed by all sight hounds.

ELKHOUND

The Elkhound (Norwegian Elkhound) hails from Norway where he hunts the elk, known as the moose in the US. The hound has to be solidly built to take on such a large form of quarry. The attitude of the Norwegians to this native breed is that he should be nimble, quick and courageous whether he is destined for the hunt or is to become a household companion. He fulfils these dual expectations.

✦ LEFT
Elkhounds are solid, and their legs and feet must be powerful to carry them.

✦ BELOW AND FAR LEFT
As well as being powerfully built to cope with hunting elks, Elkhounds need the intelligence demonstrated by these bright, sensitive eyes and sharp ears.

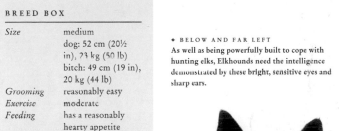

Within the group, the spitz types have pricked ears and tails that curl up over their backs. The Elkhound is a true spitz; he has another characteristic of the type – a loud voice, which he enjoys using. He is basically friendly, but intruders could be forgiven for doubting it.

The Elkhound's coat, which is basically grey, makes him weatherproof. It is a delight to clean by sponging off the worst mud, letting it dry and then brushing it vigorously.

He stands around 52 cm (20½ in) at the withers, and his body is solidly chunky at 23 kg (50 lb). To keep his powerful shape he eats well and may need careful rationing. Elkhounds tend to live to a ripe old age and are a good choice for the active family.

FINNISH SPITZ

✦ BELOW
The Finnish Spitz's outline is as
sharp as his hearing.

The Finnish Spitz (Non-sporting
Group) is the national dog of Finland,
and the Finns are very fussy about his
appearance, which is very striking. He
is bright red in colour and in early
puppyhood looks like a fox cub.
When he grows up he has stiffly
pricked ears and a tail that curls up
over his back. His coat is easy to
clean off and brush up.

He grows to a maximum of 50 cm
(20 in) but weighs at best a mere 16 kg
(35 lb). He is a pocket-sized athlete,
the nearest thing to perpetual motion,
and he loves to be part of a pack. He is
used in Finland to search out the
whereabouts of birds, most
particularly the capercaillie (a large
grouse), and is the only member of the
Hound Group whose objective is a
bird. His reaction to a successful hunt
is to tell the world in a strident voice,
which he also uses at home.

The Finnish Spitz is not greedy; he
lives a reasonably long life, giving joy
to his friends; and he expects to be
part of the household. In other words
he is a healthy extrovert and considers
that those who own him should be
similarly healthy and extrovert.
Whether the neighbours would agree
is a point to be considered.

BREED BOX	
Size	small-medium dog: 43–50 cm (17–20 in) bitch: 39–45 cm (15–18 in), 14–16 kg (31–35 lb)
Grooming	easy
Exercise	moderate
Feeding	undemanding
Temperament	noisy, needs understanding

✦ LEFT
He has a loud voice which he uses often – this is
a very characteristic pose.

✦ ABOVE
That appealing look will change quickly if
you relax.

FOXHOUND

The Foxhound (English Foxhound) rarely appears in the show-ring other than as a member of a pack. He is only likely to be a household dog while being "puppy-walked" on behalf of an official pack of Foxhounds, but this

BREED BOX	
Size	medium 64 cm (25 in), 30.5 kg (67 lb)
Grooming	minimal
Exercise	considerable
Feeding	has a very hearty appetite
Temperament	a friendly pack animal

does not mean to say that he cannot live his whole life as family dog.

A Foxhound may stand up to 64 cm (25 in) at the withers and is solid muscle and bone. He needs a great deal of food and is not fussy

about the form in which it reaches his food-bowl. He disposes of the daily ration rapidly as behoves a dog that has for generations had to race his pack-mates.

A friendly dog, he adapts to life on a collar and lead very well. He can be taught civilized behaviour, but selection over the centuries to produce the ultimate fox-finder has also bred out those dogs that are not keen on the chase. An appearance in a high-standard obedience competition is unlikely.

There is also an American Foxhound, which is taller and lighter than the English version. It evolved from the first English pack that went to America in about 1650.

GRAND BLEU DE GASCOIGNE

The Grand Bleu de Gascoigne is yet another native of France. He is best described as lanky as he stands up to 70 cm (27½ in). His devotees refer to him as having an aristocratic head style, and his low-set, fine ears are long enough to sweep the ground and

BREED BOX	
Size	medium-large maximum 70 cm (27½ in), 32–35 kg (70½–77 lb)
Grooming	minimal
Exercise	necessary
Feeding	not excessive
Temperament	gentle and acceptable

push scent into his nostrils while he is hunting his natural prey, the hare.

He is possessed of a deep, melancholy, baying voice. His coat is smooth and easily groomed. Black-mottled on a white base, it gives him an overall bluish tinge, hence his name.

With his obvious length of leg he is no slouch when he wants to run, but he has a reputation for lacking energy, not a characteristic which normally applies to a hound. He is a companionable dog, and he need not be costly to feed. Time will tell how popular he becomes.

GREYHOUND

The Greyhound is, of course, the template for what are collectively known as the sight hounds. There is a physical difference between those Greyhounds that course hares and those that are seen in the show-ring, but they all have the same instincts. The adult dogs retired from chasing the electric hare make wonderful family pets, but retain their instinct

♦ RIGHT
The Greyhound is
the fundamental
sight hound – lithe,
muscular, deep-
chested and tight-
footed.

♦ LEFT
With a searchlight
eye and unwavering
gaze, the Greyhound
is also known as a
gaze hound.

to chase. This can well mean that they may not be popular if let off the lead in public parks while surrounded by other dogs. Fortunately, though, they are easy to clean up after a long ramble down muddy lanes.

They stand as much as 76 cm (30 in) high, and they can be surprisingly heavy for such a sleek dog. Their appetites are not excessive, but exercising them is fairly demanding if they have to be kept on a lead – owners need to be fit to walk fair distances each day.

A healthy Greyhound is beautifully proportioned and a fine sight, although as in all breeds of similar style, the pups go through a gawky, loose-limbed stage.

BREED BOX	
Size	medium-large 71–76 cm (28–30 in), 36.5 kg (80½ lb)
Grooming	minimal
Exercise	essential
Feeding	medium
Temperament	affectionate and even-tempered

♦ LEFT
All colours – red, white and blue – are in favour. Anything goes as long as it is fast.

♦ RIGHT
The Greyhound is an ancient breed that may have originated in the Middle East.

HAMILTONSTOVARE

The Hamiltonstovare is alternatively known as the Swedish Foxhound. There is considerable similarity in type between this breed and the English Foxhound.

In his native country the Hamiltonstovare is a very popular hound indeed. He has a style of his own with the mixture of black on his back and neck, and his mainly rich

◆ BELOW LEFT
A white blaze down the centre of the skull and around the muzzle is the typical head-marking.

◆ BELOW
The Hamiltonstovare presents a wonderful contrast of colours in a classic pattern.

BREED BOX

Size	medium
	dog: 50–60 cm
	(19½–23½ in)
	bitch: 46–57 cm
	(18–22½ in)
	23–27 kg (59½ lb)
Grooming	easy
Exercise	necessary
Feeding	medium
Temperament	even-tempered

He has an appetite to go with his lifestyle, and he does not cause too much difficulty being cleaned up after a country ramble in mid-winter. He makes a thoroughly good canine companion for an energetic family.

brown head and legs. The white blaze on his head, down his neck, coupled with white paws and tail-tip make him instantly recognizable.

He stands around 57 cm (22½ in) at the withers, but he does not have quite as much body substance as the English version. He is a hunter with the same urgency in the chase as many other hounds; as such, he is truly a dog for the countryside, but he is very civilized if circumstances force him to become a temporary town-dweller.

◆ LEFT
Although the Hamiltonstovare is just that touch lighter framed than the English Foxhound, note the same classic white paws and tail-tip.

HARRIER

✦ BELOW
A good nose with well opened nostrils is
essential for this scent hound.

The Harrier is one of those breeds
that has been written about for
centuries. He is basically a hare-
hunter, and enthusiasts speak about
him as a specialist bred for the job.
The breed is rarely seen in Britain,
and no official standard is lodged
with the Kennel Club. In the United
States it is officially recognized,
but has no great show record.

BREED BOX	
Size	medium 48–53 cm (19–21 in), 22–27 kg (48½–59½ lb)
Grooming	easy
Exercise	necessary
Feeding	medium
Temperament	mild and kindly

✦ BELOW
A typical hound breed specifically selected
to chase the straight-running hare.

The Harrier stands in height
between the Beagle and the Foxhound
and in general terms has some of the
characteristics of both. Physically and
mentally he leans more toward the
Foxhound, as his whole inclination is
to hunt and chase. For anyone keen to
domesticate one of these dogs the best
advice is to resist the temptation.

✦ ABOVE
The origins of the old Harrier breed are
unknown, but today's dogs are thought to have
been derived from the English Foxhound by
selective breeding.

IBIZAN HOUND

The Ibizan Hound, from the Balearic Islands of the Mediterranean, is typical of the hounds portrayed in ancient art on all manner of Egyptian scrolls and friezes. He will hunt anything, from squirrels to deer, tirelessly with scant regard for the imprecations of a frustrated owner.

A finely structured dog, he does not carry much flesh. He comes in varying mixtures of white, chestnut or tawny. His coat is usually smooth, but occasionally a rougher coat is seen, sometimes only in the form of a moustache or other facial hair, which gives him a very different, slightly amusing, appearance. In either coat he feels the cold and is unsuited to living outside.

He needs good, regular feeding to ensure at least a minimal layer of fat over his ribs is maintained.

BREED BOX	
Size	medium 56–74 cm (22–29 in), 19–25 kg (42–55 lb)
Grooming	easy
Exercise	essential
Feeding	medium
Temperament	reserved and independent

SEGUGIO ITALIANO

The Segugio Italiano, also known as the Italian Hound, has been exported from his native Italy only in recent years and is not yet established in any numbers in other countries.

He stands some 59 cm (23 in) at his tallest, but there is considerable variation. He has a short coat that can be harsh or smooth, and in neither would he be difficult to groom. He is not a greedy feeder. His colour range includes black and tan and deep red through to cream.

He is generally lightly built with good musculature as befits an active hunter of considerable stamina. His temperament can be even, but early

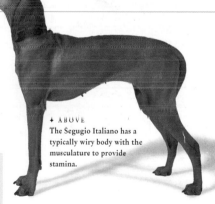

BREED BOX	
Size	medium 52–58 cm (20½–23 in), 18–28 kg (39½–62 lb)
Grooming	undemanding
Exercise	necessary
Feeding	medium
Temperament	even

exports were not enthusiastic about being handled by strangers; things are reported to have improved, but it would still be advisable not to take one on without careful research among breeder enthusiasts, of whom there are nowadays a handful in most countries.

IRISH WOLFHOUND

The Irish Wolfhound is the largest breed of dog known, if not necessarily the heaviest. A magnificent creature, he is well proportioned even for a dog that may reach 86 cm (34 in) in height and weigh a minimum of 54.5 kg (120 lb). His expression of quiet authority and his rough, harsh coat give him a look of invincibility, while

✦ LEFT
This is the largest breed of dog, but there is no air of menace, even if those jaws are believed to have cleared Ireland of wolves.

his attitude towards people is kind.

He adapts to living under most circumstances, but those who own him must reckon with the problems of transporting or lifting a dog of these dimensions, especially if he is immobilized by illness or injury. This is another breed prone to suffer from bloat, and the feeding regime must be strictly observed to prevent it.

Rearing puppies of giant breeds is a skill in itself, and the advice of an intelligent, caring breeder should be followed closely. Growth is rapid, but over-feeding can cause as many

BREED BOX	
Size:	giant dog: minimum 79 cm (31 in), 54.5 kg (120 lb) bitch: minimum 71 cm (28 in) 40.9 kg (90 lb)
Grooming:	regular
Exercise:	regular
Feeding:	very considerable
Temperament:	gently dignified

problems as too low an intake, as can any tendency to over-exercise during the Wolfhound's youth. In adulthood he will enjoy long rambles in the country, and he can achieve surprising speeds. The breed does not live to a ripe old age, but Irish Wolfhounds are such delightful dogs to live with that their devotees accept this with resignation.

✦ RIGHT AND ABOVE
This massive creature illustrates the range of chest and body sizes seen among the sight hounds.

NORWEGIAN LUNDEHUND

The Norwegian Lundehund, rare outside the Scandinavian countries, is a lightly built, spitz-type standing some 38 cm (15 in) high.

The Lundehund has a curious history. He comes from an island off the coast of Norway, and by a process of self-selection over the years he has developed the ability to climb cliffs so that he can raid puffins' nests for their eggs. This process of adaptation has resulted in him having six toes on each of his feet. The feet are turned slightly outwards, presumably to help the dog to climb the cliffs.

BREED BOX

Size	small
	38 cm (15 in)
Grooming	reasonable
Exercise	moderate
Feeding	simple
Temperament	alert and lively

◆ ABOVE
The Norwegian Lundehund's curious doubled dew-claw arrangement is particularly noticeable on the hind feet.

◆ LEFT
This attractive, though rare, breed has a gentle expression and a very appealing head.

PHARAOH HOUND

The Pharaoh Hound is surely the original Egyptian-style hound seen in temple friezes, albeit the breed now comes from Malta. A handsomely rich tan in colour with minimal white on his chest and extremities, he stands up to 56 cm (22 in) tall, not a large member of the sight-hound set by comparison with the Greyhound. This is a thoroughly tidy dog that has become reasonably popular since the early 1970s.

His short, smooth coat is extremely simple to groom but does not give much protection against the cold. He loves his exercise, is a superb mover, and is more likely to return on command than some hounds. In spite of his athleticism he is not a greedy dog.

BREED BOX

Size	medium
	20–25 kg (44–55 lb)
	dog: 56 cm (22 in)
	bitch: 53 cm (21 in)
Grooming	easy
Exercise	medium
Feeding	reasonable
Temperament	alert and intelligent

◆ LEFT
This could have come from the frieze of a temple in the Nile valley, so little has this breed altered in thousands of years.

◆ LEFT
He has the characteristic prick ears and light body of a Mediterranean hound, but the penetrating eyes show why this breed is one of the sight hounds.

OTTERHOUND

The Otterhound is a big-boned, shaggy dog that stands 67 cm (27 in) at the withers. He turns the scales at a minimum of 40 kg (88 lb), so he has a considerable presence. In 1978, after the hunting of otters became illegal in Britain, the breed was thrown a lifeline by the Kennel Club, which registered it as a separate breed. They have been

◆ LEFT
Otterhounds are no longer allowed to chase otters in Britain, so they plunge up and down rivers and streams after mink.

BREED BOX	
Size	medium-large
	dog: 67 cm (27 in),
	40–52 kg (88–115 lb)
	bitch: 60 cm (24 in),
	45.5 kg (100 lb)
Grooming	fairly demanding
Exercise	essential
Feeding	considerable
Temperament	even-tempered

registered in the US since the early twentieth century.

Otterhounds seem to amble somewhat casually, and they give the impression of being extremely laid-back in their behaviour. Owners should have a love of exercise and a relaxed view about dogs bringing twigs, mud and the like into the kitchen after a family outing.

The Otterhound is a typical pack-hound in some ways, but unusual in being shaggy, massive and well attuned to the role of a house-dweller.

◆ BELOW
The Otterhound's imposing head has intelligent, gentle eyes, and jaws capable of a powerful grip on his prey.

◆ RIGHT
At his smartest the Otterhound is still not stylish, but his genial character and adaptability make him a good choice for an energetic family with space to spare.

RHODESIAN RIDGEBACK

+ BELOW
Rhodesian Ridgebacks are bold dogs that know
no fear and have the physique to back that
attitude.

The Rhodesian Ridgeback is a solidly
built upstanding dog of considerable
presence. He is characterized by a
dagger-shaped ridge of hair along his
back from his withers to just above his
tail-root, which gives him his name.

In his native country he is a guard
dog, and his height at close to 67 cm
(26 in) coupled with a very solid frame
make him extremely powerful. His

BREED BOX

Size	medium-large dog: 63–67 cm (25–26 in), 36.5 kg (80½ lb) bitch: 61–66 cm (24–26 in), 32 kg (70½ lb)
Grooming	simple
Exercise	necessary
Feeding	fairly demanding
Temperament	aloof and dignified

quarry as a hound includes lions, and
his dignified bearing suggests that he
would not flinch from the task.

Without a difficult coat to keep
clean, he will appeal to those who want
an impressive canine member of the
household. Nobody in their right
mind would contemplate breaking
into a house in the knowledge that
there was a Rhodesian lurking within.

He enjoys his exercise and his food;
and he makes a handsome companion.

+ ABOVE LEFT
The Rhodesian's expression sometimes gives the
impression of being able to hypnotize.

+ BELOW
While these puppies are charming, they will
grow into large, powerful dogs. With their
ancestry as hunters and guards, it may not be
wise to choose one as a first dog or as a
companion for small children.

SALUKI

The Saluki or Gazelle Hound is a dog of Middle Eastern origin. He is an elegant creature coming in a variety of colours, from white through cream and golden red to black and tan and

+ RIGHT
The Saluki was much prized by the Arab sheikhs, who bred them as hunters to pursue wildlife over all manner of terrain.

BREED BOX	
Size	medium
	dog: 58.4–71 cm
	(23–28 in), 24 kg
	(53 lb)
	bitch: 57 cm
	(22½ in), 19.5 kg
	(43 lb)
Grooming	essential
Exercise	demanding
Feeding	demanding
Temperament	very sensitive

+ ABOVE
The Saluki is a sight hound, and those soft eyes are far-seeing.

tricolour. He sports a smoothly silky coat that carries longer feathering on the backs of his legs and also from the upper half of his ears. He stands as tall as 71 cm (28 in) at his withers, but he is lightly built, carrying very little fat – the dividing line between accepted and under-nourished is sometimes hard to assess. In spite of this he has great stamina in the chase.

His expression suggests he is looking into the distance, and he certainly has very acute sight. He is not a dog for a rough-and-tumble family as he is sensitive to loud voices and vigorous handling. He is admittedly highly strung, but his devotees rate him as extremely faithful to those whom he trusts.

+ RIGHT
This is a lightly built breed in which speed is of the essence, hence those powerful thigh muscles. The feet are long, especially the middle toes, which makes the dog unusual.

SLOUGHI

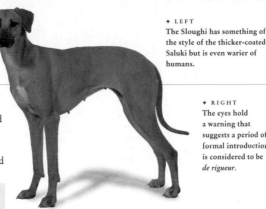

+ LEFT
The Sloughi has something of the style of the thicker-coated Saluki but is even warier of humans.

The Sloughi (pronounced "sloogi"), from North Africa has been described as a smooth-coated version of the Saluki, but in fact he is a separate breed, although of similar purpose and

+ RIGHT
The eyes hold a warning that suggests a period of formal introduction is considered to be *de rigueur*.

BREED BOX

Size	medium
	12.5–13.5 kg
	(27½–30 lb)
	dog: 70 cm (27½ in)
	bitch: 65 cm
	(25½ in)
Grooming	easy
Exercise	necessary
Feeding	undemanding
Temperament	indifferent to strangers

from the desert where he is known as a tireless hunter.

This is another breed that has never achieved great popularity. Most of those seen outside their native lands have not demonstrated the elegance that they are reputed to exhibit. There is a tendency to try to keep them lean to a degree that suggests under-nutrition.

Standing up to 70 cm (27½ in) at the withers, the Sloughi varies in colour from fawn through sable to black with tan points. His temperament with his owners is affectionate, but he has little regard for strangers. It would be as well to make careful enquiries of breeder experts before deciding to own one.

WHIPPET

The Whippet has achieved great popularity and justifiably so; he is intelligent, beautiful, gentle and easy to care for. Neat and tidy, with a magnificent turn of speed for such a

BREED BOX

Size	small
	(27½–30 lb)
	12.5–13.5 kg
	dog: 47–51 cm
	(18½–20 in)
	bitch: 44–47 cm
	(17–18½ in)
Grooming	easy
Exercise	average
Feeding	undemanding
Temperament	gentle and affectionate

small dog – 51 cm (20 in)– he is built on true sight-hound lines.

He walks close to his owner's heel, hardly ever any distance away, whether it is on a stroll down a country lane or on a purposeful walk to the local shops. He seems to fascinate all strata of owners, and his amicable temperament disguises his ability to hunt superbly.

His coat is fine and close in texture, and he comes in almost every colour mixture imaginable, with a range from

+ ABOVE
The Whippet is the smallest of the true sight hounds and one of the fastest movers.

solid colours to patches of all descriptions. He does not cost the earth to maintain, he is not a fussy eater, and temperamentally he has few equals as he seems to love people.

+ LEFT
The Whippet, one of the most companionable of all the hounds, comes in a great range of colours.

The Gundog (Sporting) Group

Dogs from the Gundog Group (Sporting) are the most recognizable of all
the breeds. The purpose of every breed in the group is to assist in hunting and
retrieving game, be it furred or feathered.

Common points include their very easy-going temperaments (although there
are slight variations) and the fact that they do not make much noise.

They range in size from the setters at 70 cm (27½ in) down to the Sussex
Spaniel at 41 cm (16 in).

One characteristic that is seen in several breeds is that the strains that are
most successful in the shooting-field are not necessarily very similar to those
that find favour in the show-ring. It would be wise to ask the breeder about this
if you are buying for a particular purpose. However, a high percentage of
gundogs of every strain retain the intelligence and willingness to please for
which they were originally selected.

◆ FACING PAGE **Pointer**

BRACCO ITALIANO

◆ LEFT AND BELOW
The Bracco's lugubrious expression is the result of an original crossing of hound and gundog (sporting) types. This is a multi-purpose dog that will fetch and carry for as long as he is asked to do so.

The Bracco Italiano originated in Italy in the early part of the eighteenth century. A mixture of hound and gundog (sporting), the original aim was to produce a pointing animal. In fact, today he is a multi-purpose dog and is used as a hunt, point and retrieve (HPR) breed. The Bracco Italiano arrived in Britain in very small numbers in the early 1990s, and Kennel Club registrations do not suggest that he is gaining in popularity. The same is true in other countries.

He measures around 67 cm (26½ in) at the tallest and has a fairly solid head and body. His fine glossy coat varies in colour from orange and white to red and white. He is an attractive looking dog and easy to clean up after a day's work in the field. He is reasonably independent for a gundog, but he is nonetheless a good worker.

His suitability as a household or family dog remains unproven.

BREED BOX	
Size	medium-large 56–67 cm (22–26½ in), 25–40 kg (55–88 lb)
Grooming	easy
Exercise	necessary
Feeding	medium
Temperament	gentle

BRITTANY

The Brittany is a relatively recent emigrant from his native France. A lively, handy-sized breed, standing some 50 cm (19½ in), the Brittany is an HPR capable of carrying hare and pheasant.

He has a flat, dense coat with a slight wave, so he is not difficult to clean up. His distinctive colour is mainly white with orange, liver, black or tricolour mixed in. He is not expensive to feed, but he can be greedy so needs some rationing. Square-built, with a relatively short neck, his tail, which he wags enthusiastically, is usually docked short. He makes a cheerful, tractable family member and revels in exercise and work.

◆ LEFT
The Brittany is a superb setting and flushing dog as well as a retriever. It is a popular sporting breed in North America.

◆ ABOVE RIGHT
The Brittany comes in all sorts of colours and patterns.

BREED BOX	
Size	small dog: 48–50 cm (19–19½ in), 15 kg (33 lb) bitch: 47–49 cm (18½–19 in), 13 kg (28½ lb)
Grooming	relatively easy
Exercise	essential
Feeding	undemanding
Temperament	energetic and busy

ENGLISH SETTER

The English Setter is a tall, handsome creature of comparatively slight build. He gives the impression that he knows he is attractive and intends to be noticed by all and sundry. As he stands 68 cm (27 in) tall, he is easily seen; he has a gloriously long, silky coat that can be a mixture of black, orange, lemon or liver with white. Like all such coats, it requires dedication to keep it clean after a day's work. The breed has a long, lean aristocratic head set on a long muscular neck.

The English Setter can be trained to work in the field with speed and intensity, quartering large tracts in search of pheasant, partridge or grouse; once his relatively long nose recognizes an exciting scent he comes to a rapid stop and setts on to the object. The sight of well-trained setters at full gallop suddenly screeching to a halt is, to say the least, memorable. There is no huge difference in shape and style between the show and working strains, but hunters have selected more for brains than beauty.

As a family dog the English Setter is a natural because of his friendly nature; however, he has a wildish streak in his make-up, even if it is not as marked as in his Irish counterpart. He needs a firm, calm hand to turn him into a house-dog, and he is not ideally suited to life in the suburbs. That said, he has a host of urban-dwelling admirers who will disagree with this personal verdict.

◆ LEFT AND FAR LEFT
The English Setter has, over the years, been bred in large numbers by top breeders who have produced their own very characteristic styles, but the soft eyes are obvious in all strains.

BREED BOX

Size	large
	dog: 65–68 cm
	(25½–27 in),
	28.5 kg (63 lb)
	bitch: 61–65 cm
	(24–25½ in), 27 kg
	(59½ lb)
Grooming	demanding
Exercise	demanding
Feeding	reasonable
Temperament	a friendly enthusiast

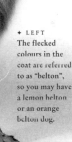

◆ LEFT
The flecked colours in the coat are referred to as "belton", so you may have a lemon belton or an orange belton dog.

◆ ABOVE
A pose adopted by so many dogs when waiting for the owner to suggest a bit of action.

GERMAN SHORT-HAIRED POINTER

The German Short-haired Pointer (GSP) has only been seen in Britain since the early 1950s, but he has made himself the most popular of the dual-purpose dogs. A handsome,

◆ ABOVE AND LEFT
This is a true sporting dog, full of athleticism – smooth lines, tight muscles and an all-seeing expression.

BREED BOX

Size	medium
	dog: 58–64 cm
	(23–25 in), 28.5 kg
	(63 lb)
	bitch: 53–59 cm
	(21–23 in), 24 kg
	(53 lb)
Grooming	easy
Exercise	essential
Feeding	medium
Temperament	highly trainable and friendly

powerfully made HPR worker, he allies a smooth, gleaming coat and a balanced, muscular frame with a keen nose and a high work-rate.

He stands as tall as 64 cm (25 in) at the withers and comes in variations of liver or black base, sometimes solid-coloured, more commonly with white ticking or spotting. The coat is short and coarse to the feel and is groomed with relative ease to keep its sheen. He has a squarish outline and his tail is customarily docked to a medium length. On the move, his muscles ripple with the style and grace of an athlete, and he requires regular exercise. He benefits from having his brain put to good use by extensive training, whether he remains a household member or finds his way to his intended role in the field. His is the sort of overall ability that it would be a pity to waste, as he is a genuine all-rounder.

GERMAN WIRE-HAIRED POINTER

The German Wire-haired Pointer, a more recent export than his Short-haired cousin, serves the same general purpose as an HPR breed. The two breeds differ not only in coat but in size, the Wire-haired being very slightly taller at 67 cm (26 in).

The outer coat is thick and harsh and the young, growing dog often

sports a moustache round his muzzle, which gives him a somewhat humorous look. The extra length of coat with a dense undercoat provides very good weatherproofing in the winter cold and enables the dog to be particularly good working in water to retrieve shot game.

There are not as many solid-coloured Wire-haireds as Short-haireds, especially in solid black, otherwise the colours are similar. Adequate exercise is vital as this is a working breed. These dogs do not enjoy being limited to a short stroll around the block.

◆ ABOVE
The GWP is heavier in body and limb than the Short-haired version.

◆ ABOVE RIGHT
The GWP is an HPR breed with a harsh, weatherproof coat.

BREED BOX

Size	medium
	dog: 60–67 cm
	(23½–26 in),
	25–34 kg (55–75 lb)
	bitch: 56–62 cm
	(22–24 in), 20.5–
	29 kg (45–64 lb)
Grooming	reasonable
Exercise	essential
Feeding	medium
Temperament	intelligent and biddable

GORDON SETTER

The Gordon Setter, from Scotland, is the heavyweight of the setter section. He stands 66 cm (26 in) tall, but he is more solidly built than any of the others. As a result he tends to move more steadily but still with considerable drive. He is a tireless worker who likes and needs his exercise; he does enjoy his food and can be heavy when fully grown.

He has a long silky textured coat of shining black with a pattern of chestnut-red tan on his muzzle and limbs. He grows slowly, as do all the setters, through a leggy, gawky stage, during which he can be the despair of his owner, but eventually he matures into a sound, dignified dog.

Grooming has to be thorough but is not over-demanding. This dog can make a good-natured companion as well as a reliable worker in the field and on the moors.

BREED BOX

Size	large
	dog: 66 cm (26 in),
	29.5 kg (65 lb)
	bitch: 63 cm (25 in),
	25.5 kg (56 lb)
Grooming	reasonable
Exercise	reasonable
Feeding	fairly demanding
Temperament	dignified and bold

◆ TOP
Setters vary in style, but no-one can fail to recognize the solid build of the Gordon...

◆ LEFT
...or the particularly powerful head and neck.

◆ RIGHT
The Gordon may not have the glamour of his English and Irish cousins, but he is a trustworthy, steady, working dog and will last all day in the field.

HUNGARIAN VIZSLA

The Hungarian Vizsla (Vizsla) is a spectacularly coloured HPR breed from Central Europe. The short, dense coat of rich red russet only needs polishing with a cloth to keep it at its glorious best.

The breed stands up to 64 cm (25 in) at the withers and weighs some 28 kg (62 lb) and is strongly built with well-muscled limbs and a noble head that is not over-fleshed. The Vizsla is a worker with a great reputation in his

BREED BOX	
Size	medium
	20–30 kg (44–66 lb)
	dog: 57–6 cm
	(22½–25 in)
	bitch: 53–60 cm
	(21–23½ in)
Grooming	easy
Exercise	medium
Feeding	medium
Temperament	lively and fearless

+ ABOVE
The sight of a Vizsla when the sun is at its zenith is a flash of the richest red.

+ LEFT
There can be few more handsome heads than this – the Vizsla is keen-eyed and has an alert, intelligent expression.

native Hungary as both a pointer of game and a reliable retriever; he takes special delight in going into water in his quest for a shot bird. As a companion he is a good, affectionate

member of the household, but he can be fairly protective so he needs a firm hand. Easily trained by those who set their mind to it, he is a truly all-purpose dog.

HUNGARIAN WIRE-HAIRED VIZSLA

The Hungarian Wire-haired Vizsla is another HPR breed, very much like the Hungarian Vizsla, with the exception that the coat is harsh. He sports definite eyebrows, which give him a sterner expression. His height is

the same, as is his weight, and he demonstrates much the same characteristics of temperament. The coat on his legs is short and harsh and possibly makes his limbs appear larger.

+ ABOVE RIGHT
The harsh coat is the same russet red as the Hungarian Vizsla.

+ LEFT
Developed in the 1930s, the Wire-haired Vizsla is a popular gundog in Canada.

BREED BOX	
Size	medium
	20–30 kg (44–66 lb)
	dog: 57–64 cm
	(22½–25 in)
	bitch: 53–60 cm
	(21–23½ in)
Grooming	relatively easy
Exercise	medium
Feeding	medium
Temperament	lively and fearless

IRISH RED AND WHITE SETTER

The Irish Red and White Setter comes as a surprise to those who have always recognized the traditional Irish Setter, often incorrectly called the Red Setter. In fact, the Red and White is reputed by the Irish to have been the original version, but he became practically unknown outside his native Ireland for almost all of the early part of the twentieth century.

His success since the start of the 1980s has been gradual as breeders have become more selective and people have begun to notice this handsome, large, red and white dog. He is similar in general appearance to the Irish Setter but has a slightly broader head and is more heavily built. He stands up to 65 cm (25½ in) at the withers and has a base colour of white with solid red patches on head and body and mottling on his limbs.

He does not eat greedily and enjoys human company. He makes a friendly family dog, but, like a number of breeds with finely textured, longish coats, needs careful attention to keep him clean and wholesome after a run in the country. He is not temperamentally as racy as the Irish Setter, but still can be quite a handful to control, and his training requires firmness and application on the part of his owners.

✦ BELOW
Irish Setters are just red to most of us, but the original was probably this dog, often with more white than red.

✦ ABOVE
These dogs have a characteristic brilliant white blaze down the top of the muzzle.

BREED BOX	
Size	large
	dog: 65 cm (25½ in),
	29.5 kg (65 lb)
	bitch: 61 cm (24 in),
	25 kg (55 lb)
Grooming	demanding
Exercise	demanding
Feeding	reasonable
Temperament	cheerful and
	biddable

✦ RIGHT
The Irish Red and White Setter is a strong, athletic dog, good-natured and affectionate and deservedly growing in popularity, but it requires patience to train him.

IRISH SETTER

The Irish Setter is known to his friends as the Mad Irishman, with a devil-may-care way about him. He is certainly beautiful, but to keep that long, silky coat of deep chestnut gleaming requires thorough and regular grooming.

He stands around 65 cm (25½ in), but the official breed standard does not contain a height clause because, according to those who have bred him all their lives, a good Irish Setter cannot be a bad height. He is actually allowed to have a small amount of white on the front of his brisket, but nowhere else.

He does not carry a great deal of flesh, but his musculature has to be powerful because he is expected to work at top speed in the shooting field. He is not expensive to feed, although he can burn up a lot of calories, and he expects to be well exercised. He can be trained to curb his wildness by those who set out to be firm, and his attitude to one and all is of sheer friendship and *joie de vivre*. The recall exercise is not easily mastered by him.

The bitches of the breed tend to have very big litters of up to sixteen puppies at a time.

+ RIGHT
The Irish Setter first appeared in recognizable form in the early eighteenth century.

+ RIGHT
Almond-shaped eyes with a soft, kindly expression characterize the Irish Setter.

+ RIGHT
The sheen on the deep chestnut coat is the reason why this is among the best known and most popular breeds in the world.

BREED BOX	
Size	large
	dog: 65 cm (25½ in),
	30.5 kg (67 lb)
	bitch: 26 kg
	(57½ lb)
Grooming	demanding
Exercise	demanding
Feeding	reasonable
Temperament	affectionate and racy

ITALIAN SPINONE

The Italian Spinone (pronounced "spin-o-ny") is yet another HPR breed that has entered Britain in the past twenty years. He stands up to 70 cm (27½ in) at the withers but weighs as much as 39 kg (82 lb).

He has a thick, wiry coat all over, and sports very distinctive eyebrows that are longer and stiffer than the rest of his hair. He also has softer hair round his cheeks and upper lips.

He can come in a variety of pastel shades of orange and brown on a white background. To complete the picture, he has a characteristic relaxed trot that appears tireless. He comes from areas where he meets both hilly terrain and marsh. His feet take a fair degree of pounding, but fortunately he is blessed with hard pads and hair between the toes. Dew-claws on all four feet tend to make his feet appear even more massive.

He has become amazingly popular in a relatively short time; his devotees speak well of his ability as an all-purpose gundog. They also rate him highly as a family companion.

BREED BOX	
Size	large
	dog: 60–70 cm
	(23½–27 in),
	34–39 kg (75–86 lb)
	bitch: 59–65 cm
	(23–25½ in),
	29–34 kg (64–75 lb)
Grooming	fairly demanding
Exercise	demanding
Feeding	reasonable
Temperament	friendly and alert

◆ ABOVE
A rough, tough all-purpose dog, the Italian Spinone's large hairy feet facilitate work in marshy terrain.

KOOIKERHONDJE

The diminutive Kooikerhondje from the Netherlands stands about 40 cm (16 in) tall and carries a medium-length coat with a slight wave in it, coloured with clear orange-red patches on a white background.

He has a kind expression, a sharply featured head with ears hanging close to the skull, a tidy, well-balanced frame on straight legs and a well-feathered tail that is carried fairly gaily. The whole bearing is that of a happy little dog who would not take a lot of grooming or feeding and will be ready for all the fun going in a family or a single person household.

◆ ABOVE
Small and supple, the Kooikerhondje's active frame makes him a good candidate for agility training.

BREED BOX	
Size	small
	35–41 cm
	(14–16 in),
	9–11 kg (20–24 lb)
Grooming	simple
Exercise	medium
Feeding	reasonable
Temperament	friendly and alert

◆ FAR LEFT
The spectacular coloration and bushy tail helped the Kooikerhondje in his traditional role of luring ducks into netting traps.

LARGE MUNSTERLANDER

The large Munsterlander is a handsome HPR breed that originated in Germany. The dog stands 61 cm (24 in) at the withers. He is muscularly built and is similar in shape and style to the setters.

He sports a longish dense coat and has a fair amount of feathering on his legs and fur on his feet, which can get muddy. He is always a basic black with

✦ RIGHT
The Large Munsterlander is a keen, all-purpose gundog with a good nose and excellent stamina.

a fair amount of white ticked with black on his body and limbs. His well-groomed coat has a glorious sheen to it when he stands in sunlight. He retains his full tail, which ends in a plume.

The Large Munsterlander enjoys exercise whether working or rambling with his family and, being a biddable sort of dog, he does not need quite the concentration required to handle a setter. This is a dog who can make a very pleasing companion for active folk.

✦ RIGHT
This breed always has a black head, but the expression is alleviated by the gleam in those golden-brown eyes.

BREED BOX	
Size	medium–large dog: 61 cm (24 in), 25–29 kg (55–64 lb) bitch: 59 cm (23 in), 35 kg (77 lb)
Grooming	reasonable
Exercise	reasonable
Feeding	reasonable
Temperament	affectionate and trustworthy

NOVA SCOTIA DUCK-TOLLING RETRIEVER

The Nova Scotia Duck-tolling Retriever comes as a surprise, if only because his name sounds highly improbable. This duck-toller does much the same job as the Dutch Kooikerhondje but uses a different method to trap susceptible ducks and other waterfowl. The constant waving of their tails lures ducks near enough for hunters to shoot them, after which the dogs retrieve them.

The breed stands around 51 cm (20 in) and has a medium-length red or orange coat with plenty of feathering, especially on the tail.

As the NSDR is blessed with a cheerful nature and enjoys being taught to be an all-round helper, he can make a good member of the household, but it remains to be seen whether his number will increase.

✦ ABOVE AND RIGHT
The main purpose of this spritely breed is to tempt waterfowl within range.

BREED BOX	
Size	small 43–55 cm (17–21½ in), 17–23 kg (37½–50½ lb)
Grooming	medium
Exercise	medium
Feeding	simple
Temperament	playful, trainable

POINTER

The Pointer is instantly recognizable. The clean-cut lines of his lean frame covered by a short, shining coat make a beautiful silhouette on grouse moor and in city parks alike, although his whole purpose in life suits him better for the countryside.

At 69 cm (27 in) he is quite a tall dog. He does not carry much surplus flesh so gives the impression of being bony. His movements are fluent and athletic. He is not a big eater; he is very easy to clean up after a day's work, and he is

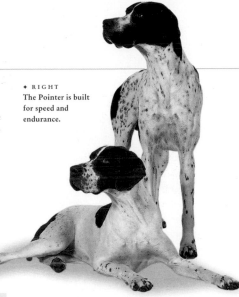

+ RIGHT
The Pointer is built for speed and endurance.

+ ABOVE
He uses his aristocratic nose to cover a great deal of moor or pasture remarkably rapidly.

relatively easy to teach reasonable manners, though he is unlikely to win a top-standard obedience competition.

While most paintings depict him as white with a number of liver or black patches, he also comes in lemon and orange patterns. A kindly, gentle dog, he should appeal to the active owner.

BREED BOX	
Size	large dog: 63–69 cm (25–27 in), 29.5 kg (65 lb) bitch: 61–66 cm (24–26 in), 26 kg (57½ lb)
Grooming	minimal
Exercise	medium
Feeding	demanding
Temperament	kind and reasonably biddable

+ RIGHT
The Pointer was developed in Britain in the seventeenth century to find and point hares for Greyhounds to chase. Dogs of a similar type are thought to have been bred in Spain around the same time.

CHESAPEAKE BAY RETRIEVER

♦ RIGHT
The Chessie is a burly dog who delights in leaping into water, whether asked to or not.

The Chesapeake Bay Retriever is a strong, muscular dog. He stands 66 cm (26 in) high, which does not make him a giant among dogs by any means, but his purpose in life is retrieving ducks from his native Bay, which is usually cold. For this he needs much subcutaneous fat and a thick, oily-feeling coat, all of which add up to a look of substance.

He comes in a colour that is somewhat unromantically described as "dead grass" (straw to bracken). He can also be red-gold or brown.

His ability to work is prodigious. He loves people and is always ready to please, but he is not meant for the idle; rather for a family that enjoys the countryside and doesn't mind having a fair amount of it brought into the

♦ ABOVE
The head-shape is not that different from that of his Labrador cousin.

BREED BOX	
Size	large and solid
	dog: 58–66 cm
	(23–26 in),
	31 kg (68 lb)
	bitch: 53–61 cm
	(21–24 in),
	28 kg (62 lb)
Grooming	fairly demanding
Exercise	demanding but
	simple
Feeding	considerable
Temperament	alert and cheerful

house along with the dog. A very stiff brush and a chamois leather will repair the worst damage to his coat, but possibly not to the best carpet or the antique chairs!

♦ RIGHT
There's no getting away from the fact that, of all the basic retrieving dogs, this one is the heavyweight. His thick, oily coat protects him in the water and dries quickly.

CURLY COATED RETRIEVER

The Curly Coated Retriever is very obviously unusual in style as his body is covered with tight, crisp curls, even down the length of his tail. The only part of the dog with smooth hair is his face and muzzle. He is most often seen in black, but liver is not uncommon either.

His height is up to 69 cm (27 in), and he is well proportioned, so his powerful shoulders and loins do not make him appear clumsy or coarse. Those who employ him as a worker swear by his intelligence and ability in water, nosing out shot birds and bringing them to hand rapidly; he is noted for his prodigious shake.

He is energetic but not a greedy feeder. He makes a good guard for a retriever, is not hard to control and makes a good family dog.

✦ ABOVE
The coat is the mark of this calm, powerful water dog, with a mass of tight curls.

BREED BOX	
Size	large
	34kg (75 lb)
	dog: 69 cm (27 in)
	bitch: 63.5 cm
	(25 in)
Grooming	fairly demanding
Exercise	demanding but
	simple
Feeding	reasonable
Temperament	friendly, confident

✦ ABOVE
The aristocratically chiselled muzzle is smooth haired.

✦ RIGHT
It is thought that the Curly Coated Retriever originated in Britain as the result of crossing the now extinct English Water Spaniel with a retrieving setter and the later Lesser Newfoundland, which arrived in Britain in 1835 with the cod fishermen.

FLAT-COATED RETRIEVER

The Flat-coated Retriever is the lightest built of all the retrievers except the rare Nova Scotia Duck-toller. He is sociable and good-humoured, always eager to please. He is most commonly black, but there are a fair number of liver-coloured dogs. The odd yellow-coloured one is frowned on by enthusiasts.

BREED BOX

Size	medium-large dog: 58–61 cm (23–24 in), 25–35 kg (55–77 lb) bitch: 56–59 cm (22–23 in), 25–34 kg (55–75 lb)
Grooming	medium
Exercise	medium
Feeding	medium
Temperament	kindly

Standing at most 61 cm (24 in) at the withers, he is not heavily built in the loins and hindquarters, hence his lighter appearance. His coat is dense and flat and positively shines with health after a good grooming. He is not a demanding dog to feed.

The Flat-coated Retriever is an excellent household dog who loves human company; his tail wags incessantly, and his intelligence is plain to see whether he is asked to work in the shooting field or play in the park.

✦ ABOVE
This retriever also has a less square foreface than others. His deep bark gives good warning of visitors or strangers.

✦ RIGHT
Flat coats originated in Britain as the result of crossing several other breeds, including the Lesser Newfoundland, and originally had wavy coats.

GOLDEN RETRIEVER

◆ LEFT
The Golden Retriever, one of the most popular dogs, is a wonderful all-purpose breed, although guarding is not his forte.

The Golden Retriever is a canine all-rounder. He can turn his talents to anything, from his natural retrieving to acting as a guide dog for the blind, a detector of drugs or explosives, a reasonably laid-back obedience worker or just being a most attractive member of a household.

He stands 61 cm (24 in) at his tallest but gives the impression of being a solid comfortable dog; he is inclined to get his snout into the trough as often as possible, and owners need to watch his waistline. There is often quite a difference in appearance between those retrievers used in the shooting field and the type that are bred for showing and the home.

The Golden Retriever has a dense undercoat with a flat wavy top-coat; the colour varies from cream to a rich golden, which is sometimes very deep.

He is easy to train, but needs to be kept interested, because he is easily bored. His ability as a guide dog for the blind demonstrates his temperament, as the work involves a great deal of steady, thoughtful walking.

He is one of the most popular household dogs because of his generous loving nature. Such popularity is often a curse because dogs are bred by people who are not always conscientious in their dedication to producing truly healthy stock. As is true of any breed of pedigree dog, the best source of supply is direct from a reputable breeder who has the welfare of the dogs he or she produces at heart.

BREED BOX

Size	medium dog: 56–61 cm (22–24 in), 34 kg (75 lb) bitch: 51–56 cm (20–22 in), 29.5 kg (65 lb)
Grooming	fairly demanding
Exercise	demanding
Feeding	demanding
Temperament	intelligent and biddable

◆ RIGHT
The Golden Retriever was developed in Britain in the late nineteenth century.

◆ ABOVE CENTRE
These dogs have generous soft muzzles that are able to carry shot birds, hares or even the newspaper without leaving a mark.

LABRADOR RETRIEVER

The Labrador Retriever is instantly recognizable. Thought to have originated in Greenland, he is a stockily built dog; his coat is short and hard to the touch; it is entirely weatherproof and basically drip-dry. At one time the black coat was the best known, but yellow (not golden) became more widely seen fifty years or more ago. Today there is quite a trend for chocolate, which is also called liver.

The Labrador stands as high as 57 cm (22½ in), which is not very tall, but he is extremely solid. Another characteristic is his relatively short, thick-coated tail, which is known as an "otter" tail. Like the Golden Retriever he is a multi-talented dog, being much favoured as a guide dog for the blind. (In fact these two breeds are regularly cross-bred to utilize their combined skills.) He is also useful in drug-searching and has been used by the army as a canine mine-detector.

✦ ABOVE
Wisdom in a canine expression is difficult to define, but the true Labrador seems to get as near as any.

BREED BOX	
Size	large
	dog: 56–57 cm
	(22–22½ in),
	30.5 kg (67 lb)
	bitch: 54–56 cm
	(21–22 in),
	28.5 kg (63 lb)
Grooming	easy
Exercise	demanding
Feeding	reasonable
Temperament	friendly and
	intelligent

Undoubtedly his greatest skill is as a retriever from water.

The Labrador seems capable of taking all the knocks of a rough-and-tumble family, which is why he rates so highly as a household member. His temperament is such that he does not seem to take offence at any insult.

He can consume any quantity of food so needs rationing if he is not to put on too much weight. He must have exercise and, although he can live in town surroundings, he should not be deprived of regular, long walks.

✦ RIGHT
With a frame like this, it is easy to see why the breed is famous for its stamina.

CLUMBER SPANIEL

The Clumber Spaniel may only stand around 42 cm (16½ in), but he is a lot of dog. Admittedly, he was never expected to rush around the fields in the manner of the Cocker or the Springer, but he has increased in weight over the years up to 36 kg (79½ lb) or even more and thus moves at a somewhat ponderous pace.

His temperament is kindly even if a trifle aloof at times, but he can be an attractive member of a household, though he should live in the country.

✦ ABOVE
These dogs will trundle through a day's shooting at a steady pace and never lose their cool.

BREED BOX

Size	short but massive 42–45.4 cm (16½–18 in) dog: 36 kg (79½ lb) bitch: 29.5 kg (65 lb)
Grooming	reasonable
Exercise	medium
Feeding	medium
Temperament	kind and reliable

✦ LEFT
A Clumber has loose skin on his forehead, and he suffers from drooping lower eyelids. Both of these things can cause veterinary problems.

His mainly white coat, with some lemon or orange marking, is close and silky in texture, but abundant in quantity. He is not difficult to groom. Despite his size, he is not a particularly greedy dog, but he does need exercise.

✦ RIGHT
The Clumber was bred at Clumber Park, Nottinghamshire, England, in the nineteenth century. He is thought to have originated in France and includes Basset Hound in his ancestry, hence the long back.

AMERICAN COCKER SPANIEL

◆ BELOW
Nobody could fail to remember a dog with a coat like this: just as well to keep the grooming requirements in mind before succumbing to the enormous charm of those eyes.

The American Cocker Spaniel is a derivation of the English Cocker Spaniel. In both countries, their own nationality is dropped in the official name of the breed.

The process of selection from the original stock has gone quite a long way. The American has a very different head-shape from the English; the muzzle is shorter and the skull is domed to the point of roundness, while the eyes are fuller and set to

BREED·BOX	
Size	small
	11–13 kg
	(24–28½ lb)
	dog: 36.5–39 cm
	(14½–15½ in)
	bitch: 33.5–36.5 cm
	(13–14½ in)
Grooming	extensive
Exercise	medium
Feeding	small
Temperament	cheerful and intelligent

look straight ahead. The other huge difference is in the coat, which is exaggeratedly long and profuse on the legs and abdomen. If left untrimmed, this coat is impractical for the working dog. As a member of a household, his coat is likely to present a regular problem if it is not kept well groomed. Prospective purchasers must take this

into account. He comes in a whole range of very handsome colours, including black, black and tan, buff, parti-colour and tricolour.

◆ RIGHT
Note the characteristic peak to the hair over the eyebrows. This is one of the most popular breeds in the US.

◆ LEFT
These dogs were developed in the US in the nineteenth century to flush and retrieve quail and woodcock.

The American Cocker Spaniel is a thoroughly cheerful dog who does not eat ravenously. He enjoys his exercise, but is easily trained to behave in a suitable manner for suburbia. As he stands a mere 39 cm (15½ in) at his tallest, he does not need a mansion but will be happy to live in one if given the opportunity.

ENGLISH COCKER SPANIEL

The English Cocker Spaniel is the original of the American breed. He stands around the same height at 41 cm (16 in), but his coat is shorter and therefore nowhere near such hard work to keep well groomed, provided adequate attention is paid to his fairly hairy feet and his longish ears. He can

♦ RIGHT
The orange-roan colour is one of a huge range that this neat dog comes in. The breed is the basis of several of the land spaniels.

♦ LEFT
Low-slung ears with long hair make regular grooming a must.

be found in whole colours such as red (gold) and black, also in black and white, and in multicolours.

A thoroughly busy dog, he is always searching and bustling around

BREED BOX

Size	small
	12.5–14.5 kg
	(27½–32 lb)
	dog: 39–41 cm
	(15–16 in)
	bitch: 38–39 cm
	(15–15½ in)
Grooming	regular
Exercise	medium
Feeding	small
Temperament	merry, exuberant

in the grass and bushes. His name comes from his ability to flush out game, particularly the woodcock. He also delights in carrying things about whether on command or purely voluntarily. He is often portrayed as the original slipper-fetching dog by his master's fireside, tail wagging furiously.

♦ ABOVE
This dog shows a differently shaped eye, but still the gentle, relaxed expression.

♦ LEFT
The Cocker's job is to flush ground game for his handler; the tight body is essential for his bustling way of moving.

ENGLISH SPRINGER SPANIEL

The English Springer Spaniel gets his name from his ability to flush birds rapidly into the air or "spring" them. A handsome dog, relatively tall for a spaniel at 51 cm (20 in), he covers much ground at a galloping pace. His coat is close and weather-resistant, and he is either liver and white or black and white. It is not hard to groom him as long as the hair round his ears is kept fairly trim.

He enjoys his food but is not greedy. He is a compulsive worker, apparently absolutely tireless. As a household companion he is similarly minded, expecting walks in either town or country, and he reckons that those walks should not be a mere stroll down to the shops. He is capable of learning all manner of games, preferably those requiring him to retrieve a ball – endlessly!

BREED BOX

Size	small-medium
	51 cm (20 in)
	dog: 21.5 kg
	(47½ lb)
	bitch: 19 kg (42 lb)
Grooming	reasonable
Exercise	demanding
Feeding	medium
Temperament	friendly and biddable

+ LEFT
The thoroughly balanced shape of the Springer means he moves rapidly and easily.

+ LEFT
The Springer has a charm that he is quite capable of using to his own ends.

FIELD SPANIEL

+ BELOW
Several breeds of dog are liver coloured – this one shows that gleaming colour at its best.

The Field Spaniel from England is easy to mistake for a Cocker with an over-long back. He stands around 46 cm (18 in) at the withers, and although he does come in black, liver or roan, the majority are a very definite liver colour. His coat is long, glossy and needs regular attention, especially around the ears.

He is a noble-looking dog, described as having rather grave eyes in his official Standard, and that is a reasonable description. He is active and biddable, making a worthy companion as a country dog, whether working or simply as a member of a household. He does not demand unreasonable quantities of food and deserves greater popularity.

+ LEFT
The Field Spaniel is a dog for the country-dwelling family – steady and trainable.

BREED BOX

Size	small
	46 cm (18 in),
	18–25 kg
	(39½–55 lb)
Grooming	reasonable
Exercise	medium
Feeding	small
Temperament	active and
	independent

IRISH WATER SPANIEL

◆ BELOW
This is a breed of great antiquity, although a clear type emerged in the nineteenth century from which today's dogs derive.

The Irish Water Spaniel is one for the connoisseur. He is tall by spaniel standards as he reaches 58 cm (23 in). The fact is that he is much more of a retriever than a spaniel. He is covered with tight liver-coloured ringlets, except for his muzzle, the front of his neck and the last two-thirds of his tail, which thus looks a bit like a whip. When he gets wet, his shake is spectacular.

◆ LEFT
The Irish Water Spaniel has a characteristic curly topknot of hair just above the eyes.

Aficionados regard him with great affection and enthusiasm and consider that he has a good sense of humour. He certainly is energetic, revelling in any amount of exercise whether he is asked to be a household companion or fulfil his traditional role.

BREED BOX

Size	medium dog: 53–58 cm (21–23 in), 27 kg (60 lb) bitch: 51–56 cm (20–22 in), 24 kg (53 lb)
Grooming	medium
Exercise	medium
Feeding	medium
Temperament	affectionate, if aloof

◆ BELOW
Grooming is no easy task, and the art must be acquired from the start.

Grooming him requires skill and knowledge of the correct technique, as well as determination. Feeding him is not a problem as he is not greedy. This is another breed that could achieve greater acclaim.

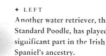

◆ LEFT
Another water retriever, the Standard Poodle, has played a significant part in the Irish Water Spaniel's ancestry.

SUSSEX SPANIEL

The Sussex Spaniel is another relatively unknown dog, but in fact is of considerable antiquity. The breed played a part in the foundations of the Field Spaniel. He stands at the most 41 cm (16 in) high, has a solid body and is possessed of a very handsome golden-liver coat.

✦ LEFT AND BELOW LEFT
This ancient breed of slow-working spaniel survived by the judicious use of other spaniel blood in breeding programmes earlier this century.

His head is somewhat broader in the skull than the Cocker, and his wrinkled brow gives him a serious look. He has massive bones for such a short-legged dog but does not need to compensate by being a greedy eater.

He makes a good member of a country household but has not yet become a family favourite.

BREED BOX

Size	small
	38–41 cm (15–16 in),
	18–23 kg
	(39½–50½ lb)
Grooming	medium
Exercise	medium
Feeding	medium
Temperament	kindly

WELSH SPRINGER SPANIEL

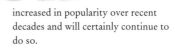

The Welsh Springer Spaniel emulates the role of his English cousin. In fact the Welsh protest that theirs is the original version. The Welsh Springer is slightly smaller, standing 48 cm (19 in) high, and is not quite as heavily built.

He is an honest, kindly dog with a true will to please, easily trainable, thoroughly enjoys human contact, and is relatively easy to groom. He is not a dog that pesters for food.

He sports a glossy, flat and silky coat of a handsomely rich dark red and white. He delights in exercise and is a fine sight on the move. This breed has deservedly increased in popularity over recent decades and will certainly continue to do so.

✦ LEFT AND ABOVE RIGHT
For sheer beauty the sheen on the warm red of the Welsh Springer Spaniel's coat in summer sunshine takes a lot of beating. The kindly expression is a mark of the breed.

BREED BOX

Size	small-medium
	17 kg (37½ lb)
	dog: 48 cm (19 in)
	bitch: 46 cm (18 in)
Grooming	reasonable
Exercise	fairly demanding
Feeding	medium
Temperament	kindly and
	intelligent

WEIMARANER

The Weimaraner is an outstanding dog. He stands tall in the gundog group at 69 cm (27 in). A highly unusual colour, the Weimaraner is nicknamed the Grey Ghost though the grey can be slightly mousy rather than the silver-grey that experts crave. Possibly his most outstanding feature are his eyes, which can be either amber or blue in colour.

This is another HPR breed originating on the European mainland. His coat is short, smooth and sleek, although there is a rare version which sports a longer coat. In the more unusual coat he is no problem to groom – it is more a matter of polishing! Even when he spends a long day in the shooting field or on a country stroll through winter mud, he does not bring the outside world into his home.

The Weimaraner is not a big feeder, although he appreciates and needs a generously filled bowl on a cold winter's day. He does need exercise, because he has a temperament that requires plenty to occupy his very active mind. He can be trained fairly easily but does not suffer fools gladly.

He has a friendly attitude to people but will act as an impressive guard if his home or his family are threatened. He is not a fawning, easy-going type of dog, even if he comes from a group that appears generally placid.

+ LEFT
The rare long-haired Weimaraner: note the undocked tail.

+ BELOW
The truly stylish Grey Ghost is built on racy lines, but with the stamina and turn of speed which emulates the thoroughbred stayer of the horse world.

+ LEFT
The Weimaraner's piercing eyes are a distinctive feature. Normally shades of amber or blue-grey, they may appear black when dilated with excitement.

BREED BOX

Size	medium-large dog: 61–69 cm (24–27 in), 27 kg (59½ lb) bitch: 56–64 cm (22–25 in), 22.5 kg (49½ lb)
Grooming	easy
Exercise	demanding
Feeding	medium
Temperament	fearless and friendly

The Terrier Group

The breeds that comprise the Terrier Group are the pest-controllers of the canine world, having been used originally to find and kill rodents of all shapes and sizes. They possess fairly similar temperaments; they have to be tenacious as well as sharp in movement and reaction. They are inclined to act first and think afterwards; they tend to argue with the dog next door and are not often the delivery man's best friend.

But a terrier which is properly introduced is a delight as far as humans are concerned. A family seeking an alert, playful, affectionate friend will be well satisfied with a member of this group. It may be thought to include one of the most popular of all dogs, the Jack Russell, although this is, in fact, a cross-breed and therefore not registered by either the British or American Kennel Club.

+ FACING PAGE **Cairn Terrier**

AIREDALE TERRIER

The Airedale, from northern England, is the largest, by some degree, of the terriers. He is a splendid fellow, with a genuine style about him that entitles him to his nickname, King of the Terriers. He stands as tall as 61 cm (24 in) and has a head with an expression suggesting total command of any situation.

The Airedale is somewhat less aggressive towards other dogs than some breeds in the group, but will not

companion and not a show-dog.

He makes a very good guard dog as he considers that his owner's property is his to look after. He has a loud voice that can be very convincing to any intruder. He is not a greedy feeder, but at the same time he is a well-built dog and naturally needs an adequate supply of nutrition.

BREED BOX	
Size	medium
	21.5 kg (47½ lb)
	dog: 58–61 cm
	(23–24 in)
	bitch: 56–59cm
	(22–23 in)
Grooming	medium
Exercise	reasonable
Feeding	medium
Temperament	friendly and
	courageous

back down if challenged. Few would dare! He is reputed to be intelligent but can be stubborn unless handled in a firm manner.

He has a black saddle and the rest of him is mostly tan; the tan can be a gloriously rich colour. His coat is harsh and dense and grows impressively but can be kept tidy with regular brushing. He sheds his coat twice a year, and at such times it is good for him to be trimmed or stripped by a professional. The experts will frown on the use of clippers, but it can be an alternative if he is destined to be a household

AUSTRALIAN TERRIER

The Australian Terrier is an alert, small dog. He stands a mere 25 cm (10 in), but there is a great deal of character packed into his small frame. His body shape is round rather than deep, but he has plenty of space for good lungs, which he needs in order to

♦ LEFT
The Australian Terrier delights in using his sharp bark to warn of a visitor's arrival; not often found in relaxed mood.

BREED BOX

Size	small 25 cm (10 in), 6.5kg (14 lb)
Grooming	reasonable
Exercise	not demanding
Feeding	small
Temperament	extroverted and friendly

be as active as he always seems to be.

He rates highly in his native land but has not yet achieved quite the same degree of popularity elsewhere. He has a relatively short top-coat, which is harsh in texture. This makes him easy to groom. He has an intelligent expression and carries his ears pricked.

He can have either steel blue on his saddle with tan on the rest of him, or an all-over red. Either way the Australian Terrier is a smart little dog who is surprisingly tractable and anxious to please. He can be very useful as a watch dog and can use his vocal chords effectively in the home. Being small, he does not cost much to feed.

BEDLINGTON TERRIER

The Bedlington Terrier is one of the most distinctive dogs of them all. Not only does he have a somewhat tucked-up loin, but he has an unusual coat, which is described as "linty". It is thick, with an unusual tendency to twist, and stands away from his skin. It needs regular tidying, which is

simple. The basic colour is blue or even sandy but most Bedlingtons appear off-white to those seeing them for the first time.

The breed hales from the northern areas of Britain, and its proper job is rabbit-chasing and catching. Nowadays

the Bedlington is also a very handy house-dog and pet. He does not have an enormous appetite, and he will find his own exercise given the chance.

His mild looks belie the fact that he is a genuine terrier in the best tradition of the group; underneath them he has considerable spirit.

BREED BOX

Size	small- medium 41 cm (16 in), 8–10.5 kg (18–23 lb)
Grooming	reasonably undemanding
Exercise	undemanding
Feeding	small
Temperament	mild

♦ RIGHT
A terrier in lamb's clothing, the Bedlington is full of courage in the house or as a rabbit catcher.

BORDER TERRIER

The Border Terrier is originally from the borders of England and Scotland and is popular as both a worker and a family dog. The fact that several veterinary surgeons own and breed Border Terriers speaks volumes for both their temperament and their freedom from problems. This is a friendly breed which appeals to many different people.

The maximum weight is just over 7 kg (15½ lb). This is a dog who is expected to work, however much he is adapted to living as a family companion. He fits that bill excellently. He has a cheeky otter-like

✦ RIGHT
The Border Terrier is described as "racy", which means giving the impression of speed without loss of substance.

head, a sound body clothed in a harsh, dense coat, and his legs will carry him across country or urban park for as long as his owner requires. The official Standard states that the dog should be

✦ BELOW LEFT
One of the most cheerful and companionable of all breeds, the Border Terrier makes an excellent family dog.

✦ BELOW
The Border Terrier has changed little since he first appeared in the late eighteenth century. He has found much favour in the show-ring but has still remained true to type. The Breed Standard describes him as having a head like an otter.

BREED BOX

Size	small
	dog: 30.5 cm
	(12 in), 6–7 kg
	(13–15½ lb)
	bitch: 28 cm (11 in),
	5–6.5 kg (11–14 lb)
Grooming	undemanding
Exercise	medium
Feeding	small
Temperament	game, friendly

capable of following a horse, hence his sufficient length of leg. He is not quarrelsome, but he is game for anything. He likes being with people.

The Border Terrier comes in a variety of colours including red, wheaten, grizzle and tan or blue and tan; he is light enough to be picked up easily, and he does not require a great deal of food. He has a lot going for him!

154

BULL TERRIER

◆ BELOW
White is the most common colour for Bull
Terriers, often with coloured markings on
the head.

The Bull Terrier is certainly one of
the odd dogs out in the terrier group.
He is not a pure terrier – his name is a
combination of bull and terrier – and,
in fact, he was originally more a dog
fighter than a small pest-controller.

The breed's shape contrasts with
other terriers. The Bull Terrier is
much more burly, he has an egg-

shaped head and a Roman nose. He
gives the impression of being ready for
anything and is nicknamed the
Gladiator of the Terriers, a description
that fits him perfectly.

The official Standard does not
speak of measurements but the experts
would accept around 45 cm (18 in) as
reasonable, while 33 kg (73 lb) is no
exaggeration of his weight. There is
also a Miniature Bull Terrier, which is
built on exactly the same lines but is
not supposed to stand above 35.5 cm
(14 in) in height.

The Bull Terrier is usually thought
of as white, but even the white ones
often have patches of red or black or
brindle on their heads. He can also
appear as black, red, fawn or brindle
with a certain amount of white, mainly

BREED BOX

Size	small–medium
	45 cm (18 in),
	33 kg (72 lb)
Grooming	easy
Exercise	medium
Feeding	medium
Temperament	even but obstinate

on his head, neck or limbs.

His coat is short and flat with a feel
of harshness about it. He is simple to
groom, by sponging the dirt off and
then rubbing him down with a cloth.

The Bull Terrier is a very active
dog. He likes his exercise and food,
and he is a grand dog to have about
the home because he loves people, but
woe betide any burglar!

The Pit Bull Terrier, originating in
the United States, was also bred for
fighting. As the result of deliberate
training for illegal dog fighting he has
been deemed dangerous and banned in
many countries.

◆ FAR LEFT
The egg-shaped head of the modern Bull
Terrier is hard as a bullet if the dog runs into
you at speed.

◆ BELOW
There is no wasted space on this attractive,
power-packed bitch – just solid quality in
the flesh.

CAIRN TERRIER

The Cairn Terrier is an engaging creature, usually blessed with a fascinating character. Coming from the Highlands of Scotland, he is one of a group of breeds that are small in stature, large in heart. He stands a mere 31 cm (12½ in). His coat, which is harsh and weatherproof, can be anything from cream, through red or grey to almost black. The essential feature is that it should end up looking shaggy even after grooming.

His prick ears atop a small sharp-featured head give him a look of alert gameness, which is absolutely justified. He bustles everywhere at great pace, tending to catch unawares any small rodents that he chases. He is a tireless fellow, with an impressively sharp voice, who delights in accompanying his human family, be it on a country walk or a shopping foray.

He lives a long life, eats whatever he is offered and has a disposition that combines a devil-may-care attitude with a great love of people.

BREED BOX	
Size	small 28–31 cm (11–12½ in), 6–7.5 kg (13–16 lb)
Grooming	medium
Exercise	reasonable
Feeding	small
Temperament	fearless

CZESKY TERRIER

The Czesky (pronounced "cheski") originated in the Czech Republic. He is a kind dog with a coat colour varying from black through dark grey to a silvery look. Sociable and relatively obedient, he tends to be less aggressive than many of the other terriers.

He stands up to 35 cm (14 in) high and is slightly longer in the back than he is tall. His coat is not shed and needs trimming regularly with attention from brush and comb. He is not greedy but eats well. He enjoys exercise as a family companion.

BREED BOX	
Size	small 35 cm (14 in), 5.5–8 kg (12–18 lb)
Grooming	medium
Exercise	reasonable
Feeding	medium–small
Temperament	cheerful, but reserved

DANDIE DINMONT

The Dandie Dinmont is another terrier whose appearance comes as something of a surprise. He has an expression that can only be described as soulful, with large round eyes peering out of an equally large head which is covered with what seems to be a huge soft cap or top-knot of hair. He comes in two distinct colours, a

+ ABOVE
The Dandie Dinmont was named after one of Sir Walter Scott's characters.

+ LEFT
The Dandie Dinmont is more docile than other terriers but has a surprisingly deep and loud bark.

BREED BOX	
Size	small
	dog: 28 cm (11 in),
	10 kg (22 lb)
	bitch: 20.5 cm (8 in)
	8 kg (18 lb)
Grooming	medium
Exercise	reasonable
Feeding	small
Temperament	independent and
	affectionate

reddish brown through to fawn, which is dubbed mustard, and a bluish grey dubbed pepper.

He is longer in his body than he is high at the withers; he may weigh up to 10 kg (22 lb) so is not a heavy dog. He is also not a big eater. He thrives on human companionship and certainly makes an attractive household member. He never looks as if he would do anything in a hurry, but he can be roused to action by the sight of any rat or squirrel unwise enough to invade his territory.

+ BELOW
A faithful houshold member, the Dandie Dinmont has gentle eyes, a soulful expression and is good with children.

SMOOTH FOX TERRIER

The Smooth Fox Terrier is a smart, alert dog. He stands about 38 cm (15 in) at the withers and always gives the impression of being right up on the tips of his toes. A lethargic dog of this breed would be most unusual. He is typical of all the square-built terriers, ready to stand his ground and argue with any dog who may challenge him, but not the one to start proceedings.

BREED BOX

Size	small–medium
	39.5 cm (15½ in)
	dog: 7.5–8 kg
	(16½–17½ lb)
	bitch: 6.5–7.5 kg
	(14–16½ lb)
Grooming	undemanding
Exercise	medium
Feeding	medium
Temperament	friendly and fearless

The Smooth Fox Terrier will take all the exercise offered but will not spend his time nagging his owner to fetch his lead. He carries enough flesh to have a well-covered frame but does not run to fat unless over-fed and under-exercised. He is not a dog to leave loose near livestock unless he has been very well schooled. He is easy to maintain in an urban area and will keep the rodent population down.

Grooming his basically white coat, with tan or black markings, is simple – use a stiff brush followed by a comb and finish off with a cloth. This regular routine will keep him looking very trim all his long life.

✦ LEFT
Most breeds of terrier came from somewhere in the British Isles; this one is the original hunt terrier used alongside packs of foxhounds.

✦ RIGHT AND ABOVE RIGHT
The sharp outline and the way in which colour appears in distinct patches on an otherwise all-white dog is typical. This is a tough, no-nonsense breed.

WIRE FOX TERRIER

The Wire Fox Terrier is the rough-haired version of the Smooth Fox Terrier, with the same aptitude for rat-catching. He measures up to 39 cm (15½ in) and is square-built. His harsh wiry coat is white, usually with a black saddle and black or tan markings or a combination of the two. The coat grows thick and he should be trimmed fairly regularly. This is probably best done by a professional, but it is perfectly possible for an owner to learn the art, given a good teacher. Well trimmed, he is a very smart dog indeed.

+ RIGHT
The Wire is the wire-haired version of the Smooth, with the same balanced body, short back and sharp features.

BREED BOX

Size	small–medium
	39 cm (15½ in),
	8 kg (17½ lb)
Grooming	medium
Exercise	medium
Feeding	medium
Temperament	friendly and fearless

+ ABOVE
The small, dark eyes are full of fire and intelligence.

The Wire Fox Terrier is not a greedy dog and does not run to fat unless he is given insufficient exercise. A very good house-dog, he will guard his domain noisily. He imagines that his family is there purely to provide him with company and fun, whether they live in town or country.

+ LEFT
The Wire Fox Terrier is a bold dog who can be noisy and wilful. He loves digging.

+ RIGHT
The breed may be derived from the old black-and-tan Rough-haired Terrier of Wales and northern England.

IRISH TERRIER

The Irish Terrier is a handsome dog, standing up to 48 cm (19 in) at the withers; he sports a harsh and wiry coat of a sandy red colour, which may on occasion tend to be a paler wheaten

tone. He gives the impression of being long in the leg, and he certainly is not burly of body.

As a result of not being thick-set, he does not need a lot of food to sustain his frame; he enjoys exercise, but this should be under strict control if there are likely to be other dogs about. He is a first-class dog for people of all ages and makes a fine house-dog.

His coat grows in a less bushy fashion than the Airedale's, and it is not hard to keep him looking neat, though he needs an occasional smartening trim by a professional groomer, unless his owner decides to take a course in the art.

BREED BOX

Size	medium
	dog: 48 cm (19 in),
	12 kg (26½ lb)
	bitch: 46 cm (18 in),
	11.5 kg (25 lb)
Grooming	medium
Exercise	medium
Feeding	medium
Temperament	good with people, fiery with dogs

✦ ABOVE LEFT
This dog bristles through and through with a love of action. He is still used as a working terrier in Ireland and is popular for field trials and lure coursing in the US.

✦ BELOW
The Irish Terrier, from southern Ireland, is one of the oldest of the terrier breeds. In the 1880s it was the fourth most popular breed in England. The Irish Terrier Club of America was founded in 1896.

✦ BELOW
Those handsome jaws contain one of the finest sets of teeth found in any dog.

GLEN OF IMAAL TERRIER

The Glen of Imaal Terrier from Ireland is the shortest of the Irish terrier breeds. He stands roughly 36 cm (14 in) at the withers, and his back is long in proportion. His coat is wiry and not over-long. He comes in blue, brindle or wheaten.

The Glen of Imaal is a native of

◆ LEFT
This is the only Irish breed of terrier that stands low to ground.

◆ BELOW
The Glen of Imaal has a surprisingly laid-back expression for a terrier.

County Wicklow and has a roughness about him that disguises a surprisingly quiet dog for a terrier. He is not common even in his own homeland, but numbers have increased over the past decade. He is not a striking dog but has a happy, game way of going which makes him an attractive family companion dog.

He does not need a great deal of grooming, and he is not a greedy eater. He enjoys his exercise but does not expect excessive attention.

BREED BOX	
Size	small
	35–36 cm (14 in),
	16 kg (35 lb)
Grooming	medium
Exercise	medium
Feeding	medium
Temperament	game but docile

KERRY BLUE TERRIER

The Kerry Blue Terrier comes from Ireland. He starts life with a black coat, but this should change to blue in some eighteen months. It is a softer, silkier coat than is common on the average square-built terrier, said to resemble astrakhan, and it does not shed. He is normally kept trimmed to a strikingly neat outline, and this is considered a "must" by the devotees of the breed. The trimming should make him look as if he carries a neat beard.

He is tall for a terrier at 48 cm (19 in), and deeper and wider in the chest than the Irish Terrier. The Kerry Blue considers himself a superior being, and he requires a good helping of his daily food. He has a way of going when he is on his lead that is almost a strut, but he can go like the wind off it. He likes people and exercise; he is relatively easily trained but does not appreciate other dogs taking liberties.

BREED BOX	
Size	medium
	dog: 46–48 cm
	(18–19 in), 15–17
	kg (33–37½ lb)
	bitch: 46 cm (18 in),
	16 kg (35 lb)
Grooming	medium
Exercise	medium
Feeding	medium
Temperament	game

◆ BELOW
Tall and powerful, the Kerry Blue acts as if he was born to be a champion, ready to take on the world at a moment's notice.

LAKELAND TERRIER

The Lakeland Terrier, from the Lake District of north-west England, is another of the group of square-built terriers. Standing 37 cm (14½ in) at the withers, he has a dense, harsh coat that can be all kinds of colours, from red through wheaten to liver, blue or black, with black and tan and blue and tan as alternatives. Grooming him is not a huge task, but as his coat grows relatively thick, it would be wise to have him professionally trimmed every now and then or possibly learn to do the job yourself. In between, the use of an ordinary brush and comb will suffice.

✦ RIGHT
The Lakeland Terrier has sufficient length of leg to cover rough terrain.

He is an agile dog who loves freedom and exercise. A tireless working terrier, he delights in joining a family and taking part in any activity that is going on; and he is not over-noisy.

BREED BOX	
Size	small–medium 37 cm (14½ in) dog: 7.5 kg (16½ lb) bitch: 7 kg (15½ kg)
Grooming	medium
Exercise	medium
Feeding	medium
Temperament	friendly and self-confident

MANCHESTER TERRIER

The Manchester Terrier is a fair height, 41 cm (16 in), and looks as if he has a bit of Whippet in his make-up. He is jet black and tan in colour and his coat is smooth, shining glossily after a good, hard polish with a cloth.

✦ LEFT
There is an obvious likeness in this stylish pair.

✦ ABOVE
This breed is well loved by many devotees. With its Whippet connection, it is an unusual type for a terrier.

He does not eat a great deal and might give the uninitiated the impression that he is a dilettante in his approach to life, but he was bred as a ratter and, given the chance in modern society, will prove he still retains his old skills.

He is a sporting sort who delights in family activity whether in town or country. He is not aggressive either to man or dog, and he makes a good companion for anyone who likes a dog to be a bit out of the ordinary.

BREED BOX	
Size	small–medium dog: 41 cm (16 in), 8 kg (18 lb) bitch: 38 cm (15 in), 7.5 kg (16½ lb)
Grooming	easy
Exercise	reasonably undemanding
Feeding	undemanding
Temperament	companionable and relatively quiet

NORFOLK AND NORWICH TERRIERS

Both Norfolk, here, and Norwich are small, solid terriers and great diggers.

The Norfolk Terrier and its older cousin, the Norwich Terrier, each bearing the name of its place of origin in England, are breeds of extremely similar type and style. They are eager, bustling, little dogs, low to the ground and thick-set in body. The essential difference is that the Norfolk Terrier's ears drop forward at the tip, whereas the Norwich Terrier's ears are pricked.

Their aim in life is to hustle foxes, badgers, rats, and anything that moves in the countryside, except farm animals and people. In fact, they are both capable of keeping their family companions on the move, but from in front rather than behind.

They stand a mere 25 cm (10 in) at the withers, with hard, wiry coats that tend to be rougher round neck and shoulders. The coat is red, wheaten, black and tan or grizzle, and it gives the impression that it is warm and thorn-proof. It does not present much of a problem when it comes to grooming, and after a country walk or a busy session down a handy hole, the coat is returned to its rough neatness very simply.

The two breeds are exhibited at shows separately in spite of the fact that there is little or no difference between them except the ear carriage. In either guise, aficionados have adopted the attitude that docking of the tail is

optional, and more and more are being seen with this appendage left as nature decreed it.

Both terriers are good rough-and-tumble dogs with kindly personalities, who will not go round looking for a fight.

✦ ABOVE
There's a gleam in this Norfolk's eyes that speaks of fun and frolic.

BREED BOX

Size	small
	25 cm (10 in),
	6.5 kg (14 lb)
Grooming	simple
Exercise	medium
Feeding	undemanding
Temperament	alert, friendly and
	fearless

✦ LEFT
This alert expression is the hallmark of the Norwich with its prick ears.

✦ BELOW
Wearing the look of a fun-loving breed, this is the Norwich at its sharpest.

PARSON JACK RUSSELL

The Parson Jack Russell Terrier is descended from the type of Fox Terrier favoured by a famous sporting parson from the West Country of England in the second half of the nineteenth century. Parson Jack developed what he considered to be the ideal hunt terrier, one that stood about 36 cm (14 in) and weighed in the region of 6.5 kg (14 lb), easy enough to carry on his saddle and capable of going to earth to bolt a hunted fox.

Devotees have continued to breed this size of terrier, which is quite different from the shorter-legged version, the popular Jack Russell seen in stable-yards, farmyards and family homes. The Jack Russell, which is a type rather than a pure breed, is a dimunitive rascal characterized by short and somewhat twisted forelegs.

The Parson comes in both smooth and rough coats, usually with a predominance of white with tan, lemon or black markings in the area of the head or the tail-root. These dogs make lively companions for lively households. They are easy to feed and groom, not difficult to teach good manners and view the human race with reasonable grace.

BREED BOX

Size	small-medium 28–38 cm (11–15 in) 5–8 kg (11–18 lb)
Grooming	undemanding
Exercise	medium
Feeding	medium
Temperament	cheerful, bold

◆ ABOVE
The Parson combines dedication as a worker with a playful nature. He makes a good house dog but requires plenty of exercise.

◆ BELOW
This is a balanced terrier; the rough-coated type is very much as the famous sporting parson bred it.

◆ ABOVE
These dogs have a sparkling eye and an intelligent-looking head.

SCOTTISH TERRIER

The Scottish Terrier has been popular for many years but is not seen quite as frequently as it was some fifty years ago. He stands some 28 cm (11 in) at the withers and gives the impression of being a neat, powerful dog for his size. He has a harsh, wiry and weatherproof coat that benefits from being kept tidy whether professionally or otherwise.

The Scottie has fairly large prick ears and carries a good deal of coat on his longish muzzle in the form of a beard.

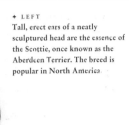

♦ LEFT
Tall, erect ears of a neatly sculptured head are the essence of the Scottie, once known as the Aberdeen Terrier. The breed is popular in North America.

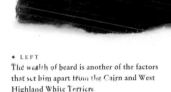

♦ LEFT
The wealth of beard is another of the factors that set him apart from the Cairn and West Highland White Terriers.

♦ BELOW
Solid and thick-set, the Scottie is surprisingly agile and active for such a short-legged dog.

BREED BOX	
Size	small
	8.5–10.5 kg
	(19–23 lb)
	dog: 28 cm (11 in)
	bitch: 25.5 cm
	(10 in)
Grooming	medium
Exercise	undemanding
Feeding	reasonable
Temperament	bold and friendly

Most people would know him as black or very dark brindle, but he does come in wheaten as well on occasion. His well-boned legs look almost thick-set and his deep frame makes him appear close to the ground. He moves with a smooth level gait, as if he is very important, and, though normally gentle, is not a dog with which to pick a fight.

SEALYHAM TERRIER

The Sealyham Terrier is a small, sturdy terrier from rural Wales. He should not grow taller than 31 cm (12 in) at the withers, and the length of his body should be slightly greater.

He has a longer coat than some terriers, but it is also wiry. As it is basically white with small patches of lemon or badger usually on his head and ears, it is not simple to keep clean in the breed's natural country home,

+ LEFT
The Sealyham is named after the Welsh village from which he originated. He has a marked independence of nature.

BREED BOX

Size	small
	31 cm (12 in)
	dog: 9 kg (20 lb)
	bitch: 8 kg (18 lb)
Grooming	medium
Exercise	undemanding
Feeding	reasonable
Temperament	alert and fearless

especially if the weather is wet. He does benefit from occasional professional attention.

The Sealyham can be a trifle cautious with strangers, but he is a superb companion or house-dog and a very effective alarm-raiser. He is known as a self-sufficient dog, who makes his own entertainment.

+ ABOVE
The curtain of hair conceals a pair of very bright eyes that miss nothing.

+ LEFT
A sturdy body on short legs tends to make it difficult to keep his coat clean, but the Sealyham does like living country-style.

SKYE TERRIER

The Skye Terrier has developed from the same root-stock as the Scottish Terrier. He is a very long dog, being only 26 cm (10 in) at the withers but twice that from stem to stern.

BREED BOX	
Size	small-medium dog. 25–26 cm (10 in), 11.5 kg (25 lb) bitch: 25 cm (10 in), 11 kg (24 lb)
Grooming	demanding
Exercise	medium
Feeding	medium
Temperament	distrustful of strangers

The coat is hard and straight as well as long, and covers his eyes. It needs constant attention, which can be demanding, so he is something of a specialist's dog. The Skye Terrier is cautious of those he does not know, while being very loyal to his own family. He is certainly a good watchdog and very striking to look at.

✦ ABOVE
Most Skyes have prick ears, gracefully fringed with hair.

✦ BELOW
From contemporary records it seems that this long-haired dog with his flowing coat is much the same as he was nearly four centuries ago.

✦ ABOVE
These game dogs were originally used to seek out otters, badgers and weasels in the rocks and burrows of their native islands off the West coast of Scotland.

SOFT-COATED WHEATEN TERRIER

The Soft-coated Wheaten Terrier, as his name implies, sports a soft and silky coat that is always wheaten in colour. He stands up to 49 cm (19 in) at the withers. He came from Ireland originally, where he was a hunter, a guard, a herder and a companion to farmers. In 1943 he was registered with the Kennel Club in Britain, and in 1973 with the American Kennel Club. Today he is recognized as an attractive pure-bred dog.

He has a good-natured temperament: he loves people and seems to get on well with other dogs. He enjoys plenty of exercise, the rougher the better. In spite of the length of his coat, it is not hard to keep in order. He needs as little trimming as possible, and he only eats enough to keep his prodigious energy levels up to par.

+ LEFT
The breed retains its happy-go-lucky charm even in full show trim.

+ ABOVE
It is hardly surprising that the breed is sometimes referred to affectionately as a "mop-head".

BREED BOX

Size	medium dog: 46–49 cm (18–19 in), 16–20.5 kg (35–45 lb) bitch: 45.5 cm (18 in), 16 kg (35 lb)
Grooming	medium
Exercise	medium
Feeding	medium
Temperament	good-natured and spirited

+ RIGHT
This square-built, power-pack of a dog is full of confidence and humour. He makes a delightful companion.

STAFFORDSHIRE BULL TERRIER

The Staffordshire Bull Terrier is not just a breed; it is a cult. The devotees of this smooth shiny-coated dog from central England often appear to be blind to the existence of any other sort. The breed is renowned for its courage, and certainly if any dog would be willing to defend owner and house to the death, this is the one. All he asks in return is adequate rations and a lot of love.

Officially the Staffie measures up to 41 cm (16 in) tall, but many bigger dogs are seen. His head is fairly big without being exaggerated. He views life as if it is entirely for his benefit. His body is built on the lines of a muscled midget, and he walks with a swagger – for prodigious distances if invited. He can be groomed in a minute, not only because he is short-coated but brimming with vitality into the bargain. He comes in red, fawn, black or brindle with varying amounts of white. The colours can be predominantly in patches, sometimes over his eyes.

BREED BOX

Size	small–medium
	dog: 35.5–41 cm
	(14–16 in), 12.5–
	17 kg (27½–37½ lb)
	bitch: 35.5 cm
	(14 in), 11–15.5 kg
	(24–34 lb)
Grooming	easy
Exercise	medium
Feeding	medium
Temperament	fearless, dependable

WELSH TERRIER

The Welsh Terrier is a square-built breed from Wales, referred to by diehards as being built like a miniature Airedale, standing up to 39 cm (15½ in) tall. He has a coat of the same abundantly wiry type, and it requires the same professional care. He also comes with a similar black saddle and tan head and legs.

Perhaps slightly thicker set than the Lakeland, he has that breed's style of standing right up on his toes. He enjoys exercise; he delights in his family and all their occupations, including any form of game. Above all, he is as biddable as any in the Terrier Group, and he is not fussy over food.

BREED BOX

Size	small-medium
	39 cm (15½ in),
	9–9.5 kg (20–21 lb)
Grooming	medium
Exercise	medium
Feeding	easy
Temperament	happy and fearless

♦ LEFT
This is an old breed that was originally known as the Old English Wire-haired Black and Tan Terrier. It is possible that the Welsh and the Lakeland Terriers have common ancestry from pre-Roman Britain.

♦ ABOVE
The set of the ears betokens intelligence and alertness.

♦ LEFT
Standing four-square on tight paws, this is a neat, cheerful, workmanlike dog and a good rat-catcher.

WEST HIGHLAND WHITE TERRIER

The West Highland White Terrier, or "Westie", has pushed his way steadily up the popularity charts, and this is no wonder; he is a handy size to pick up and carry when necessity requires it; he has an outgoing manner; he loves people and, though he will not buckle under when challenged, he does not go out of his way to pick a quarrel with other dogs.

He stands a mere 28 cm (11 in) at the withers, but he packs a great deal of spirit into his small frame. He is not as stocky as the Scottish Terrier. As his name implies, the Westie's coat is white and can get dirty very easily; he therefore needs a regular bath or a form of dry-cleaning with the use of chalk. The coat is also harsh and recovers its quality surprisingly quickly after a shampoo, but Westies do need a trim every now and then to keep them looking neat.

He will use his sharp voice to warn off strangers and so is a good guard. He makes a great family friend or a companion *par excellence* for someone living on their own.

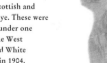

BREED BOX

Size	small
	28 cm (11 in)
	dog: 8.5 kg (19 lb)
	bitch: 7.5 kg
	(16½ lb)
Grooming	medium
Exercise	undemanding
Feeding	easy
Temperament	active and friendly

+ ABOVE
The Westie shares common ancestry with the Cairn. They were selectively bred to the white by the Malcolm family of Poltalloch in Argyleshire, Scotland.

+ BELOW
The Westie has a merry expression and loves company and attention. A devoted family member, his small size will not prevent him from protecting hearth and home.

+ LEFT
The various predecessors of today's Westies were known as Poltalloch, Roseneath, White Scottish and Little Skye. These were merged under one name, the West Highland White Terrier, in 1904.

The Utility (Non-Sporting) Group

The Utility (Non-Sporting) group includes dogs of all shapes, sizes and functions, from the Dalmatian and the Leonberger at the large end of the scale to the Tibetan Spaniel and the Lhasa Apso at the small.

There are two common explanations for the composition of the group. The first is that the breeds cannot be fitted into any of the other five groups, which is quite an unflattering way of looking at things. The second is that they are all companion dogs, which may sound politer but also suggests that the members of the other groups are not companions! To complicate matters, not all countries include the same breeds in this group. For example, the Japanese Akita is classed as a utility breed in Britain but as a working breed in the United States.

Looking through this section will undoubtedly give you some sympathy for those who had to solve the problem of how to classify such a varied assortment.

◆ FACING PAGE Schnauzer

BOSTON TERRIER

The Boston Terrier is a strikingly handsome dog. He is often described as the national dog of America, although his short muzzle confirms that he has Bulldog in his ancestry.

He stands around 38 cm (15 in) tall; he can vary considerably in weight around the 9 kg (20 lb) mark, but he is easily handled and picked up. His coat is short and shiny, and can be kept that way with the minimum of fuss. As his colour scheme requires brindle or black with white markings, he is instantly recognizable.

The Boston Terrier is compactly built with a square-shaped head and wide-set, intelligent eyes and prick ears. He is both dapper and boisterous, without being too short bodied; strong-willed but nevertheless a thoroughly good-natured house-dog.

♦ RIGHT
Today's Boston Terriers are the result of a cross between the Bulldog and the English White Terrier (now extinct).

♦ BELOW
Intelligence and watchfulness are the Boston's hallmarks.

♦ LEFT
Boston Terriers were originally bigger and heavier, but careful selective breeding has produced the clean-cut dog of today.

BREED BOX	
Size	small–medium lightweight: under 6.8 kg (15 lb) middleweight: 6.8–9 kg (15–20 lb) heavyweight: 9–11.3 kg (20–25 lb)
Grooming	simple
Exercise	undemanding
Feeding	undemanding
Temperament	determined

♦ ABOVE
The Boston Terrier has a characteristically short muzzle and a square head.

BULLDOG

The Bulldog, often referred to as the British Bulldog to distinguish him from any other, is instantly recognized by all who see him.

He has a friendly, if stubborn nature. His devotees will not hear a word against him, but those who fancy taking one on must understand his special needs. His physical characteristics, for example, mean that a walk should not be conducted at a

BREED BOX

Size	small-medium dog: 25 kg (55 lb) bitch: 22.5 kg (50 lb)
Grooming	simple
Exercise	undemanding
Feeding	medium
Temperament	affectionate and determined

great pace, especially in the heat of the day. The shape of his head and his breathing apparatus mean that he can easily become short of breath; he can, on occasion, put in a surprising burst of speed, but over-exertion on a hot day can, and does, have serious side-effects. In addition, he tends to breathe noisily.

The Bulldog was bred to get to grips with bulls by grabbing their noses with his front teeth. The design of jaw for which he was bred, in the days when bull-baiting was legal, has been considerably exaggerated in recent times, even though it is no longer necessary to fulfil that role.

His coat is short and easily kept clean; he can be all manner of colours from red through fawn to white or pied. He is a massively built dog,

giving the impression that his muscles have been built up like those of a human weight-lifter. He weighs 25 kg (55 lb), sometimes more, and he eats as befits his size. He is a superb guard dog and he adores children. He is reasonably good with other dogs as he simply appears to ignore them; but he can give a show of aggression towards strangers, human or canine, if provoked.

CANAAN DOG

The Canaan Dog is a relatively recent export from the deserts of the Middle East, hailing predominantly from Israel. He retains much of the semi-wild and has yet to settle into modern western society. He is a true canine athlete standing up to 61 cm (24½ in) at the withers and is built on the lines of a racing hunter rather than a heavy plodder, so he is not a greedy dog.

His coat, which is of medium length, is easily groomed; it ranges in colour from red to sand or may be either black or white. He has good guarding instincts as well as those of the hunter. He is one of the anomalies in the Utility Group, being more of a Working dog in his lifestyle.

The Canaan Dog's origins indicate that he needs plenty of exercise and likes his freedom; he is versatile but needs time to prove his adaptability to western concepts of obedience.

BREED BOX	
Size	medium–large 51–61 cm (20–24 in), 18–25 kg (39½–55lb)
Grooming	undemanding
Exercise	demanding
Feeding	medium
Temperament	alert and distrustful of strangers

CHOW CHOW

The Chow Chow is an example of a spitz breed, with his square-built frame, tightly curled tail and prick ears. He is unusual in that he has a very laid-back temperament, seldom rousing himself to move at any considerable speed. His movement is stilted and stiff-legged. The inside of his mouth and his tongue are black.

He stands up to 56 cm (22 in) at his tallest, and he is thick-set in body. He does not eat heartily considering his apparent bulk, but this is partly exaggerated by the thickness of his very plush coat, which can be black, red, blue, fawn or cream. It is not an easy coat to groom effectively and requires regular attention.

The Chow Chow originated in China, where he performed all kinds of functions, from guarding and companionship right through to ending up as a possible source of food for humans! He is a loyal dog to his owners but does not respond well to strangers.

At one time he was considered bad-tempered. Nevertheless, he attracts a host of admirers, but he does need careful attention from those who do not know the breed well.

BREED BOX	
Size	small–medium dog: 48–56 cm (19–22 in), 27 kg (59½ lb) bitch: 46–51 cm (18–20 in), 25 kg (55 lb)
Grooming	demanding
Exercise	undemanding
Feeding	medium
Temperament	independent but loyal

DALMATIAN

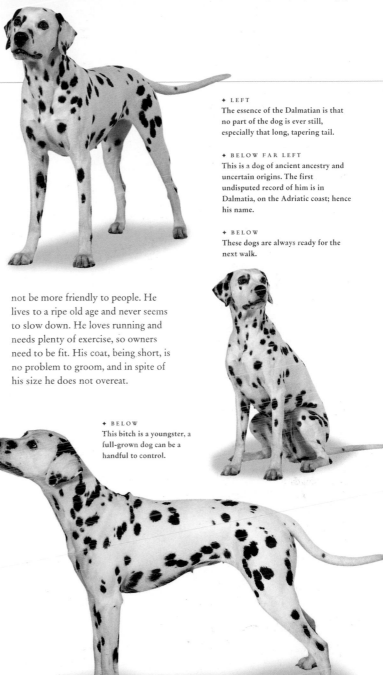

The Dalmatian is as distinctive a breed as any. With his white base colour and plethora of spots, either black or liver, all over his head, body and limbs, he is the original "spotted dog". He has been known in Britain for well over a century and was originally used as a carriage dog; he has a penchant for

running between the wheels, quite undaunted by the close proximity of flashing hooves. In the US he was used to control the horses that pulled fire appliances and is still a well-known fire house mascot.

The Dalmatian is a handsome dog up to 61 cm (24 in) in Britain, 58.5 cm (23 in) in the US. He could

not be more friendly to people. He lives to a ripe old age and never seems to slow down. He loves running and needs plenty of exercise, so owners need to be fit. His coat, being short, is no problem to groom, and in spite of his size he does not overeat.

♦ LEFT
The essence of the Dalmatian is that no part of the dog is ever still, especially that long, tapering tail.

♦ BELOW FAR LEFT
This is a dog of ancient ancestry and uncertain origins. The first undisputed record of him is in Dalmatia, on the Adriatic coast; hence his name.

♦ BELOW
These dogs are always ready for the next walk.

♦ BELOW
This bitch is a youngster, a full-grown dog can be a handful to control.

BREED BOX	
Size	large dog: 58.5–61 cm (23–24 in), 27 kg (60 lb) bitch: 56–58.5 cm (22–23 in), 25 kg (55 lb)
Grooming	easy
Exercise	demanding
Feeding	medium
Temperament	outgoing and friendly

FRENCH BULLDOG

The French Bulldog is the French version of the British Bulldog. He has a similar square face but without the exaggeration of the shortened muzzle. He carries his large ears erect, well-up on his skull. His dark eyes are full of expression, usually kindly but capable of a glint which suggests that he does not suffer fools gladly.

+ LEFT
French Bulldogs can move very much faster than their solid frame might suggest.

He can weigh up to 12.5 kg (27½ lb) but enjoys his food, so his diet must be controlled. He comes in dark brindle, fawn or pied, and his coat is short, close and shiny, so easily groomed. He is compactly built with a slight concave curve over his loins, and like his British cousin he has a short tail, which can be corkscrew-shaped.

He rushes about when taking exercise, but finds hot days hard going, tending to breathe noisily when under severe stress. He makes a charming house-dog and gives the impression that he would guard hearth and home with his life.

+ ABOVE
The large upright ears tend to swivel to pick up every sound.

+ ABOVE
These dogs both have pied coloration; the most desired pattern comes with a neat central band down the forehead.

+ LEFT
French Bulldogs are one of the few breeds that have their loins higher than their withers; this helps them to launch themselves vertically, as if on springs.

BREED BOX	
Size	small-medium 30.5–31.5 cm (12–12½ in) dog: 12.5 kg (27½ lb) bitch: 11 kg (24 lb)
Grooming	easy
Exercise	undemanding
Feeding	undemanding
Temperament	cheerful and intelligent

GERMAN SPITZ

The German Spitz has two recognized varieties in two different sizes. In its country of origin there are, in fact, five different sizes ranging from the Wolfspitz, which stands around 53 cm (21 in) to the Pomeranian, which is the smallest at less than 20 cm (8 in).

The two recognized varieties are the middle size and the next size down, officially christened the German Spitz (Mittel), measuring between 30 and 38 cm (12–15 in), and the German Spitz (Klein) measuring 23–29 cm (9–11½ in).

Apart from the size variation the Mittel and the Klein are identical; they are prick-eared, sharp-featured dogs with compact bodies and tightly

✦ ABOVE
A pair of perky Kleins with intelligent eyes and good bone structure.

✦ LEFT
No matter which size, a German Spitz carries a great deal of coat which needs a great deal of grooming. This one is a Mittel.

✦ RIGHT
A typical spitz head.

curled tails. They have thick, harsh-textured coats that keep them warm in the coldest of winters. They come in every variety of colour, from chocolate to white, as well as in all sorts of combinations. Their coats look marvellous after a thorough grooming, but they are not for the lazy owner.

They are sturdy, cheerful creatures, capable of raising a merry chorus to warn of the arrival of a stranger but delighted when the stranger turns out to be a friend. They will join in all the family fun and make good companions for all ages.

BREED BOX	
Size	small
	Mittel: 30–38 cm
	(12–15 in),
	10.5–11.5 kg
	(23–25 lb)
	Klein: 23–29 cm
	(9–11½), 8–10 kg
	(17½–22 lb)
Grooming	demanding
Exercise	medium
Feeding	undemanding
Temperament	happy and lively

✦ ABOVE
A coat like this Klein's will cope with the bitterest of winter weather.

JAPANESE AKITA

The Japanese Akita, or simply Akita, is included in the working group by some countries. The Japanese Akita is striking; no other word fits such a powerfully built dog. He stands up to 71 cm (28 in) at the withers and his legs and body are designed on lines that would do credit to a champion bull. The Japanese bred him as a fighting dog, and his temperament, certainly among the males, is often awesome and need to be watched.

He attracts people with his brilliant colour schemes, which range from white through brindle and pinto to grey. Whatever colour he is, his thick, plush coat shines. That coat needs grooming to bring out the best in it. The typical spitz shape of pricked ears, which are hooded, wedge-shaped head, taut, compact body and curled tail are all there in the dog, but in no other spitz breed are they so expressive. He needs a lot of exercise as he is all muscle; he needs control as he is bossy and very intelligent; he needs feeding to go with his bulk but is not greedy. He is not always an ideal family dog.

If he is the dog that fits the lifestyle, he is superb. Rather than asking, "Is this the dog for me?" the question should be, "Am I the person for the dog?"

+ ABOVE
The Japanese Akita comes in a series of very striking colours and patterns.

BREED BOX	
Size	large
	50 kg (110 lb)
	dog: 66–71 cm
	(26–28 in)
	bitch: 62–66 cm
	(24½ –26 in)
Grooming	medium
Exercise	demanding
Feeding	medium
Temperament	courageous and
	dominating

JAPANESE SHIBA INU

The Japanese Shiba Inu (Shiba Inu) stands up to 39.5 cm (15½ in). He is much the same shape as the Akita, including the hooded ears that tip sightly forward continuing the topline of his neck. He has the same plush feel to the coat, but comes in less striking colours, including red, black, black and tan, and brindle, which do not have quite the same brilliance.

His temperament is not so dominating, though his intelligence is just as obvious; a Shiba will think his way through to getting what he wants. He is not noisy but will spot the invader of his owner's property without making a scene about it.

He loves his family and joining in all activities, but he is not a restlessly demanding dog. He is trainable and enjoys learning.

+ ABOVE
The Shiba Inu is the smallest of the Japanese breeds and of ancient origin.

+ LEFT
The Shiba Inu's plush coat comes in a variety of colours. Note the hooded ears.

BREED BOX	
Size	small
	8–10 kg (18–22 lb)
	dog: 39.5 cm (15½ in)
	bitch: 36.5 cm
	(14 in)
Grooming	reasonable
Exercise	reasonable
Feeding	reasonable
Temperament	bright and
	intelligent

JAPANESE SPITZ

The Japanese Spitz arrived in Europe less than twenty years ago but is already well established. Standing about 36 cm (14 in) tall, he is a neat, sharply outlined dog with a stand-off coat that is never anything but

♦ ABOVE
The pointed muzzle should be neither too thick nor too long.

brilliant white. Considering the thickness of his coat, he is not too difficult to groom or even to keep clean, although it will obviously need regular attention.

He is not over-noisy indoors or out, but makes a good sentry. He is capable of being an extremely companionable and nimble character whether with a large family or a single householder. He is not greedy but is not a picky feeder for what, at first sight, looks like a dainty dog.

♦ BELOW
Three delightful Japanese Spitz, with their coats gleaming like freshly fallen snow. It's possible that these small, nimble dogs have the same ancestry as the Samoyeds.

BREED BOX	
Size	small
	30–36 cm
	(12–14 in),
	5–6 kg (11–13 lb)
Grooming	medium
Exercise	medium
Feeding	undemanding
Temperament	affectionate and alert

KEESHOND

◆ LEFT
The Keeshond is a very solidly built, hardy dog that can live happily in the toughest of weather conditions. He was used as a guard and vermin catcher in his native Holland.

The Keeshond comes from Holland, where he guards farms and barges, and is also known as the Dutch Barge Dog. He is another spitz with smallish pricked ears, a compact body and the most tightly curled tail of all the spitzes. He stands around 46 cm (18 in) and is solidly built; he can be a greedy feeder and needs rationing if he is not to put on excess weight.

His harsh coat is thick, and he comes in what is officially called silver-grey – in fact, he sports long guard-hairs that have black tips. He withstands freezing temperatures and snow, regarding them with contempt, and considers central heating in his owner's house to be a sign of weakness! Grooming him is hard work, but his is the sort of coat that well rewards those who are conscientious and dedicated.

He loves human company and the exercise which goes with a busy family, but he is not demanding. He has sharp hearing and responds noisily to the arrival of visitors or the intrusion of strangers.

◆ BELOW
Thoroughly trusting and cheerful, the Keeshond loves people.

BREED BOX

Size	small–medium dog: 46 cm (18 in), 19.5 kg (43 lb) bitch: 43 cm (17 in), 18 kg (39½ lb)
Grooming	demanding
Exercise	medium
Feeding	medium
Temperament	friendly and vociferous

◆ LEFT
The coat does not look like this one unless someone has made a great effort.

LEONBERGER

Make no mistake, the Leonberger is a
whole lot of dog: he can stand as tall as
80 cm (32 in). He derives from the
town of Leonberg in Germany, and he
has traces of several large breeds in his

♦ LEFT
His size means he is
not really suited to
town or flat
dwelling.

ancestry. As could be expected from
his bulk, he needs a great deal of
feeding to sustain him.

His inclusion in the Utility
Group is questionable because
he has far more in common
with members of the Working
Group. He is a friendly dog, but
he can give a good account of himself
if asked to guard his home. His coat is

of medium length and is not all that
hard to groom except there is so much
of it. The colour range is from reddish
brown through golden to a lighter
yellow, but most specimens have a
black mask on their cheerful faces.

His attitude to exercise reflects his
attitude to life and people. He is
accommodating and easygoing. He
does not see much point in hurrying
anywhere, preferring to amble
amiably. He is also a good swimmer
in any weather and, given his size,
is best suited to country life. He
is first and foremost an easy,
genial companion.

♦ ABOVE
These are powerful, self-confident dogs but
entirely good-natured.

♦ ABOVE
The closer you get to a Leonberger the
kinder the expression.

♦ BELOW
Leonbergers move deliberately, with a
long-striding gait, and a great deal faster
than their size might suggest.

BREED BOX	
Size	very large 34–50 kg (75–110 lb) dog: 72–80 cm (28–32 in) bitch: 65–75 cm (25½–29½ in)
Grooming	fairly demanding
Exercise	medium
Feeding	demanding
Temperament	kindly

LHASA APSO

The Lhasa Apso is a native of Tibet, where these dogs were originally kept as indoor guards. With their intelligence and sharp hearing, they were ideally suited to the task. Their long, hard coats protected them from the severities of the climate. These days a Lhasa Apso can be glamour personified, the colour of the coat ranging from gold to grey, but that show-ring gleam is not achieved without regular shampoos and lots of hard work.

The Lhasa Apso stands around the 25 cm (10 in) mark at his withers, but he sports a back that is a little bit longer than his height, though not so exaggeratedly as to make him prone to a weakened spine. His appetite is appropriate to his small size.

His head, under all the hair that often covers his face, is much more like that of one of the smaller terriers than one would expect. He is tough in cold weather, and he will cheerfully walk for miles. He has an independent nature and is wary of strangers, although very affectionate with his owners. He makes a delightful family companion.

✦ ABOVE
The long hair falling over the Lhasa Apsos' eyes protected them from the wind and glare in their native Tibet.

BREED BOX

Size	small
	25–28 cm
	(10–11 in), 6–7 kg
	(13–15½ lb)
Grooming	demanding
Exercise	undemanding
Feeding	undemanding
Temperament	companionable but haughty

✦ ABOVE LEFT
With the hair swept back from the eyes, the Lhasa Apso has a soulful expression.

✦ LEFT
Lhasa Apsos must be seen on the move to realize just how active the dog under that mass of coat really is.

MINIATURE SCHNAUZER

The Miniature Schnauzer (Terrier Group), one of three Schnauzer breeds, gives the impression that he should be banded together with the square-built members of the Terrier Group, which indeed he is in the US. Standing around 36 cm (14 in) in a coat that is harsh and wiry, his must be one of the most stylish outlines of any dog.

To achieve the look that you see in the show-ring takes a professional touch; for the companion at home, all that is required is a good instructor

♦ LEFT
Combing the whiskers and leg hair every day will keep him looking neat.

and a wire-glove. The breed comes in black, black and silver or, most commonly, in what is officially termed "pepper and salt", but to most people would be a dark grey.

What makes the Schnauzer family so distinctive is their ears, which are set up high on their heads and tip forward towards the temple; in addition, they tend to grow luxurious eyebrows and beards.

The Miniature Schnauzer gives the impression of doing everything on the double; he enjoys exercise but does not grumble if he is not out and about all the time. He is not noisy. He

makes a handy-sized companion for people of all ages, from the busy family to the senior citizen who needs a friend; possibly the best Utility breed from the companion point of view.

BREED BOX

Size	small-medium dog: 36 cm (14 in), 9 kg (20 lb) bitch: 33 cm (13 in), 7.5 kg (16½ lb)
Grooming	straightforward
Exercise	medium
Feeding	undemanding
Temperament	alert and intelligent

♦ ABOVE LEFT
The Miniature Schnauzer is reliable, robust and agile but, above all, adaptable.

♦ BELOW
Black is an officially recognized colour for the Miniature Schnauzer, although there are not many of them.

♦ RIGHT
The likeness to a terrier is obvious. Apart from the Schnauzer, the Affenpinscher and the Miniature Pinscher played a part in its development.

POODLES

The Poodle comes in three sizes, Standard, Miniature and Toy, and a number of whole colours. Some countries place the Toy Poodle in the Toy Group. The breed has certain unusual features, chief among which is that the coat is single and does not shed. It is often recommended as a suitable dog for those people who suffer from an allergy to dog hair or dust.

The Poodle's intelligence is renowned; he can be taught all manner of skills, from water-retrieving to circus tricks. He appears to enjoy performing, and the praise and laughter that result.

The Poodle's shape is common to all three heights, with a proud, chiselled face and skull, an elegant neck, and a sound body and legs; the tail is often docked to half its normal length, but this is not compulsory.

The largest, which is referred to as the Standard Poodle, has a minimum height of 38 cm (15 in); the Miniature between 28 and 38 cm (11–15 in); the Toy should measure less than 28 cm (11 in). Most Standards are considerably taller than the minimum height officially allowed.

The Standard tends to be a real tomboy of a dog, racing about field or park, but returning rapidly if reasonably well trained. The Miniature and Toy sizes are equally happy extroverts but better suited to town

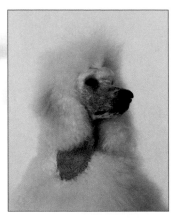

✦ ABOVE
An old breed from Germany, the Standard Poodle was originally a water-retrieving dog.

✦ LEFT
This is the best known show cut, and is meant to protect the dog's chest, kidney and leg joints.

BREED BOX	
Size	three sizes Standard: over 38 cm (15 in), 30–34 kg (66–75 lb) Miniature: 28–38 cm (11–15 in), 6 kg (13 lb) Toy: maximum 28 cm (11 in), 4.5 kg (10 lb)
Grooming	demanding
Exercise	medium
Feeding	straightforward
Temperament	sparky and cheerful

◆ BELOW
Underneath the huge coat is a dog that measures less than 38 cm (15 in) high.

◆ RIGHT
The Miniature Poodle trimmed and groomed for a show. Companion animals do not need to be trimmed like this, although regular attention is still essential.

◆ LEFT AND RIGHT
Apricot is not a common colour for a Toy but is very attractive at its best. Usually it tends to lighten as the dog gets older, but this one is still a rich colour.

◆ BELOW
The Toy Poodle has the same herding, guarding and water-retrieving background as the Standard. These chocolate, black and apricot Toys are very neatly groomed.

life. They can be picked up easily.

The range of colours includes white, cream, apricot, blue, silver, chocolate and black. Grooming is a specialist job. Left untouched the harsh-textured coat will grow to extraordinary lengths. Some form of trimming is essential at regular intervals, and the choice of cut varies from the simple "lamb" to the so-called "lion". Professional demonstration is necessary, even if an owner chooses to learn a do-it-yourself technique.

At one time, the Toys were accused of being finicky feeders, but well-bred specimens are as hardy as either of the larger sizes. The Poodle, whatever the size, is a companion dog *par excellence*.

SCHIPPERKE

The Schipperke hails from Belgium. He is a spitz-type dog of around 36 cm (14 in) in height. His erectly pricked ears and his not over-long neck, combined with a stocky body, give him a compact look. He is usually docked, but if left alone, his tail tends to curl up and over his back in true spitz fashion.

He sports a densely harsh coat, which is black, and less frequently cream or fawn-gold. It is very simple to groom and keep shining with a brush and a rough cloth. He is a brisk mover and delights in exercise over any distance. He is an easy-going character who will eat what he is given. He makes a very good house-dog as he has a sharp bark coupled with sharp hearing.

BREED BOX	
Size	small 22–36 cm (9–14 in), 5.5–7.5 kg (12–16½ lb)
Grooming	easy
Exercise	medium
Feeding	medium
Temperament	intelligent and amiable

SCHNAUZER

The Schnauzer (Standard Schnauzer, Working Group) is the middle size of the Schnauzer family. He stands up to 48 cm (19 in) at the withers and is a handsome compact dog who appears fiercer than he actually is. He is in his element as a companion to a busy

♦ LEFT
Prominent eyebrows and whiskers are the hallmarks of the Schnauzer breeds.

household, for which he provides a very useful warning signal at the approach of visitors, whether friend or foe, with a loudish, sharp bark.

He has the same short, harsh coat as the Miniature, and it comes in some of the same colours, i.e. pepper and salt as well as black. Grooming is no problem even after a muddy walk. He loves exercise and does not refuse however much is offered, especially if children are included in the equation. He does not run to too much flesh provided his daily intake of food is regulated.

BREED BOX	
Size	medium dog: 48.5 cm (19 in), 18kg (39½ lb) bitch: 45.5 cm (18 in), 16 kg (35 lb)
Grooming	straightforward
Exercise	medium
Feeding	medium
Temperament	alert and reliable

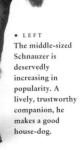

♦ LEFT
The middle-sized Schnauzer is deservedly increasing in popularity. A lively, trustworthy companion, he makes a good house-dog.

SHAR PEI

The Shar Pei, also known as the Chinese Shar-Pei, is a breed of great distinction. He has become well known because of his unusual appearance, with his wrinkly skin and frowning expression.

His head-shape is rectangular with little taper from occiput to nostrils, and his lips and muzzle are well padded. He has inherited a tendency to be born with in-rolling eyelids (entropion), and this can cause

problems. He is born with very wrinkled skin and unfortunately the wrinkles remain into his adult life; skin problems can occur as a result. The earliest exports were not blessed with the most perfect of temperaments.

+ ABOVE
The loose skin and wrinkles are abundant in puppies but may be limited to the head, neck and withers of an older dog.

Those who like the breed obviously appreciate the Shar Pei's unusual appearance, while those who find him ugly will steer clear. He stands up to 51 cm (20 in) tall and is powerfully built, mounted on reasonably firm legs.

In any country where there is a very small pool of breeding stock, faults will multiply. The breed has improved over the past ten or fifteen years, but it would be wise to decide on the selection of such an unusual dog only after long, careful consideration of its qualities and detailed discussions with responsible long-term devotees of the breed.

+ FAR LEFT
The Shar Pei has a large head and a well-padded muzzle.

+ LEFT
The Shar Pei almost became extinct in its native China following the prohibition of dogs. Breeders in Hong Kong kept the Shar Pei line going.

BREED BOX

Size	medium 46–51 cm (18½–20 in), 16–20kg (35–44 lb)
Grooming	medium
Exercise	medium
Feeding	medium
Temperament	independent but friendly

SHIH TZU

The Shih Tzu (Toy Group) originated in China. He has a host of admirers who greatly appreciate his wide-eyed expression and his distinctly cavalier attitude to the world about him. He views that world from a fairly small frame which is only some 26.5 cm (10½ in) high, but he gives the impression of mental superiority in no uncertain terms.

He has a long, dense coat, which rewards hard work and gets distinctly ragged if neglected. He comes in a glorious variety of colours, often with a white blaze to his forehead, and he carries his high-set tail like a banner over his back. He definitely enjoys being part of the family, but does not suggest that he is anxious to partake in long, muddy tramps across the fields. He takes a fair deal of cleaning up if he does feel an urge towards outdoor forays in mid-winter.

◆ BELOW
Shih Tzus are sturdy, bouncy extroverts that make delightful family companions.

◆ ABOVE
The golden head typifies a breed that is totally convinced of its superiority.

BREED BOX

Size	small
	dog: 26.5 cm (10½ in)
	bitch: 23 cm (9 in)
	4.5–7.5 kg
	(10–16½ lb)
Grooming	demanding
Exercise	reasonable
Feeding	reasonable
Temperament	friendly and independent

◆ ABOVE
The hair grows upwards on the bridge of the nose, giving the distinctive "chrysanthemum" look.

◆ LEFT
This beautiful coat gives a very good idea of the work involved in grooming a Shih Tzu to show standard.

TIBETAN SPANIEL

The Tibetan Spaniel (Non-Sporting Group) is a neat, tidy dog standing only 25.5 cm (10 in). His coat is longish and silky but does not take as much grooming to keep it looking good as you would at first expect.

He turns up in all sorts of colours, but a golden-red is the most common.

He also comes in a mixture of fawn and white. He has slightly bowed front legs, but this should not be an excuse for him to be grossly unsound.

His nature is accommodating in the household, being happy-go-lucky. He takes naturally to climbing over garden rockeries with gay abandon or rushing around the garden with his family. He does not spend his time looking for food, and he makes a delightful household companion.

+ LEFT
An unfussy breed that does not demand endless grooming.

+ BELOW
The Tibetan Spaniel's original purpose was to act as a companion and watchdog in the monasteries of Tibet.

BREED BOX

Size	small 25.5 cm (10 in), 4–7 kg (9–15½ lb)
Grooming	medium
Exercise	undemanding
Feeding	reasonable
Temperament	Loyal and independent

TIBETAN TERRIER

The Tibetan Terrier (Non-Sporting Group) is a profusely coated, square-built dog, standing as high as 40 cm (16 in). His coat is fine, although with hard brushing it can be made to gleam like silk. He comes in a range of colours from white to black, including golden. He loves people, enjoys plenty of exercise and is extremely nimble and energetic. He eats well, but not greedily. He will act as quite an impressive guard to house and family.

+ ABOVE
A terrier does not usually have such a shiny coat as this, but the Tibetan is, in truth, more of a guard dog.

+ RIGHT
The coat needs regular grooming, which, together with his boundless energy and enthusiasm, means this good-natured dog may be rather overwhelming.

BREED BOX

Size	small-medium 35.5–40 cm (14–16 in), 8–14 kg (18–31 lb)
Grooming	fairly demanding
Exercise	demanding
Feeding	medium
Temperament	outgoing and intelligent

The Working Group

The Working Group has the largest number of breeds and numbers of dogs within breeds. For this reason, in the US and some other countries they have been split into two groups – Working and Herding. These distinctions have been noted in the descriptions of each breed.

The undivided Working Group includes both herding and working, the latter being those breeds that guard, haul and rescue.

The sizes range from the very large Great Dane and the Mastiff, through the middle-sized German Shepherd Dog and the smaller Shetland Sheepdog, to the tiny Lancashire Heeler.

They are mostly extremely predictable dogs, bred for many generations for definite purposes. They have been selected for their trainability and have active minds. Their standard of obedience and their energy go a long way towards accounting for their popularity. Even trained dogs with active minds and bodies can easily become mischievous or difficult to control if they are left too much to their own devices. On the whole they are dogs that need occupation to fill their waking hours.

✦ FACING PAGE **Bullmastiff**

ALASKAN MALAMUTE

The Alaskan Malamute is a big dog; he does not stand as tall as some other giant breeds – 71 cm (28 in) – but he is massively built as befits a dog that is designed to pull heavy weights over snow-covered terrain for vast distances in sub-zero temperatures.

+ LEFT
The heaviest of the sled dogs, the Alaskan Malamute has a distinctly watchful air.

BREED BOX	
Size	giant
	38–56 kg
	(84–123½ lb)
	dog: 64–71 cm
	(25–28 in)
	bitch: 58–66 cm
	(23–26 in)
Grooming	medium
Exercise	demanding
Feeding	demanding
Temperament	reasonably amenable

He can weigh well in excess of 56 kg (123½ lb). Temperamentally he is normally friendly to people, but he can take umbrage with other dogs; a Malamute in full cry after a canine foe is an awesome sight and requires strength and experience in those who have to apply the brakes.

This is a superbly built, handsome breed. His relatively short, harsh, dense coat can be any shade of grey through to black, or from gold through red to liver, with areas of white on his underbelly, mask, legs and feet.

The breed was developed over many generations in Alaska and the Arctic fringes of Canada as a "workhorse", and he uses his ability to pull to great effect when he is on the end of a lead. He needs training from early puppyhood to be controllable in a household situation, so training classes are essential.

He enjoys his food and needs a great deal of exercise from those capable of handling such a giant; he is a delightful dog for those who are ready for a challenge.

+ RIGHT
The Alaskan Malamute is a powerful, dignified dog. Named after the Mahlemuts, an Innuit tribe, he was used as a draught animal long before Alaska became an American state.

+ ABOVE
This dog displays a thoroughly handsome and trusting expression, but he is not one to treat in a casual fashion.

ANATOLIAN SHEPHERD DOG

The Anatolian Shepherd Dog comes from Turkey. He is known to his familiars as the Karabash, the Turkish term for his best-known marking, which is cream to fawn in colour and sporting a black mask and ears.

Many European and Asian countries use two distinct types of dog with flocks of sheep. One is for herding and the other for guarding. Shepherd dogs are there to protect flocks against marauding wolves – and marauding humans in the form of rustlers! The Anatolian's height at a top level of 81 cm (32 in) puts him into the range of the awesome; he weighs accordingly. He therefore takes a good deal of feeding.

His coat is short and dense but is not hard to keep tidy. He likes his exercise, but as his ancestors were expected to amble about with the shepherd as the flocks moved from pasture to pasture, he is not often in a hurry.

This breed needs understanding; he will make a good family dog, but the

+ ABOVE
This is a breed of ancient origin that is regarded as a national emblem in its Turkish homeland.

family must make up its collective mind that his purpose in life is to guard; a few generations of living a softer life has not obliterated the results of careful selection since this mastiff type evolved.

BREED BOX	
Size	giant dog: 74–81 cm (29–32 in), 50–64 kg (110–141 lb) bitch: 71–79 cm (28–31 in), 41–59 kg (90½–130 lb)
Grooming	easy
Exercise	demanding
Feeding	demanding
Temperament	bold and independent

+ BELOW
A family group, all complete with the prized black mask that gives the breed the popular name of Karabash.

AUSTRALIAN CATTLE DOG

The Australian Cattle Dog (Herding Group) is a relatively recent immigrant to Britain and North America. He is a true working dog, whose alternative name in his country of origin is the Queensland Heeler.

Heelers persuade cattle to move by taking a quick nip at their heels, a practice not without danger of rapid retaliation! Good cattle-ranching Heelers have selected themselves effectively by their ability to survive the flashing bovine hooves. They are equally agile in the household situation, revelling in all the exercise they can get. They are loyal and biddable.

A robust breed standing a maximum 51 cm (20 in), the Australian Cattle Dog packs a lot of solid muscle into what is a relatively small frame. The official colours of the short, dense coat are blue mottled or red speckled, but they have to be seen to be properly appreciated. They are easy dogs to keep and groom.

BREED BOX

Size	small-medium 16–20 kg (35–44 lb) dog: 46–51 cm (18–20 in) bitch: 43–48 cm (17–19 in)
Grooming	easy
Exercise	medium
Feeding	medium
Temperament	alert and trustworthy

AUSTRALIAN SHEPHERD DOG

The Australian Shepherd Dog (Herding Group) originated in the United States. The Australians claim no credit for him. Exactly how he got his official name is not clear, but the important thing to recognize is that he is a soundly made working dog of considerable charm.

He stands up to 58 cm (23 in) high and has a medium-length coat that is not difficult to groom. He comes in various colours – blue merle, red merle, black or red, all with tan in his head area and on his lower legs.

He is an athletic sort who gives the impression of being capable of working with farm stock most effectively, and who greets friend and stranger openly and without aggression. He needs exercise to keep him fit but will not pester to go out.

BREED BOX

Size	medium-large 46–58 cm (18–23 in), 16–32 kg (35–70½ lb)
Grooming	reasonable
Exercise	demanding
Feeding	medium
Temperament	even-tempered

BEARDED COLLIE

The Bearded Collie (Herding Group) possesses bewitching eyes! He can make the toughest heart melt just by standing still and looking soft; hence his enormous increase in popularity over the last three decades. Standing up to 56 cm (22 in) at his withers, he

◆ BELOW
The Bearded Collie has pure Scottish ancestry and retains the basic instincts of a worker.

◆ LEFT
These keen observant eyes are one of the breed's most attractive features.

moves with athletic grace on legs and feet which, like his whole body, are covered with a harsh, shaggy coat underlaid by a soft, close undercoat.

The coat takes plenty of effort to groom as it is capable of picking up a good deal of the countryside in which he greatly prefers to spend his days. Colours range from all shades of grey, through black, blue and sandy, all

with white on head, brisket and lower limbs; he is rounded off with the typical beard after which he takes his name.

The Bearded Collie looks what he is – a cheerful, fun-loving rogue – and has converted well from his original role as a farm worker to make a superb companion and family friend.

BREED BOX	
Size	medium
	18–27 kg
	(39½–59½ lb)
	dog; 53–56 cm
	(21–22 in)
	bitch: 51–53 cm
	(20–21 in)
Grooming	demanding
Exercise	demanding
Feeding	medium
Temperament	lively, cheerful

◆ BELOW
Quiet while lying waiting, these dogs will move like a flash when the order is given.

BELGIAN SHEPHERD DOG

The Belgian Shepherd Dog (Herding Group) stands as high as 66 cm (26 in) at his tallest, so he is quite sizeable, but he does not carry a great deal of bulky muscle. He is an agile, swift-moving, elegant dog, with a graceful head and neck.

He has been selected over many decades to act as both herder and guard, so he is not instantly friendly to everyone.

There are three distinct coat types and four colour patterns. They originated as variants from different areas of Belgium. The two with long, straight top-coats are the Groenendael, black (Belgian Sheepdog), and the Tervueren, which is red, fawn or grey, with a black overlay (Belgian Tervueren). The smooth-coated version is the Malinois, which is the same colour as the Tervueren (Belgian Malinois), while a harsh, wiry coat, usually reddish fawn, fits the Laekenois.

An active, working breed, these dogs require plenty of exercise and training. Failure by owners to occupy such intelligent minds can easily lead to the development of mischievous habits. This is a breed for those with the will and the time to enjoy the company of a canine all-rounder.

+ ABOVE
A wiry-coated Laekenois looks very different from the other varieties of Belgian Shepherd Dog.

BREED BOX

Size	medium–large 56–66 cm (22–26 in), 27.5–28.5 kg (60½–63 lb)
Grooming	medium
Exercise	demanding
Feeding	medium
Temperament	reserved

+ ABOVE
The Laekenois has hair growing around his eyes, but it should not obscure them.

+ LEFT
The Groenendael has a long-haired black coat, sometimes with frosting – white or grey hairs – around the muzzle.

+ LEFT
In Belgium these dogs are classified as separate breeds. In the US the Groenendael is the Belgian Sheepdog, and the Laekenois is not recognized.

◆ BELOW
For many devotees, the most glamorous of all
the Belgian Shepherd Dogs is the Tervueren.

◆ LEFT
The Tervueren has a black mask
on his face and black ears.

◆ RIGHT
The only smooth-coated
Belgian Shepherd Dog is
the Malinois.

◆ LEFT
In spite of the
difference in coat
type and colour, all
four dogs are the
same basic shape.

BERGAMASCO

The Bergamasco is one of the most
recent exports from Italy; like so
many others, he has long been used as
a herding dog and a guard dog in the
mountains, and he has strong
protective instincts. It is
too early to give much
indication of how well
he will settle in as a member of a
family household.

He stands up to 62 cm (24½ in)
high and can weigh as much as 38 kg
(84 lb). He is solid and powerful,
expects exercise, not necessarily at
a great pace, and will eat
appropriately for his size.

His most distinctive
feature is his coat, which can
be solid grey or black with any
shade of grey and a certain
amount of white; light fawn is
also seen. The coat itself is
abundant and harsh.

BREED BOX	
Size	large
	56–62 cm (22–
	24½ in), 26–38 kg
	(57½–84 lb)
Grooming	demanding
Exercise	demanding
Feeding	medium
Temperament	cautious, intelligent

◆ BELOW
Grooming may be a
problem with this breed.

◆ LEFT
The Bergamasco's coat, described as
greasy to the touch, makes him appear
unkempt, but also keeps him warm and
dry. It tends to form loose mats.

BERNESE MOUNTAIN DOG

The Bernese Mountain Dog is a
handsome, affable fellow. At his tallest
he reaches a height of 70 cm (27½ in)
and he is built on sturdy lines. His
laid-back temperament allied to a great
love of his food means he tends to be
overweight.

His coat is soft and wavy and
responds to vigorous brushing by
producing a real sheen. It is basically
black with patches of reddish brown,
a striking white blaze on the head
and a white cross on the chest. He is
an intelligent, trainable dog, full of
bonhomie and courtesy which makes
him a very suitable member of a
country household. This is not a dog
for the town dweller.

He was originally a draught dog
and will pull a light cart with evident
enjoyment.

◆ RIGHT
The white blaze and
cross on the head
and chest are
characteristic of this
handsome Swiss dog.

◆ LEFT
The massiveness of
the bone of the leg
and the power of the
shoulders show why
the Bernese is a
favourite for pulling
dog-carts.

BREED BOX	
Size	large
	40–44 kg (88–97 lb)
	dog: 64–70 cm
	(25–27½ in)
	bitch: 58–66 cm
	(23–26 in)
Grooming	medium
Exercise	medium
Feeding	medium–large
Temperament	good-natured

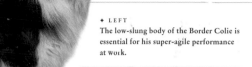

BORDER COLLIE

The Border Collie (Herding Group) is the classic farm dog. He is neat; he is agile; he thinks on his feet, and if his owner does not occupy his mind with useful training he will get into mischief, because his brain is always active.

Ideally he stands some 53 cm (21 in) at his withers, though he may look lower to ground as he travels at speed in a form of permanent crouch. His eyes show keen

♦ LEFT
The low-slung body of the Border Collie is essential for his super-agile performance at work.

BREED BOX

Size	small–medium dog: 53 cm (21 in), 23.5 kg (52 lb) bitch: 51 cm (20 in), 19 kg (42 lb)
Grooming	medium
Exercise	demanding
Feeding	medium
Temperament	very alert and trainable

To put it bluntly, he does not suffer fools gladly, and he is not averse to taking a swift nip at those who do not get his point, in the same way that he will liven the reactions of the sheep or cattle which are his natural flock.

♦ LEFT
This is the sharp expression of what is, by common consent, the most trainable breed of them all.

♦ BELOW
Working dogs from the Scottish borders, this is a breed that needs to be constantly occupied if destructive behaviour is to be avoided.

intelligence and his type is the favourite for those who wish to compete at top level in obedience competitions.

His coat is usually moderately long but is relatively easy to groom as long as the tangles are dealt with on a regular basis. He comes in all kinds of colours with white, but the commonest base colour is black. He demands exercise for his muscles just as much as for his brain. He makes an ideal family dog for the grown family, but he is not best suited to be a nursemaid to the very young, though no doubt such heresy will raise a few protests.

201

BOUVIER DES FLANDRES

The Bouvier des Flandres (Herding Group) is a powerful and rugged-looking dog. His basic role in life is herding both cattle and sheep, but over the years he has adapted to town life to a surprising degree. He has found favour with police forces not only in his native Belgium, but in Britain and several other countries.

He stands up to 68 cm (27½ in) and weighs solidly to match; he sports a coat which is coarse both to touch and to view. He also carries a beard and moustache, which add to his fairly fearsome appearance; coupled with a colour that ranges from fawn through brindle to black, he might be thought forbidding, but, in fact, he is a trustworthy character and fully deserves his increasing popularity as a house-companion for those who enjoy a strong dog.

BREED BOX	
Size	large
	dog: 62–68 cm
	(24½–27½ in),
	35–40 kg (77–88 lb)
	bitch: 59–65 cm
	(23½–25½ in),
	27–35 kg (60–77 lb)
Grooming	fairly demanding
Exercise	medium
Feeding	medium
Temperament	calm and sensible

✦ ABOVE
Bouvier des Flandres are solid and stable dogs. That, combined with their size and forbidding expression, has encouraged several police forces to train them for service.

✦ BELOW
Despite his expression the Bouvier des Flandres is an aimiable dog unless provoked.

✦ RIGHT
The Bouvier was once a cattle dog in its native Belgium and was also used to pull carts. He is balanced in body and limb, a true power-pack.

✦ ABOVE
The ears are small and high set.

BOXER

The Boxer is one of the canine world's characters! He is rightly recognized by his vast army of devotees as an extrovert. He is intelligent but needs to be convinced that his owner knows best – any other relationship is liable to be a disaster.

He stands up to 63 cm (25 in) high, and his supple limbs and body are well covered with muscle. He is full of stamina; he considers that his family household are his to guard, and woe betide anyone who does not recognize the fact.

His coat is simple to keep clean and neat; his colour ranges from red-fawn through various shades of brindle, with degrees of white. Some Boxers are born entirely white; a percentage of these are deaf from birth and as a result, many breeders put them down.

He is not a particularly greedy dog, but his appetite needs control if he is not to become overweight. His concept of exercise is that life is to be lived at speed. He can be trained to be obedient, but those who set out to

+ LEFT
Originating in Germany, the Boxer's ancestors were used for hunting wild boar and deer. Today he has one of the most distinctive shapes of all dogs.

harness this canine power-pack need to realize what they are facing.

His pugnacious upturned chin gives him the appearance of a pugilist; he does not start fights frequently, but he never backs down if challenged.

BREED BOX	
Size	medium
	dog: 57–63 cm
	(22½–25 in), 30–32
	kg (66–70½ lb)
	bitch: 57–59 cm
	(21–23½ in), 25–
	27 kg (55–59½ lb)
Grooming	easy
Exercise	demanding
Feeding	medium
Temperament	biddable and
	fearless

+ ABOVE
Nothing gets past those flashing eyes. The Boxer is one of the best guarding breeds.

+ RIGHT
A rare sight – a relaxed Boxer – but he will still react in a flash if he needs to.

BRIARD

The Briard (Herding Group) is from France. He has a Gallic charm about him which captivates a good number of folk. He has a rugged appearance, subtly combined with a slightly dapper look. At up to 68 cm (27 in) tall, he is a big dog, but underneath the long, wavy coat he is not a heavyweight.

The coat comes in black, slate grey or varying shades of fawn. It needs regular grooming, especially as the breed thoroughly enjoys exercise in town or country and can bring the great outdoors back indoors on returning home. The Briard is one of a mere handful of breeds that not only

BREED BOX

Size	large dog: 62–68 cm (24½–27 in), 38.5 kg (85 lb) bitch: 56–64 cm (22–25 in), 34 kg (75 lb)
Grooming	demanding
Exercise	demanding
Feeding	demanding
Temperament	lively and intelligent

is born with double hind dew-claws but should retain them. This gives his feet a very hairy appearance, which adds to his tendency to act rather like a floor-brush.

Briards are trainable; all that is needed is determination and patience. The dog must have total confidence in his owner. When he plays, he plays rough. He is good with children, but perhaps not with toddlers; they may get knocked over. This, of course, is true of many breeds, but it would be wise to remember that this handsome dog started off as a guarding dog for flocks of nomadic sheep.

BULLMASTIFF

The Bullmastiff evolved from crossing the Old English Mastiff with the Bulldog, to produce a very effective guard dog. In an age in which several large guarding breeds have been imported into Britain from mainland Europe, the original role of the Bullmastiff as a gamekeeper's assistant has tended to be forgotten.

He stands as much as 69 cm (27 in) high and weighs up to 59 kg (130 lb), which means he is both big and powerful. He is not to be trifled with; he does not suffer fools gladly, so he merits ownership by those who appreciate his cardinal virtue, utter faithfulness, and can handle a dog of independent nature.

He has a close fitting, hard coat, which can be brindle, fawn or red. He does not take a great deal of effort to keep clean and neat. He is muscular all over. His head is reminiscent of the old-fashioned Bulldog of the nineteenth century, which had a longer nose than in modern times. He does not therefore suffer the breathing problems that beset some brachycephalic breeds and enjoys exercise without being over-demanding.

This original gamekeeper's dog can achieve a truly awesome turn of speed in spite of his size.

+ LEFT
The power of the jaw is obvious.

+ BELOW LEFT
As befits a reliable guard dog, the Bullmastiff is noted for his alertness.

+ BELOW RIGHT
This is an extremely strong dog that may be stubborn and over-protective; not one for the novice owner.

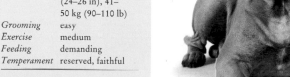

BREED BOX

Size	large to giant dog: 63.5–69 cm (25–27 in), 50–59 kg (110–130 lb) bitch: 61–66 cm (24–26 in), 41–50 kg (90–110 lb)
Grooming	easy
Exercise	medium
Feeding	demanding
Temperament	reserved, faithful

ROUGH COLLIE

The Rough Collie (Collie, Herding Group), from Scotland, has a dignified and intelligent expression. The Rough Collie stands up to 61 cm (24 in) high. He has three basic coat colours: cream to gold sable, tricolour and blue merle, which is a clear silver-blue splashed

BREED BOX

Size	medium–large dog: 56–61 cm (22–24½ in), 20.5–29.5 kg (45–65 lb)
Grooming	demanding
Exercise	medium
Feeding	medium
Temperament	friendly

with black. All three include white to some degree. The breed has a considerable history as working sheepdogs, but has not been used in this fashion to any great extent for a long time. Consequently the old, fast-moving Collie is not so obvious, and the dogs we see today tend to be a trifle idle. They do, however, make wonderful pets and household companions.

SMOOTH COLLIE

The Smooth Collie (Collie, Herding Group), also from Scotland, is simply the Rough Collie without the long coat. His coat is short and flat. He comes in the same colour variations as the Rough, although blue merles are more obvious in the Smooth.

The Smooth Collie is, if anything, more active than the Rough, and he expects more exercise. He makes an excellent household member but has never achieved the popularity levels of the "Lassie" dog, maybe because his short coat lacks film-star glamour.

◆ ABOVE RIGHT
The Smooth has moderately large ears, carried semi-erect when alert.

◆ LEFT
The Smooth version of the better known Rough Collie revealing the shape the coat hides.

BREED BOX

Size	medium–large measurements as the Rough Collie
Grooming	simple
Exercise	medium
Feeding	medium
Temperament	gay and friendly

DOBERMANN

◆ LEFT
Well controlled, the Dobermann is as good
a guard dog as any.

The Dobermann (still known in the US as the Doberman Pinscher) originates from Germany and is a tough, fast-moving guard dog. He was bred selectively by Herr Louis Dobermann as an all-purpose tracking/police dog. He is built on clean, powerful lines and reaches ideally 69 cm (27 in) at the withers.

His short, close-lying coat responds to polishing with a true gleam. He is most commonly seen as black, with tan colouring on the muzzle, forechest, legs and feet; but the black can be replaced by red or blue, or even, more rarely, with fawn.

He is energy personified, and at one time had a reputation for being

bad-tempered. Careful, sensible selection and training has altered this to a very large extent, but he is still a dog that needs to know who is going to be the boss in any family or work-place. As a house-dog, he ranks with any breed for faithful performance. He demands exercise as a right and needs a sizeable amount of food as a result.

◆ RIGHT
A soft expression is the result of leaving the ears uncropped, as in the UK.

◆ RIGHT
This elegant and powerful breed has an enormous following throughout the world but frightens some people.

BREED BOX	
Size	large
	dog: 69 cm (27½ in), 37.5 kg (83 lb)
	bitch: 65 cm (25½ in), 33 kg (73 lb)
Grooming	simple
Exercise	demanding
Feeding	medium–demanding
Temperament	alert and biddable

ESKIMO DOG

The Eskimo Dog (American Eskimo Dog) is one of a group of husky types. He is smaller than the Alaskan Malamute, but thicker set than the Siberian Husky. He was bred to haul fairly weighty sleighs over snow for the Inuit people ; temperament was not important. He is the classic dog portrayed in books on polar exploration; he had to fight for his very existence.

It is important to recognize such facts, as this dog stands 68 cm (27 in) high and weighs up to 47 kg (104 lb). When he decides to pull on lead or harness he does just that, he pulls. He has a thick double coat of any known dog colour, and grooming him is hard work.

He eats well and voraciously. Training him takes time and patience.

✦ LEFT
The Eskimo Dog follows very much in the tradition of the polar exploration dogs, willing to lie for hours waiting for the next task.

✦ ABOVE
These dogs display a watchful eye and a somewhat reserved attitude to people.

✦ LEFT
The coat protects against the rawest of cold weather – essential for the hard-working role for which he was bred.

BREED BOX	
Size	medium–large dog: 58–68 cm (23–27 in), 34–47 kg (75–104 lb) bitch: 51–61 cm (20–24 in), 27–41 kg (59½–90½ lb)
Grooming	demanding
Exercise	demanding
Feeding	demanding
Temperament	wary and alert

ESTRELA MOUNTAIN DOG

The Estrela Mountain Dog is a sturdy, sizeable dog of the mastiff type, which comes from the mountainous regions of Portugal.

This is a well-mannered breed with a delightfully shambling way of going. He regards people as friends and enjoys living with a family. He also enjoys exercise as befits his size, at a top level of 72 cm (28½ in) at his withers. He eats well but is not greedy.

His coat is usually fairly long and comes in fawn, brindle or wolf grey, but the general impression is of a large benign dog with a dark muzzle. Grooming him is not a huge problem. He has a loud bark and will give a good account of himself if his household is threatened, but he is not a difficult dog to handle, being relatively amenable to training.

✦ ABOVE
The benign expression of eye is the key to the personality.

BREED BOX	
Size	large–medium
	30–50 kg
	(66–110 lb)
	dog: 65–72 cm
	(25½–28½ in)
	bitch: 62–68 cm
	(24½–27½ in)
Grooming	medium
Exercise	medium
Feeding	medium
Temperament	loyal but stubborn

✦ ABOVE
The Estrela Mountain Dog looks what he is – massive and kindly.

✦ LEFT
The Estrela is not a dog to delight in cramped accommodation; he needs space.

FINNISH LAPPHUND

The Finnish Lapphund is yet another spitz type from the Nordic countries. Standing an average 47 cm (18½ in), he is a handsome dog with a bright expression, wide-set prick ears, and a tail carried over the back.

A solidly made dog, his profuse, coarse outer coat requires regular grooming. The coat colours may be any of a variety all over, but shades other than the main tone are seen on the head, chest and tail-tip, giving him a striking and attractive appearance.

He could make a useful companion/watchdog for any household as he is sensible and of good stature. He is rare outside his native country of Finland.

BREED BOX	
Size	medium–small 46–52 cm (18–20½ in), 20–21 kg (44–46 lb)
Grooming	fairly demanding
Exercise	medium
Feeding	medium
Temperament	calm and intelligent

+ TOP
The Finnish Lapphund is a typical spitz-type, originally used to herd reindeer.

+ ABOVE
This sharp, intense look befits his character exactly.

+ LEFT
The breed is not often seen outside Finland but is a sensible size for a small family home.

GERMAN SHEPHERD DOG (ALSATIAN)

The German Shepherd Dog (Herding Group) must be the best known breed of them all. His breeding and training have led to his renown as a herding sheepdog, a leader of the blind and as a police dog. Police forces, the armed services, prison officers, drug officers and private protection agencies all over the world employ the GSD.

There are considerable variations in what is regarded as the ideal shape for this multi-purpose dog. Traditionally, the dog is a proud, powerful creature, standing an average 63 cm (25 in), with a body length slightly greater than its height. Coat lengths vary; some enthusiasts state that a medium length coat is the only acceptable version, while others accept a long-haired type. Colours include black, black and tan, and sable. White and cream dogs do occur, but raise loud, horrified protests from many aficionados, something to bear in mind if the ultimate intention is to show the dog. All such matters of taste aside, the fact remains that, at his best, the GSD is an intelligent, trainable dog with a pleasant, loyal disposition and makes a first-class household member. He needs exercise and, on occasion, may need to be stimulated in that direction as he can be wilfully idle. On the other hand, most need to have their energies directed into useful pursuits as the GSD, in common with so many breeds in the Working Group, originated as a shepherd dog.

BREED BOX	
Size	large dog. 60–66 cm (24–26 in), 36.5 kg (80½ lb) bitch: 55–60 cm (22–24 in), 29.5 kg (65 lb)
Grooming	medium
Exercise	demanding
Feeding	medium
Temperament	steady, highly trainable

+ TOP RIGHT
The eyes show the breed's intelligence – the GSD does not miss a trick.

+ RIGHT
A handsome all-purpose dog that enjoys walking.

GIANT SCHNAUZER

The Giant Schnauzer is the largest of the three Schnauzer varieties. This big dog is very similar in shape to his smaller cousins, being a clean-cut, square-built dog that can stand as high as 70 cm (27½ in) at his withers. He is found in the same colours – black or pepper and salt – as the smaller ones, but naturally he is a more imposing looking animal.

At one time employed as a cattle-droving dog, he has become popular as a household guard dog in Germany and Britain. He also has a role as a

+ LEFT
The Giant Schnauzer has a distinctively moulded head and huge eyebrows.

+ ABOVE
This is a no-nonsense breed used in Europe for police work. It is not aggressive unless provoked.

police dog in Europe because he is highly trainable and loyal.

He needs regular trimming, he enjoys family life, he does not eat a vast amount considering his size, and his beard and moustache give him the sort of expression that will impress those with felonious intent.

+ RIGHT
In some countries the Giant Schnauzer's ears are cropped.

BREED BOX	
Size	large dog: 65–70 cm (25½–27½ in), 45.5 kg (100 lb) bitch: 60–65 cm (23½–25½ in), 41 kg (90 lb)
Grooming	medium
Exercise	medium
Feeding	medium
Temperament	bold and good- natured

+ LEFT
The Giant Schnauzer will keenly defend his territory. It is not a breed to be treated casually.

GREAT DANE

The Great Dane is a true giant among dogs; he stands an absolute minimum of 76 cm (30 in), but the adult male should be considerably taller. His coat is short and dense, and therefore relatively easy to keep neat and sleek.

He has five official colours, which are jealously guarded by the breed enthusiasts – brindle, fawn, blue, black and harlequin, the latter being a basic white with all black or all blue patches that give the appearance of being torn at the edges. Any other colour is a freak, and it is unwise to pay extra money on the suggestion that "this unusual colour is very rare and therefore is more valuable".

BREED BOX

Size	giant dog: minimum 76 cm (30 in), 54 kg (119 lb) bitch: minimum 71 cm (28 in), 46 kg (101½ lb)
Grooming	simple
Exercise	medium
Feeding	demanding
Temperament	kindly but dignified

He is a strong, deep-chested dog but is truly a hound used for chasing wild boar in his native country, which is Germany, not Denmark. He can be trained to be reasonably obedient

✦ ABOVE RIGHT
The Dane is remarkably gentle for such a huge creature.

because he is intelligent. He likes both exercise and his creature comforts; he recognizes the pleasure of occupying the major part of the hearth in front of a roaring fire. For those who see him as the dog of all dogs and can afford his large appetite, he is a must; but, like all giant dogs, he has a regrettable tendency to have a shortish life span.

✦ RIGHT
This brindle bitch takes up a lot of space – she won't curl up easily in a small house.

✦ ABOVE
The Dane's head is big, carried high, giving the impression of strength.

HOVAWART

The Hovawart (pronounced "hoffavart") is a guard dog from the Black Forest region of Bavaria. He wears a medium length coat, which can be black and gold, a goldish blond or, on occasion, black by itself. He stands up to 70 cm (27½ in), but he is not a heavy-bodied dog.

He has yet to make his mark outside of Bavaria, but he is trainable, enjoys family life, and does not demand vast amounts of exercise or food. He is possessed of a good nose, so he will follow a scent, which suggests that he could become a canine all-rounder.

BREED BOX

Size	medium–large dog: 63–70cm (25–27½ in), 30–40 kg (66–88 lb) bitch: 58–65 cm (23–25½ in), 25–35 kg (55–77 lb)
Grooming	medium
Exercise	medium
Feeding	medium
Temperament	alert, intelligent, wilful

✦ ABOVE RIGHT
The black and gold colour gleams on this fit, athletic native of the Black Forest.

✦ RIGHT
A friendly look in a breed that enjoys human company.

✦ BELOW
The Kuvasz comes from a cold climate, hence his thick coat.

HUNGARIAN KUVASZ

The Hungarian Kuvasz (Kuvasz) has quite a presence in the United States. He is of the style seen in many European countries acting, as a guard or herder; he is cautious of strangers.

A prospective owner requires considerable experience of handling difficult dogs before introducing the Hungarian Kuvasz into normal household circumstances.

He stands up to 75 cm (29½ in) tall, wears a medium-length, thick coat, which is pure white and reasonably groomable. He requires a fair amount of exercise, is of burly build and eats accordingly.

✦ LEFT
This brilliant white dog never relaxes his guard. He is thought to have found his way to Hungary with nomadic Turkish shepherds sometime during the Middle Ages.

BREED BOX

Size	large 66–75 cm (26–29½ in), 30–52 kg (66–115 lb)
Grooming	medium
Exercise	medium
Feeding	demanding
Temperament	trainable, wary

HUNGARIAN PULI

The Hungarian Puli (Puli, Herding Group) is a herding dog, and typifies the cliché "once seen, never forgotten". His coat varies from black, through grey and fawn to apricot. It grows massively into a weather-resistant equivalent of the Eskimo's parka. It will withstand cold and wet. As the dog matures the coat tends to form into cords.

These cords are not to be confused with the mats that are the sign of an idle owner. The coat takes a great amount of hard work to keep in order. The cords cover the dog literally from head to toe and include the face and tail. There is, indeed, very little visible of the dog beneath the coat. When the dog moves the cords swing *en masse*

◆ RIGHT
A mid-European dog with a highly distinctive corded coat which swings like a loose rug as he goes on his energetic way.

BREED BOX	
Size	small
	dog: 40–44 cm
	(16–17½ in), 13–
	15 kg (28½–33 lb)
	bitch: 37–41 cm
	(14½–16½ in),
	10–13 kg
	(22–28½ lb)
Grooming	very demanding
Exercise	medium
Feeding	undemanding
Temperament	lively but reserved
	with strangers

rather like a curtain. The Hungarian Puli is a fast-moving energetic creature who loves exercise and people. He is a great barker and therefore an effective burglar alarm. This is a dog for the devotee.

KOMONDOR

◆ RIGHT
In spite of the coat over his eyes, the Komondor misses nothing.

The Komondor is another dog from Hungary, where he guards flocks and farms. He has a huge, corded coat that reaches the ground in the adult. It is white immediately after the dog has been bathed and dried; drying him is a

◆ RIGHT
This is a dog for the wide open spaces and those with time to maintain him.

long drawn-out process. His whiteness tends to be rapidly compromised by contact with the countryside. His average height is 80 cm (31½ in), and he weighs about 50 kg (110 lb), so he is an awesome chap once roused. His ancestry is as a farm dog; bringing such a dog into a town atmosphere is totally misguided. His basic instinct is to guard, and to trifle with a dog of such dimensions is risky, to put it mildly. This is definitely a dog only for those who understand what they are taking on.

BREED BOX	
Size	giant
	dog: minimum 65
	cm (25½ in), 50–
	51 kg (110–112½ lb)
	bitch: minimum
	60 cm (23½ in), 36–
	50 kg (79½–110 lb)
Grooming	very demanding
Exercise	medium
Feeding	medium
Temperament	wary, protective

LANCASHIRE HEELER

The Lancashire Heeler is a stylish little dog. He stands a mere 30 cm (12 in) high and is slightly longer than he is tall. His forelegs tend to be slightly bowed, but this should not be excessive. As his name implies, he was used on farms to herd cattle and he still does when required.

His coat is not truly short, but it does not grow to any great length. He is always black and tan and a thorough, brisk grooming will have him shining in no time at all. He enjoys exercise, but he does not make an issue of it. He makes a terrific household companion and appears to love children and joining in games.

He has a sharp bark which is louder than one might expect from such a small package, he eats well and is highly biddable.

+ LEFT
A small and active dog that adapts easily from droving to being part of a household. The original Lancashire Heelers were used to drive cattle by nipping at their heels, much like the Welsh Corgi.

BREED BOX

Size	small
	6.5 kg (14 lb) dog:
	30 cm (12 in)
	bitch: 25 cm (10 in)
Grooming	easy
Exercise	medium
Feeding	undemanding
Temperament	happy and
	affectionate

+ ABOVE
The prick ears betoken the dog's readiness to join in any form of fun.

+ LEFT
Short legs carry a powerful little body; this breed will clear the house of rats just as a bonus.

MAREMMA SHEEPDOG

The Maremma Sheepdog is Italy's
version of the nomadic flock-guarder.
As such this is a dog that has derived
from generations of working guard
dogs. He stands as high as 73 cm
(29 in), but he is not heavily built.

He has been seen in Britain, but not
the US, for some twenty years in

◆ LEFT AND BELOW FAR LEFT
This dog's ancestry means that he requires
plenty of exercise as well as discipline.

steadily increasing numbers, and his
temperament has gradually altered
from the initial sharpness which was
to be expected from this type of
import. Now he is a fairly trainable

dog of good basic intelligence, even if
still a trifle aloof with strangers.

He carries a medium-length coat
that fits him closely; it is white with a
slight touch of fawn. He has an alert
expression that denotes
the watchfulness of his
ancestry. He is a
worker and requires
exercise to keep him
the fit, muscular creature
that his breeding has made him.

◆ BELOW
An expression that suggests that he is not a
fawning dog; he will take his time to admit
strangers to the bosom of his family.

BREED BOX	
Size	large
	dog: 65–73 cm
	(25½–29 in), 35–45
	kg (77–99 lb)
	bitch: 60–68 cm
	(24–27½ in),
	30–40 kg (66–88 lb)
Grooming	medium
Exercise	demanding
Feeding	medium
Temperament	lively, active

MASTIFF

The Mastiff is often referred to as the Old English Mastiff. He stands up to 76 cm (30 in) and is built on massive lines. Giant dogs such as this grow remarkably quickly and require care in feeding; they do eat a lot and can be expensive to rear. In addition a dog

✦ RIGHT
The hindlegs are not always well formed, so care has to be taken in selecting a sound puppy.

✦ BELOW LEFT
The breed is usually good-natured but nevertheless has massive jaws in a very solid head.

that weighs as much as many an owner requires determination as well as ability to control it. Although the Mastiff is not demanding as regards exercise, he still needs an adequate amount of freedom.

This dog has a short-lying coat that is reasonably easy to keep in order. The colour varies from apricot-fawn to a dark brindle-fawn, always combined with a black mask and ears.

Fortunately he has a calm temperament – if not he would be dangerous.

BREED BOX	
Size	giant 70–76 cm (27½–30 in), 79–86 kg (174–189½ lb)
Grooming	simple
Exercise	medium
Feeding	demanding
Temperament	steady

NEAPOLITAN MASTIFF

The Neapolitan Mastiff has the usual mastiff square-shaped head and muzzle, powerful body, and strong limbs. In addition he sports a quantity of loose skin around jowls

and dewlap, coupled with pendulous lips, which give his head a huge appearance.

His short, dense coat is tight fitting on body and limbs; it is usually black or blue-grey, but occasionally brown shades are seen. He enjoys exercise but is not over-demanding in this respect; he does boast a fairly large appetite. He is undoubtedly courageous and protective of owner and property. His devotees state that he will only use his full force on command, which comes as a relief to those who do not own him.

Grooming him is not a great problem, although, like so many breeds that have loose jowls, he dribbles, and when he shakes his head he may prove a trifle anti-social.

✦ ABOVE
The Neapolitan Mastiff may be descended from the war and fighting dogs of Ancient Rome.

✦ LEFT
The skin folds down the neck are there to protect vital structures from attack.

BREED BOX	
Size	giant 65–75 cm (25½–29 in), 50–70 kg (110–154 lb)
Grooming	undemanding
Exercise	medium
Feeding	fairly demanding
Temperament	devoted guard

NEWFOUNDLAND

✦ BELOW
The Newfoundland has immense charm and a sense of humour.

The Newfoundland is a massive cuddly bear of a dog. His large face radiates *bonhomie*. He is a water-dog *par excellence* to the extent that his fanciers warn purchasers that if they do not want to be forcibly rescued from water, they should not go swimming with a Newfoundland! He is known to everyone as "The Newfie".

He can stand up to 71 cm (28 in) high, not all that tall by some standards, but his body is built on generous lines as are his legs, which end in feet with webs between his toes to help him swim strongly at speed. He weighs up to 69 kg (152 lb) and eats to match.

He has an all-embracing coat which has a slightly oily feel to it. Not surprisingly, this renders it totally waterproof. The colour can be black, brown, or white with black markings, which is generally known as Landseer (because Sir Edwin Landseer included Newfoundlands of this marking in many of his paintings).

In spite of being an aquatic dog, he has his own style of movement on *terra firma* – he tends to roll in a charming, nautical fashion. He expects exercise, but prefers it to be in water; then, when he gets back home, he has an engaging habit of shaking vigorously. This is a dog for the whole family, but not for the house-proud or the flat-dweller.

BREED BOX	
Size	giant
	dog: 71 cm (28 in),
	64–69 kg (141–
	152 lb)
	bitch: 66 cm (26 in),
	50–54.5 kg
	(110–120 lb)
Grooming	fairly demanding
Exercise	aquatically
	demanding
Feeding	demanding
Temperament	delightfully docile

✦ ABOVE
The rather deep-set eyes give an expression of benign relaxation.

✦ ABOVE
A house needs plenty of room to accommodate a Newfie.

✦ LEFT
The lung space is evident even in a front view of this master-swimmer among dogs.

NORWEGIAN BUHUND

The Norwegian Buhund is a neatly shaped spitz. He has erect ears on an intelligent head and a lively attitude to life. He measures around 45 cm (18 in), so he is not at all an imposing dog, but he has an air of alertness about him that makes people pay attention.

BREED BOX	
Size	medium–small 41–46 cm (16– 18 in), 24–26 kg (53–57 lb)
Grooming	undemanding
Exercise	medium
Feeding	undemanding
Temperament	energetic and fearless

+ RIGHT
This is the archetypal outline of a spitz; all neatness and expectancy. He was once used as a sled-dog in his native country.

+ RIGHT
The Norwegian Buhund is an easy dog to keep clean; he gives the impression of disliking getting very muddy.

+ LEFT
This is a breed of energetic dogs that may be initially wary of strangers but fits family life well.

His coat is close and harsh; the commonest colour is a wheaten gold, but dogs with black and wolf-sable coats are seen. The coat is short enough to require no great skill or time to keep groomed.

He is a herder in his native Norway, and good hearing allows him to react swiftly as a guard. He gets on well with his family but is somewhat reserved with those he does not know. He thoroughly enjoys exercise and is relatively biddable, so his bustling style can be kept under control when loose in field or park.

OLD ENGLISH SHEEPDOG

The Old English Sheepdog (Herding Group), nicknamed the Bobtail, is another of those breeds that could be classified as distinctive the world over. He has evolved from a practical, working-style sheepdog into a stylized show-dog; his use in commercial advertising has led to a growth in popularity, sadly to the breed's overall detriment.

He stands around 61 cm (24 in) high, but his huge, fluffed-up coat makes him look somewhat taller. The owners who exhibit their dogs have to put in hours of work in order to maintain them in show-ring style. Left ungroomed for any length of time, the harsh-textured coat can become

matted to a degree that leaves little alternative but to clip.

He is a cheerful extrovert and makes a good family companion, provided the family is committed to the dog's exercise and can cope with

his occasionally explosive nature. He will join in every possible activity with enthusiasm. He is capable of being a first-class guard of his owner's property, with a highly distinctive bark to emphasize his presence.

+ LEFT
Old English Sheepdogs are known as Bobtails because their tails are customarily docked.

+ BELOW LEFT
This breed goes back at least 150 years, possibly longer.

+ BELOW RIGHT
The higher rump end is the result of grooming the hair upwards.

BREED BOX

Size	large
	dog: minimum
	61 cm (24 in),
	36.5 kg (80½ lb)
	bitch: minimum
	56 cm (22 in),
	29.5 kg (65 lb)
Grooming	very demanding
Exercise	medium
Feeding	medium
Temperament	friendly and outgoing

PINSCHER

The Pinscher, originally from Germany, is best described as a midway stage between the Dobermann and the tiny Miniature Pinscher. He wears the same short, dense coat in the same basic black-and-tan colour combination of the Dobermann, with the same alternatives of red, blue and fawn with tan.

He is a sharp-outlined dog, with an alert-looking head and expression, and a neat, muscled body. He moves with nimble athletic strides. As he stands

<table>
<tr><td colspan="2">BREED BOX</td></tr>
<tr><td>Size</td><td>medium–small
43–48 cm (17–19 in)</td></tr>
<tr><td>Grooming</td><td>easy</td></tr>
<tr><td>Exercise</td><td>medium</td></tr>
<tr><td>Feeding</td><td>undemanding</td></tr>
<tr><td>Temperament</td><td>active and confident</td></tr>
</table>

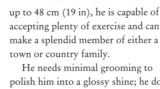

◆ LEFT
The Pinscher is a very bright breed with clean-cut features and bright eyes.

up to 48 cm (19 in), he is capable of accepting plenty of exercise and can make a splendid member of either a town or country family.

He needs minimal grooming to polish him into a glossy shine; he does not ask for excessive food, and he possesses a sharp voice and an intelligent mind, which makes him a handy watchdog.

◆ ABOVE
This red-coat version positively shines to prove the dog's health.

◆ LEFT
Although he can be distrustful of strangers, the Pinscher is responsive to training and makes a good family member.

◆ LEFT
A charming
sheepdog from
Poland with a
friendly
attitude, which
has brought
him great
popularity.

POLISH LOWLAND SHEEPDOG

The Polish Lowland Sheepdog is thought to be descended from the ancient Asian herding dogs. It nearly became extinct during World War II, but since then careful breeding has ensured its survival. Standing around 52 cm (20½ in), he has a cheerful look about his well-haired face, and he is a truly active working herder.

He has been often compared to a smaller version of the Bearded Collie; both breeds are also extremely intelligent and trainable. He is good-natured to the extent that he makes a thoroughly balanced family companion and children's playmate.

He needs plenty of exercise and can be boisterous; his coat is long and harsh, with a density to his soft undercoat that guarantees he will find cold winters no problem after his native Poland. Grooming has to be thorough, but the breed is very tolerant.

◆ BELOW
The Polish Lowland Sheepdog
is usually born without a tail.
His long thick coat needs
regular grooming.

BREED BOX

Size	medium–small dog: 43–52 cm (17–20½ in), 19.5 kg (43 lb) bitch: 40–46 cm (16–18 in)
Grooming	demanding
Exercise	demanding
Feeding	medium
Temperament	alert, biddable

PORTUGUESE WATER DOG

◆ LEFT
These dogs
are similar
to the
Poodle but
without
such a
refined
head.

The Portuguese Water Dog is commonly mistaken for the Standard Poodle; he stands up to 57 cm (22½ in), has a profuse coat, and is brown or black in basic coloration. He has not got the refined head of the Poodle, but he does have a traditional trim, clipped from behind the rib-cage.

His tail is not docked but is clipped except for a sizeable plume at the end. This trim is based on his role as a swimmer; he has been taught by Portuguese fishermen to retrieve lost nets. These dogs have exaggerated webs on their feet to help them to swim.

He is reputed to be stubborn, so he requires firm handling. He adores freedom of exercise, and he makes a good family dog with a cheerful attitude.

◆ BELOW
Note the powerful
body and unusual
tail-carriage.

BREED BOX

Size	medium–large dog: 50–57 cm (20–22½ in), 19–25 kg (42–55 lb) bitch: 43–52 cm (17–20½ in), 16–22 kg (35–48½ lb)
Grooming	demanding
Exercise	demanding
Feeding	medium
Temperament	tireless and amenable

PYRENEAN MOUNTAIN DOG

♦ LEFT
The Pyrenean Mountain Dog is massive and requires a firm handler. A steady-moving dog with very considerable dignity, he can be quite reserved with strangers.

The Pyrenean Mountain Dog, also known as the Great Pyrenees, is a solidly built animal measuring as much as 70 cm (27½ in) and weighing up to 60 kg (132 lb). He is another of the

BREED BOX	
Size	giant dog: 70 cm (27½ in), 50-60 kg (119-132 lb) bitch: minimum 65 cm (25½ in), 40 kg (88 lb)
Grooming	demanding
Exercise	medium
Feeding	demanding
Temperament	confident and genial

flock-guarding dogs of the European nomad shepherd; with his coarse-textured white coat he merges into the flock. As a domestic house-dog he requires regular grooming; bathing him is no easy task.

The modern Pyrenean has more of the permitted badger coloration, especially on head and ears, than twenty or thirty years ago. He is

another breed that grows large double hind dewclaws, which help him in snow-covered terrain.

He does not require excessive exercise and normally moves at a dignified amble in park or pasture. He makes a good household member, his basic temperament having become more gentle as a result of generations of selective breeding worldwide.

PYRENEAN SHEEPDOG

The Pyrenean Sheepdog is a very recent introduction to Britain and is not registered in the US. He stands up to 48 cm (19 in) high and appears neat in general outline with a lean body. His coat is

fairly harsh with a somewhat windswept look; it is supported by a thickish undercoat. Colour can vary from fawn through grey to merle and black or black and white.

He is a smallish dog for an all-purpose flock-guarder, but he gives an impression of speed and enjoys exercise. It is too early to predict his suitability as a general family dog.

♦ LEFT AND ABOVE
This second breed from the Pyrenees is totally different in looks. Both breeds work with sheep but perform in contrasting styles.

BREED BOX	
Size	medium–small 38–48 cm (15–19 in), 8–15 kg (18–33 lb)
Grooming	medium
Exercise	medium
Feeding	undemanding
Temperament	alert, wary

ROTTWEILER

The Rottweiler, from Germany, is a handsome and striking breed. The males can stand as tall as 69 cm (27 in), and they are solidly built of hard muscle.

Unfortunately their popularity has not done the breed good service as the ease of selling any standard of Rottweiler proved too attractive for

unscrupulous dealers. It was predictable that such a powerful dog would be all too capable of inflicting great damage if he attacked humans, and in the late 1980s this happened. The numbers of Rottweilers being bred dropped dramatically, and this dangerous situation levelled off. The

breed is very intelligent, but there is a considerable difference in temperament between the dog and the bitch, the latter in general being calmer and her reactions easier to predict.

BREED BOX	
Size	large
	dog: 63–69 cm
	(25–27½ in),
	50 kg (110 lb)
	bitch: 58–63.5 cm
	(23–25 in),
	38.5 kg (85 lb)
Grooming	simple
Exercise	medium-demanding
Feeding	demanding
Temperament	courageous,
	trainable

The coat is invariably of medium-short length and black and tan in colour. Grooming is rewarding; it produces a magnificent shine very easily. Exercise is essential because of the muscular nature of the breed. He likes his food and expects plenty.

This is a breed for experienced dog owners who will devote time and attention to the dog. He merits much of the enthusiasm he engenders but needs good control.

◆ ABOVE
The powerful muzzle shows why the breed has earned respect as a guard.

◆ TOP RIGHT
An average-sized, strong, agile dog, the Rottweiler is not for the nervous owner or for newcomers to dogs.

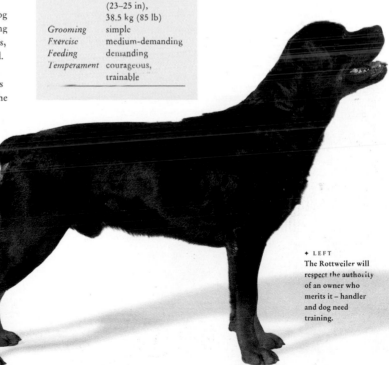

◆ LEFT
The Rottweiler will respect the authority of an owner who merits it – handler and dog need training.

ST BERNARD

The St Bernard is yet another instantly recognizable breed. He stands tall, but it is his massive frame that makes him so remarkable. He originated in the mountains of Switzerland and is traditionally depicted with a miniature brandy-barrel attached to his collar as

+ RIGHT
These dogs were first taken to the famous Hospice in the Swiss Alps by the monks as guards and companions in the seventeenth century.

BREED BOX	
Size	giant maximum 91.5 cm (36 in) dog: 75 kg (165½ lb) bitch: 68 kg (150 lb)
Grooming	medium-demanding
Exercise	medium
Feeding	demanding
Temperament	steady and benevolent

he locates the traveller stranded in deep snow.

Everything about the modern St Bernard is huge, right down to his feet. He has a great breadth of skull and huge jaws. His lower lip tends to droop at the outside corner, which means that he drools a fair amount.

His limbs are big-boned, so rearing the young is expensive and needs to be well understood. Exercise in the puppy should be increased very slowly as he grows to ensure that the minimum strain is put on tender tissues. Exercise in the adult is usually a gentle progression, though a St Bernard pulling on his lead can be a struggle for the handler. Grooming is not

a problem except that there is a lot of coat to be dealt with. The coat is normally medium length, but there is a short-coated St Bernard. The colour can be orange, red brindle or

mahogany brindle with white markings, or white with any of the above as coloured patches.

Temperamentally the breed is trustworthy and benign, which is just as well, since the rare occasion when a St Bernard does erupt is awesome to view. This is an attractive breed, but those who fall for him should consider carefully how well they can cope.

+ ABOVE RIGHT
It is all too easy to fall for the delightful charm of the youngster.

+ LEFT
St Bernards are massive dogs with truly powerful bones in the forelegs.

SAMOYED

The Samoyed is the "Laughing Cavalier" of dogdom, with his brilliant white colour and his typical spitz expression. He stands up to 56 cm (22 in) high, and he is very slightly longer than tall. His coat is harsh and stand-off, in a basic white, but many of the breed carry varying amounts of

+ LEFT
This is a happy-go-lucky breed with never a nasty thought, though plenty of mischievous ones.

biscuit, which is a light reddish fawn.

Grooming is hard work, but Samoyeds are tolerant and will submit for hours, if necessary, to lying on their sides while the owners brush and comb them. The breed has a history as a sled-dog and has hairy, flat feet to enable it to cope with ice that would otherwise pack into the spaces between the pads.

He enjoys exercise, but needs human company; he is a super member of a family household, but still manages to be a great companion to those who live alone. He is not a huge eater, in spite of his energetic lifestyle. His only real drawback is his tendency to bark noisily, especially when he is enjoying himself, which is most of the time.

+ FAR LEFT
Samoyeds have a smiling and cheerful expression.

+ BELOW
Under the coat, there is usually a muscular frame that fits well into a sled-harness, given the opportunity. The breed originated with the Samoyeds, a nomadic tribe of northern Asia.

BREED BOX

Size	medium-large dog: 51–56 cm (20–22 in), 23 kg (50½ lb) bitch: 46–51 cm (18–20 in), 18 kg (39½ lb)
Grooming	very demanding
Exercise	medium
Feeding	medium
Temperament	alert and smiling

SHETLAND SHEEPDOG

The Shetland Sheepdog (Herding Group) is a diminutive version of the Rough Collie, although few companion dogs are genuinely as small as the official top height permitted for show dogs, which is around 37 cm (14½ in). In fact, this very attractive little dog has all the instincts that his name implies and, although today he is very much a family dog, he is still capable of reacting as a worker.

+ RIGHT
The slight tilt of the head, as if asking a question, is typical of the Sheltie.

+ BELOW RIGHT
This miniature version of the Rough Collie is a worker in its own right.

BREED BOX

Size	small
	9 kg (20 lb)
	dog: 37 cm (14½ in)
	bitch: 35.5 cm
	(14 in)
Grooming	demanding
Exercise	medium
Feeding	undemanding
Temperament	affectionate and
	responsive

He carries a long, straight top-coat that can be coloured sable, tricolour, blue merle, black and white, and even black and tan. The undercoat is thick, so it requires thorough grooming fairly frequently if it is not to become matted and impossible to cope with.

He is an alert dog and will take a great deal of exercise if it is offered but can just as easily make a first-class companion for an elderly person. He is watchful and capable of giving tongue when the occasion demands it.

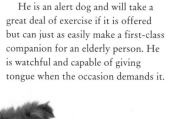

+ BELOW
Shelties are sturdy, cheerful and easy to train. They are also photogenic!

SIBERIAN HUSKY

The Siberian Husky is the racer of the sled-dog world. It may seem a hard thing to say about what, in many ways, is a very charming dog indeed, but he lives only to pull a sledge! He stands up to 60 cm (23½ in) at the withers, he

is lean at his muscular best, and he has a head that is distinctly reminiscent of a wolf, but with a kinder look.

His coat is fairly long and will keep him warm in the most bitter cold. He can come in virtually any colour or pattern of colours. His eyes are the most remarkable feature of his face as they too can vary in colour, even to the extent of one being brown and the other blue. If that was not odd enough, dogs are found whose individual irises can show two halves of different hues.

His attitude to people is of extreme tolerance; to his own kind he can be very domineering, and there is a distinct pecking order in a racing pack. It is possible to persuade the odd one to walk on a loose lead and even obey basic commands, but it simply is not his idea of how a dog should behave. People who keep them usually exercise them in front of a sledge if snow is available or by pulling a wheeled rig on forest tracks. Husky racing events take place all over Britain, America and Europe. Think carefully before choosing him as a companion animal.

✦ ABOVE
These dogs can jump a good height from a standstill.

BREED BOX

Size	medium-large dog: 60 cm (23½ in) 23.5 kg (52 lb) bitch: 53.5 cm (21 in), 19.5 kg (43 lb)
Grooming	medium
Exercise	very demanding
Feeding	demanding
Temperament	friendly but reserved

✦ ABOVE
The Siberian Husky rarely lowers his pricked ears.

✦ RIGHT
Originally draught dogs with the Inuit people, half a dozen Siberian Huskies attached to a racing sledge will give an exciting ride.

✦ LEFT
Note the strength of the legs, which keep racing Huskies on the move.

SWEDISH LAPPHUND

The Swedish Lapphund is built on very similar lines to the Finnish Lapphund. He may stand up to 51 cm (20 in) and is of typical spitz construction. His coat is weather resistant and of medium length; it is a mixture of black and brown with an

+ RIGHT
This stout-framed dog has a coat fir to withstand Scandinavian weather.

+ BELOW
The Swedish Lapphund has a relatively gentle character.

occasional touch of white on his chest or feet. He is not difficult to groom.

He appears to be a friendly, intelligent dog. His temperament would appeal to a family household as he enjoys exercise and is not greedy. He is not, as yet, well known outside his native country.

BREED BOX	
Size	medium-small 44–51 cm (20 in), 19.5–20.5 kg (43–45 lb)
Grooming	medium
Exercise	medium
Feeding	medium
Temperament	active and friendly

SWEDISH VALLHUND

The Swedish Vallhund looks and acts very much like a grey or yellowish Corgi. He is built on similar lines, standing a mere 35 cm (14 in) tall, but somewhat longer in body than height.

His job is to herd and he does this, as do the Corgis, by nipping at the heels of cattle that are not as quick to move as required.

He is cheerful with sharply erect ears and is steadily gaining in popularity, although not registered in the US. He makes an excellent family companion as he delights in exercise and human friendship.

His coat is reasonably short, harsh and easy to keep in shape. He comes in grey, greyish brown and varying shades of yellow with reddish brown thrown in.

+ ABOVE
If you're looking for real intelligence in a dog's expression, it is to be found in this charmer.

BREED BOX	
Size	small dog: 33–35 cm (13–14 in) bitch: 31–33 cm (12½–13 in) 11.5–13 kg (25½–28½ lb)
Grooming	undemanding
Exercise	medium
Feeding	undemanding
Temperament	friendly and eager

+ RIGHT
The Swedish Vallhund is a low-to-ground, heeler type, agile, nimble and very biddable.

TIBETAN MASTIFF

The Tibetan Mastiff is an unusual member of the mastiff world because he has a longish coat. He has a genial expression, but odd specimens can be touchy. On the whole they are likeable creatures with coats of varying colours, ranging from black, through black and tan, to gold and grey.

He stands up to 66 cm (26 in), which means he is not a giant, but his body is solidly made. He is also unusual for a mastiff in that he carries his tail high and over his back. He is a useful guard dog and enjoys his exercise, but those who choose him should be ready to handle a powerful dog.

✦ ABOVE
A genial eye may belie a distrustful temperament – not a dog for the casual.

✦ ABOVE
Well suited to his native Tibet, he needs thorough grooming if he is destined to live indoors.

✦ RIGHT
Most European mastiffs are descended from this breed, which was saved from extinction last century.

BREED BOX

Size	large
	66 cm (26 in)
	64–82 kg
	(141–181 lb)
Grooming	fairly demanding
Exercise	medium
Feeding	demanding
Temperament	aloof and protective

WELSH CORGI (CARDIGAN)

The Welsh Corgi (Herding Group) comes in two separate versions: the Cardigan and the Pembroke. The Cardigan Corgi stands ideally 30 cm (12 in) at the withers; he is relatively long-cast on sturdy, short legs. He is unlike his Pembroke cousin in that he carries a full tail, which is long and very well coated. He is not hard work to groom, nor is he greedy.

Colour-wise he can be almost any dog colour, though white should not predominate. He has large, erect ears and an intelligent eye. He does not bustle about very rapidly and is

+ LEFT
Cardigan Corgis come in a range of colour schemes and have large ears set well back.

prepared to take life as it comes, though when working with cattle he has to be nimble enough to nip a heel and avoid the retaliatory kick.

As a member of a household he has a curiously benign attitude, but can raise the alarm vociferously if his territory is invaded.

+ BELOW FAR LEFT
A watchful expression is typical of this ancient breed.

+ ABOVE
Blue eyes only occur in blue merle dogs.

BREED BOX	
Size	small
	30 cm (12 in)
	dog: 11 kg (24 lb)
	bitch: 10 kg (22 lb)
Grooming	medium
Exercise	medium
Feeding	undemanding
Temperament	alert and steady

+ LEFT
The Cardigan is solidly built on short sturdy legs.

WELSH CORGI (PEMBROKE)

The Pembroke (Herding Group) is the better known version of the Corgi. He customarily sports a docked tail. He stands 30.5 cm (12 in) at the withers and has a longish body. He is sturdily built with a sharp, bright expression and prick ears.

He has a straight dense coat of medium length and is not difficult to

◆ LEFT
The better known Corgi – the Pembroke – usually comes in red and white.

BREED BOX

Size	small
	25.5–30.5 cm
	(10–12 in)
	dog: 10–12 kg
	(22–26½ lb)
	bitch: 10–11 kg
	(22–24 lb)
Grooming	medium
Exercise	medium
Feeding	medium
Temperament	workmanlike and active

groom once he has dried off after a country walk. The most common colour is red with white markings, but he does come in sable, fawn or even black and tan.

He is traditionally a cattle-drover, hence his occasional tendency to nip the heels of humans rather than cattle. His slightly doubtful temperament of previous times seems to have improved over the last decade.

He is a popular household dog with families who enjoy his brisk, energetic attitude to life, but he has a slight tendency to over-eat so he needs rationing on occasion.

◆ ABOVE
This is a practical and adaptable breed, friendly and full of stamina.

◆ BELOW
This young dog displays all the charm of a breed whose purpose is to walk cattle, even if he isn't very big.

◆ ABOVE
His foxy head should show an intelligent and alert expression.

The Toy Group

The Toy Group is made up of breeds that are among the smallest of all.
The largest are the ever-popular Cavalier King Charles Spaniel, the Chinese
Crested Dog and the Lowchen, while at the other end of the scale are the
Pomeranian and the Chihuahua. Height measurements are not given in many of
the Kennel Club's official Breed Standards; rather, these tend to give ideal
weights or weight ranges.

The name Toy is in some ways misleading; admittedly some of the breeds
tend to appear to be animated playthings, but their temperaments suggest that
they are anything but. The breeds included have some common factors, such as
the ability to be picked up and carried easily, but they vary widely in size, type
and behaviour. The misconception to avoid is that they are all dear little things
who behave impeccably and do not take any effort to look after.

✦ FACING PAGE **Yorkshire Terrier**

AFFENPINSCHER

The Affenpinscher, originally from Germany, is a dog that makes people laugh. He is said to resemble a monkey facially, and certainly his twinkling eyes give his expression a thoroughly mischievous glint. He stands up to 28 cm (11 in) high and weighs 3–4 kg (6½–9lb).

He has a coat that is harsh in texture and generally looks pretty untidy, so grooming him is not an over-serious business. He is game for fun and is capable of taking part in family activities as his muzzle is not so exaggeratedly short as to interfere with his breathing to any real extent.

He is normally black all over, although a grey coloration does sometimes appear. As a house companion, he is one of the best because he is fearless and delights in confronting any intruder.

◆ LEFT
A sense of mischief prevails whenever two or more Affenpinschers are gathered together.

◆ BELOW
The tail is often left undocked and curls gently over the back when the dog is moving.

BREED BOX	
Size	small 24–28 cm (9½–11 in), 3–4 kg (6½–9 lb)
Grooming	medium
Exercise	medium
Feeding	undemanding
Temperament	lively and self-confident

◆ BELOW
The coat is rough and of uneven length over the body – shaggy in some places, shorter in others. This is a truly hairy specimen.

◆ ABOVE
The greying effect produces a remarkable facial study.

AUSTRALIAN SILKY TERRIER

The Australian Silky Terrier, known variously as the Sidney Silky or just the Silky, is a mixture produced from cross-breeding the Australian Terrier and the Yorkshire Terrier. The result is a sharp-featured, silky-coated dog that stands some 23 cm (9 in) high at the withers.

One would expect any animal produced by mating one from Australia with one from Yorkshire to

+ LEFT
A compact dog, Silkies may have been bred primarily as household companions, but they are also pretty good rat-catchers.

+ BELOW LEFT
At times Silkies can put on quite a serious expression, not accurate evidence of their true temperament.

+ RIGHT
Silkies should have small, cat-like feet and no long hair on the legs.

BREED BOX

Size	small
	23 cm (9in),
	4 kg (9 lb)
Grooming	medium
Exercise	medium
Feeding	undemanding
Temperament	alert and friendly

be only too capable of holding his own, so the term "silky" should never mislead anyone into thinking it denotes anything soft. Not a bit of it – he is full of character!

His coat, which is fairly long and straight, comes in blue and tan or greyish blue and tan, and with minimal brushing can become glossy. He is intended as a household companion and does the job splendidly.

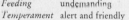

+ RIGHT
In silhouette the essential sharpness of outline and the fixed gaze become obvious – a good mixture of toy and terrier.

BICHON FRISE

The Bichon Frise (Non-Sporting Group) originated in the Mediterranean area and is dazzlingly white in colour. He is as sure of his own importance as any dog could be.

He stands up to 28 cm (11 in) high and is slightly longer in the back than

♦ LEFT
A modern glamour star – with a coat trimmed like topiary; very stylish but hard work to maintain.

BREED BOX	
Size	small
	23–28 cm (9–11 in),
	3–6 kg (6½–13 lb)
Grooming	demanding
Exercise	medium
Feeding	medium
Temperament	a friendly extrovert

he is tall. He carries his tail curled high over his back, and his natural coat should be fine and silky with soft corkscrew curls. The canine topiarists have got hold of him, and the corkscrew curls are not seen in the show-ring today. There is no necessity to have his curls scissored off – it costs money and is not obligatory! But he still needs grooming.

He is spritely and enjoys family games; he is another Toy who can cope most adequately with the rush of life's rich pattern in a busy household.

BOLOGNESE

The Bolognese, who has recently started to spread from his native Italy, is a small white dog with a square compact build. He has a distinctive white coat, which is described as flocked and covers the whole dog, head and all.

♦ RIGHT
The Bolognese is a fairly similar dog in type, but with a coat that is not cosseted except to keep it clean and tidy.

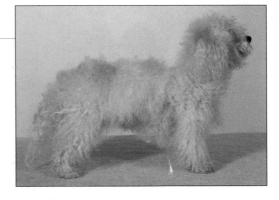

BREED BOX	
Size	small
	25–31 cm
	(10–12 in),
	3–4 kg (6½–9 lb)
Grooming	fairly demanding
Exercise	medium
Feeding	undemanding
Temperament	happy, alert, initially
	reserved

He stands up to 31 cm (12 in) and, as he is expected to be exhibited in the natural state, he tends to give the impression of a rough-and-ready character, which is unusual in a Toy breed. He does not have an exaggerated trim especially for the show-ring.

His body and legs are well muscled, and he gives the impression of enjoying plenty of free exercise. He comes from the same root stock as the Bichon Frise so is an intelligent dog. He also has the same large, round eyes with black rims.

Those looking for a pleasant, small dog, who is not too tiny, might well consider having a look at the cheerful Bolognese as a household companion.

CAVALIER KING CHARLES SPANIEL

The Cavalier King Charles Spaniel (the Cavalier) is a popular Toy dog with everyone. Built on the lines of a small gundog, he has a charm for the elderly as well as the young family. He seems to love people and he does not find fault with other dogs.

His weight range is 5.5–8 kg (12–18 lb), which is a wide enough range, but as a breed they do tend to get even heavier. The Cavalier's placid nature and friendliness often induces people to give him injudicious titbits that encourage obesity!

He has a good-looking head and a well-balanced body. He can appear in a series of colours, from ruby (red), black and tan, and tricolour (black and white with tan markings) to Blenheim, which is a mix of rich chestnut and white, often with a lozenge of chestnut in the centre of a white patch down the middle of his head.

He enjoys exercise and is built on elegant, athletic lines; indeed, he needs it in view of his hearty appetite. He is not difficult to groom as his coat can be kept tidy with normal brush-and-comb techniques; a true favourite.

◆ LEFT
A neat breed, ideal for anyone who wants an active and cheerful companion.

◆ BELOW
The charm of the Cavalier's expression is beautifully caught in this head-study

BREED BOX	
Size	small
	32 cm (13 in),
	5.5–8 kg (12–18 lb)
Grooming	medium
Exercise	medium
Feeding	medium
Temperament	very friendly

◆ BELOW
The Cavalier is in fact a miniature spaniel, combining all the qualities of a Toy and a Gundog.

CHIHUAHUA

The Chihuahua probably originated in South America and indeed is named after a Mexican state. He comes in two versions, one of which is smooth-coated, the other long-coated. Apart from their coat, they are identical, tiny dogs of tremendous spirit. They weigh up to 3 kg (6½ lb), but lighter specimens are generally preferred in the show-ring. The Smooth Coat has a soft, glossy covering of a coat, while the Long Coat is never coarse and is relatively easy to keep neat. The Chihuahua is very proud of his tail, which he carries high like a flag. It typifies the breed's personality.

All colours are accepted, but fawn to red with white is the most frequently seen.

They are brave dogs, putting up with pain remarkably stoically, but not accepting cheek or insult from dogs vastly larger than themselves. They do not appreciate humans who invade their homes without permission, yelling defiance and threatening mayhem as they race to defend their home and family.

Rearing a young Chihuahua puppy requires care in moving about; a high-stepping human can very easily trample on such a tiny creature, so Chihuahua breeders soon learn to use a shuffling method of walking. The breed, however, is not a weak or delicate one; in fact, the opposite is true. Both versions enjoy exercise and are extremely game, but families with young children must supervise the interaction between puppy and child carefully and constantly.

BREED BOX	
Size	very small 15–23 cm (6–9 in), 1–3 kg (2–6½ lb)
Grooming	medium
Exercise	undemanding
Feeding	undemanding
Temperament	spirited and intelligent

✦ ABOVE
The large, round, bright eyes set wide apart are a hallmark of a spritely breed.

✦ LEFT
The Chihuahua is a well-proportioned little dog ready to take on anything.

CHINESE CRESTED DOG

The Chinese Crested Dog comes in two versions, one is largely devoid of hair, the other covered with a veil of long soft hair. The hair colour in both cases is white to silvery white.

◆ LEFT
The Chinese Crested Powder-Puff, at one time seen as an outcast by breeders, now recognized as essential to the future of a very unusual breed.

BREED BOX

Size	small
	dog: 28–33 cm
	(11–13 in)
	bitch: 23–30 cm
	(9–12 in)
	maximum 5.5 kg
	(12 lb)
Grooming	unusual
Exercise	medium
Feeding	medium
Temperament	cheerful and friendly

The Powder Puff is heavier in build than the racy-looking Hairless. Grooming of either type is not demanding; the Hairless dogs feel the cold, although their skin is thick, smooth and tough, and they need extra attention in cold weather. The Chinese Crested dogs are hardy, friendly and affectionate creatures, who are also intelligent and perform well as watchdogs in a family household.

◆ RIGHT
The Hairless version has a crest on the head and neck, a plume on the end of the tail and thick hair on the feet and lower legs.

ENGLISH TOY TERRIER

The English Toy Terrier comes in only one colour pattern, and that is the traditional combination of black and tan. His coat is short, dense and responds with a good gloss to a brisk polishing with a cloth. This neat dog stands an ideal height of 30 cm (12 in) and weighs around the 3 kg (6½ lb) mark, so he is well named.

He has dark, sparkling eyes, and his prominent ears are described by the cognoscenti as candle-flame in shape. To watch him move is a joy if he is sound, because he goes extremely smoothly and easily like a much larger dog in style.

He is friendly and affectionate by nature, and he makes a thoroughly charming companion, with a touch of the terrier in him.

◆ LEFT AND ABOVE RIGHT
Yet another remarkable tiny dog, he makes up for his lack of size by possessing a mighty yap.

BREED BOX

Size	small
	25–30 cm
	(10–12 in),
	2.7–3.5 kg (6–8 lb)
Grooming	simple
Exercise	undemanding
Feeding	undemanding
Temperament	alert and terrier-like

GRIFFON BRUXELLOIS

The Griffon Bruxellois (Brussels Griffon) from Belgium is one of the characters of the Toy Group. He is truly bright and cheerful. With a monkey-like expression and his usual harsh coat of red, he has the equivalent of canine cheek. There is a smooth-coated version, which is equally pert, and both can come in other colours.

◆ LEFT
These dogs sport a walrus moustache.

◆ BELOW
Two of a kind, both harsh in coat, with the less common black colour in front.

BREED BOX

Size	small
	18–20 cm (7–8 in),
	2.2–4.9 kg (5–11 lb)
Grooming	medium
Exercise	undemanding
Feeding	undemanding
Temperament	lively and alert

family, but he also makes a cheerful and fearless companion for those who live on their own. He does not take much grooming, but professional stripping on occasion in the rough-coated form is not a bad idea.

He weighs anything from 2.2–4.9 kg (5–11 lb), but the middle of that range is the most usual. He has a bit of the terrier about him, so he thoroughly enjoys his exercise with a boisterous

◆ ABOVE
A typical smooth-coated head with a bright observant eye.

◆ RIGHT AND LEFT
The smooth-coated type has a solid body on neat legs and is not too difficult to keep clean and tidy.

ITALIAN GREYHOUND

The Italian Greyhound, at his best, is a true miniature of the classic Greyhound. He is graceful and nimble in his movements. He weighs 2.7–4.5 kg (6–10 lb), so there is not much of him. Breeders have to steer a fine line between producing a slightly coarse animal or an all too delicate one.

His coat is short and glossy, and his skin is fine; he does not take too kindly to cold weather and will wrap himself up in a blanket quite deliberately. Grooming only requires a piece of silk rubbed over him daily to keep him shining rather like a porcelain model. The colours seen are black, blue, cream, fawn, red and white or any of those broken with white areas. He holds his ears in a quizzical fashion when really interested.

His bones are fine and therefore fairly easy to break. His muscles can be quite impressive, but, in truth, too many dogs appear spindly. This is an elegant, ancient breed, but those who fancy owning one should study them carefully before rushing out to buy the first one offered. He is not suited to life in an energetic family household, until children are old enough to understand the problems of his lightweight stature.

BREED BOX	
Size	small 25.5 cm (10 in), 2.7–4.5 kg (6–10 lb)
Grooming	easy
Exercise	undemanding
Feeding	undemanding
Temperament	intelligent and vivacious

JAPANESE CHIN

The Japanese Chin is a pretty dog by any standards. He has a round shaped head with large eyes that show the white in the inner corners, giving him a permanent look of surprise. His coat is profuse, long and silky, and comes only in black and white or red and white. The ideal weight is 1.8–3.2 kg (4–7 lb), so he is a true Toy, but confident with it.

He gives the impression of having a slightly superior air, but also of being delighted to meet people. In spite of its length, his coat is not difficult to control as long as grooming is regular and thorough. He enjoys a scurry round the garden or a walk round the local park, but is not enthusiastic about long country hikes. More a dog for a quiet existence than a family companion; not suitable for young children.

BREED BOX	
Size	very small maximum 18 cm (7 in), 1.8–3.2 kg (4–7 lb)
Grooming	undemanding
Exercise	undemanding
Feeding	undemanding
Temperament	cheerful and good-natured

KING CHARLES SPANIEL

The King Charles Spaniel is also
known as the English Toy Spaniel. He
is similar to the Cavalier but has a
shorter nose and a more domed head.
He has a long, silky coat, which comes
in the same colour range as the
Cavalier – black and tan, ruby,
Blenheim and tricolour – and is
equally rewarding to groom.

He is more reserved than the
Cavalier but has the same kindly and
intelligent disposition. He weighs
between 3.6 and 6.3 kg (8–14 lb). He
makes a genuine, devoted companion
but does not need too much exercise
or food.

✦ LEFT
Easily mistaken for
the better-known
Cavalier King
Charles Spaniel, but
with a slightly more
snubbed nose. The
Cavalier was
developed from this
breed.

✦ BELOW
Another breed that is no longer docked, the tail
in its natural state is well feathered and not
carried high.

✦ ABOVE
The large dark eyes and long well-feathered ears
give him an appealing look.

BREED BOX

Size	small
	3.6–6.3 kg (8–14 lb)
	dog: 25.5 cm (10 in)
	bitch: 20.5 cm (8 in)
Grooming	medium
Exercise	undemanding
Feeding	medium
Temperament	gentle and affectionate

LOWCHEN

The Lowchen or Little Lion Dog is an interesting dog, which originated in Europe. He stands up to 33 cm (13 in) at the withers, so he is not one of the tiny Toys.

He carries a long silky coat of any colour, which forms a mane, and he derives his alternative name from the fact that he is trimmed to resemble a lion; the coat of the body is clipped from behind the last rib and the whole length of the tail except for a plume on the end. Grooming is obviously a real job, but he does not need anything out of the ordinary to keep him neat.

He is active and playful. He gets on very well with children so makes a satisfactory household pet.

+ ABOVE LEFT
A somewhat grave expression belies the fact that the dog can be a real live wire.

+ BELOW
The Lowchen needs clipping to maintain the leonine hind-end and the trimmed tail.

BREED BOX

Size	small 25–33 cm (10–13 in), 3 kg (6½ lb)
Grooming	fairly demanding
Exercise	medium
Feeding	medium
Temperament	intelligent and affectionate

MALTESE

The Maltese (previously known as the Maltese Terrier) is an extremely stylish little dog. He stands up to 25 cm (10 in) tall. His round eye-rims are black and act as a contrast to the whiteness of his long, silky coat – white all over, though occasional lemon markings appear. Grooming such a coat to achieve constant effect is time-consuming, but the results are very rewarding.

He is one of the neatest movers in the Toy Group; at full trot he seems to sail along with his coat billowing around him. He obviously loves exercise and appears to derive enormous pleasure and humour from human company. Any suspicion that he is delicate is totally misplaced; he is surprisingly hardy and spirited. His trusty, lively nature is endearing.

+ LEFT
The all-white coat and the round dark eyes is something breeders have striven to maintain for many centuries, but they have not made a softie of the dog in the process.

BREED BOX

Size	small (10 in), 2–3 kg (4½–6½ lb)
Grooming	very demanding
Exercise	undemanding
Feeding	undemanding
Temperament	very good-natured

MINIATURE PINSCHER

The Miniature Pinscher (or Min Pin) is the smallest version of the pinscher breeds. He stands up to 30 cm (12 in) high at his withers and wears a hard, short coat that is easily groomed to shine. He comes in black, blue or chocolate with tan, and also various solid shades of red.

He carries his neat ears either pricked or half-dropped on a stylish head. He is sturdy in body and definite in his way of going, which is like that of a Hackney pony. He gives the impression that he loves being loose in a garden or park; he has quick reactions and makes a useful household watchdog.

✦ RIGHT
The large erect ears are very striking in this red-coloured dog, which has his tail undocked.

BREED BOX

Size	small 25.5–30 cm (10–12 in), 3.5 kg (7½ lb)
Grooming	easy
Exercise	medium
Feeding	undemanding
Temperament	alert and courageous

✦ BELOW
The front view shows the neat, straight legs – a toy in stature, athletic in style.

✦ LEFT
This dog has the customary docked tail.

✦ ABOVE
The black and tan coat is the one most often seen.

PAPILLON

The Papillon, or Butterfly Dog, is very attractive. He stands up to 28 cm (11 in) tall on neat, trim legs, and, underneath an easily brushed long, silky coat, he has a surprisingly strong body.

The coat is a basic white with patches of a variety of colours except liver. The traditional markings on his

head and large erect ears, with a neat white stripe down the centre of his skull and on to his nose, produce a combined effect resembling the body and open wings of a butterfly, which is how he was given his name.

He can be trained to a high level of obedience and delights in exercise with a household but is not suited to live with very young children in case he gets trodden on.

♦ LEFT
The white line down the forehead is said to represent the body of a butterfly, from which the Papillon derives his name.

♦ BELOW FAR LEFT
The tall, fringed ears represent the butterfly's wings.

♦ BELOW
The whole dog is neatly covered with long, silky hair, but beneath all the glamour is a highly intelligent and trainable animal.

BREED BOX	
Size	small 20–28 cm (8–11 in), 2–2.5 kg (4½–5½ lb)
Grooming	medium
Exercise	medium
Feeding	undemanding
Temperament	lively and most intelligent

PEKINGESE

The Pekingese has his roots in ancient
China. Tradition tells us that he
derives from the palaces of the Tang
Dynasty, and this seems to be firmly
engrained in his character, although he
shows glimpses of a humorous nature
on occasion. With a huge personality
inside a relatively small body, he is a
dog for the devotee.

He has an ideal weight of around
5 kg (11 lb), with the bitches tending
to be heavier than the dogs. Inside an
apparently small framework are
heavily boned legs.

◆ ABOVE
Modern Pekes also have very pretty heads and
this picture shows the true beauty of the Peke's
expression with lustrous, soft eyes.

He has a broad head and a very
short muzzle, which can lead to severe
breathing problems; careful selection
is necessary to breed healthy Pekes,
and there are no short cuts to getting
it right.

Exercise is a matter over which
Pekes are not ecstatic. They tend to
move with a dignified and leisurely
roll; consequently country walks are
out. The coat, which can be of
virtually any hue except albino and
liver, is long and profuse. It needs
regular and dedicated attention to
achieve a creditable result.

BREED BOX

Size	small
	18 cm (7 in)
	dog: maximum
	5 kg (11 lb)
	bitch: maximum
	5.5 kg (12 lb)
Grooming	demanding
Exercise	undemanding
Feeding	demanding
Temperament	loyal and aloof

◆ BELOW
Pekes were at one time carried by ladies of the
Chinese court and referred to as "sleeve dogs".

POMERANIAN

The Pomeranian is the smallest of the five sizes of German Spitz. He weighs up to a mere 2 kg (4½ lb), with the bitches being slightly heavier. His abundant stand-off coat is normally a whole colour such as orange, black or cream through to white. Regular grooming is necessary to achieve the overall look of a ball of fluff.

The margin between the sturdiness, which even this tiny breed should possess, and a shell-like delicateness is a fine one, and some breeders find it

✦ LEFT
The Pomeranian at his best is a dog to charm the hardest heart; this tiny character has all the courage of a lion in his eyes.

✦ LEFT
Pomeranians should have an expression of intelligence and complete confidence.

✦ BELOW
A family trio in the best of coats; but do not buy a Pom until you have tried grooming one yourself.

difficult to achieve. Poms exhibit a tremendous amount of energy, pirouetting gaily on the ends of their leads. They are capable of producing a barrage of fairly shrill yapping, which may deter burglars – and interrupt conversation!

BREED BOX

Size	very small 22–28 cm (8½–11 in) 1.8–2 kg (4–4½ lb)
Grooming	demanding
Exercise	undemanding
Feeding	undemanding
Temperament	intelligent and extrovert

PUG

The Pug is robust. He weighs up to 8 kg (17½ lb) and is packed tightly into a sturdy, compact frame. He wears a short and smoothly glossy coat, which comes most commonly in fawn but can appear in apricot, silver or black. He traditionally has a black mask. He is easily kept tidy.

He carries his tail tightly curled into a roll on the top of his back, and when he is in his most perky state of

◆ LEFT
An ancient breed of miniaturized mastiffs, Pugs were once the companions of Buddhist monks. They arrived in Europe with the Dutch East India Company and became the favoured dogs of the House of Orange.

alertness, he gives the impression that he is leaning forward towards whatever his large lustrous eyes are gazing at.

He is a dog who tends to make people smile when they see him, because he is so convinced of his own importance. For such a stocky dog he can move fast. His slightly short nose sometimes causes him problems in hot weather as it restricts his breathing, but breeders tend to select for the wide nostrils, which will enable him to exercise as freely as he wishes.

◆ ABOVE
The stern expression of the Pug belies his real sense of fun.

BREED BOX	
Size	small
	25–28 cm
	(10–11 in), 6.3–8 kg
	(14–17½ lb)
Grooming	undemanding
Exercise	medium
Feeding	medium
Temperament	lively and cheerful

◆ RIGHT
The tightly curled tail balances the snub nose exactly, to produce a very tidy little dog.

◆ ABOVE
The Pug is adaptable, sociable and good-natured and makes a good family dog.

YORKSHIRE TERRIER

The Yorkshire Terrier is a breed of two distinct types. The tiny dog, seen immaculately groomed in the show-ring, weighs up to 3.1 kg (7 lb). The jaunty dog seen on a lead in the street or racing joyfully around the park is the same dog, but often twice the size. The fact is that the long steel blue and bright tan hair that bedecks the glamour star of the shows would break off short if he ran loose. But the spirit of the true Yorkshire tyke is the same inside whatever the outward appearance.

Grooming the household companion, a dog that is immensely popular throughout the world, is easily accomplished with ordinary skills. As a home-loving animal, the Yorkie is tough, ready to play with the children or dispatch any rat unwise enough to invade his owner's dwelling.

✦ ABOVE
This Yorkie is groomed to perfection as befits a top dog.

✦ ABOVE
Companion Yorkies wear their coats shorter than these show dogs and do not require the same amount of artistry.

BREED BOX	
Size	very small maximum 3.1 kg (7 lb) dog: 20.5 cm (8 in) bitch: 18 cm (7 in)
Grooming	demanding
Exercise	medium
Feeding	undemanding
Temperament	alert and intelligent

✦ RIGHT
This elegant display shows canine grooming at its most spectacular.

INDEX

ACKNOWLEDGEMENTS

The publishers would like to thank the following dog owners and breeders for their kind help with photography:

THE HOUND GROUP:
Afghan Hound: Mrs Pascoe; Basenji: S Woollard; Basset Hound: P Walden; Basset Fauve de Bretagne: J Aldrich; Grand and Petit Basset Griffon Vendeen: Mrs Y Dean & Miss C Gutherless, R Phillips; Beagle: P Walden; Bloodhound: Mrs E Richards; Borzoi: Mr B O' Callaghan; Dachshunds: T Thomas, Mrs G E Taylor, J White, W Harris, M Endersby; Deerhound: S Finnett & H Heathcote; Elkhound: Mrs J Hibbert; Finnish Spitz: B K & B A Williams; Foxhound: J Goode; Grand Bleu de Gascoigne: E Bradic; Greyhound: J White; Hamiltonstovare: Mrs D Cooke; Harrier: Minehead Harriers; Ibizan Hound: A Wilde; Pharoah Hound: P Ayling; Irish Wolfhound: Miss A Bennett; Norwegian Lundehund: Mrs G E Sansom; Segugio Italiano: A Wilde; Otterhound: J Ashworth; Rhodesian Ridgeback: J Ellis; Saluki: Miss T Larkin; Sloughi: Miss S Harper & Mr R Read; Whippet: J White.

THE GUNDOG GROUP:
Bracco Italiano: Mr & Mrs J Shaw; Brittany: Mr & Mrs M Beaven; English Setter: F Grimsdell; German Short-haired Pointer: P Robinson; German Wire-haired Pointer: Mr R Major; Gordon Setter: Mr P F Tye; Hungarian Vizsla: K Bicknell; Hungarian Wire-haired Vizsla: R Thompson; Irish Red and White Setter: Mrs P E Brigden; Irish Setter: M Gurney; Italian Spinone: C Fry; Koikerhondje: Mrs Whybrow; Large Munsterlander: Mrs Trowsdale; Nova Scotia Duck-tolling Retriever: Mr & Mrs D Hardings; Pointer: Mr & Mrs M Welsh; Chesapeake Bay Retriever: C Mayhew; Curly Coated Retriever: Mrs C Pilbeam; Flat Coated Retriever: L Irwin; Golden Retriever: C Fry; Labrador Retriever: C Coode; American Cocker Spaniel: Mrs Petty; Clumber Spaniel: Mrs Reynolds; English Cocker Spaniel: B Harris, S Oxford; English Springer Spaniel: Mr & Mrs D Miller; Field Spaniel: Mr & Mrs N R & J Park; Irish Water Spaniel: Mr M Ford; Sussex Spaniel: Mrs C M Mitchell; Welsh Springer Spaniel: J Luckett Roynon; Weimaraners: Mrs Shall, Mrs B Adlington.

THE TERRIER GROUP:
Airedale Terrier: Mary Swash; Australian Terrier: B & V Hodgson; Bedlington Terrier: Mr B Reeves; Border Terrier: L Aldrich; Bull Terrier: P Larkin; Cairn Terrier: D Winsley & K Holmes; Czesky Terrier: B Rice-Stringer; Dandie Dinmont: Mrs Draper-Andrews; Smooth Fox Terrier: Mrs Winstanley; Wire Fox Terrier: D Chads; Irish Terrier: Mr K Anderson; Glen of Imaal Terrier: Mrs R Welch; Kerry Blue Terrier: Mr Watson; Lakeland Terrier: Mr & Mrs J Wright; Manchester Terrier: Mrs Eva; Norfolk Terrier: A Broughton; Norwich Terrier: D Jenkins; Parson Jack Russell: Mrs A Hughes; Scottish Terrier: Miss C Chapman; Sealyham Terrier: D Winsley & K Holmes; Skye Terrier: Mr & Mrs D Miller; Soft-coated Wheaten Terrier: Mrs Checketts; Staffordshire Bull Terrier: Alec Waters; Welsh Terrier: S Poole; West Highland White Terrier: Mr R Wilshaw.

THE UTILITY/NON-SPORTING GROUP:
Boston Terrier: Mr & Mrs Hounslow; Bulldog: Mr G Payne; Canaan Dog: Mr & Mrs E Minto; Chow Chow: Mrs M Bennett; Dalmatian: Miss C Hicks; French Bulldog: Mrs Stemp, Mrs Trigg; German Spitz: Mr, Mrs & Miss Bennett, S Edgson; Japanese Akita: J Feeney; Japanese Shiba Inu: M Atkinson & L Lane; Japanese Spitz: S Sparks; Keeshond: Mrs P Luckhurst; Leonberger: G Smith & J Feehan; Lhasa Apso: G Lock; Miniature Schnauzer: Mrs M R Bonnamy, Mrs T Jeffries; Poodles: Mrs A Corish, Mr & Mrs M Beaven, Mrs L Ellis; Schipperke: M Deats; Standard Schnauzer: Mrs Hatterell-Brown; Shar Pei: C Cavanagh; Shih Tzu: Mrs V Goodwin; Tibetan Spaniel: Mr & Mrs Minto; Tibetan Terrier: Mrs Draper-Andrews.

THE WORKING GROUP:
Alaskan Malamute: J Al-Haddad, A Allen; Anatolian Shepherd Dog: Anatolian Shepherd Dog Club of Great Britain; Australian Cattle Dog: Ms S Smyth; Australian Shepherd Dog: Mrs Fry; Bearded Collie: Mrs C Bennet; Belgian Shepherd Dogs: F Cosme & J Collis, Mr & Mrs M Ralph, S B Wyre & E Richardson, K M McIlherene; Bergamasco: S Band & C McCarthy; Bernese Mountain Dog: A Wells; Border Collie: F Cosme & J Collis; Bouvier des Flandres: C Pierpoint; Boxer: Mrs Cobb; Briard: E Pitt; Bullmastiff: Mrs J Gunn; Rough Collie: Mrs Burtenshaw; Smooth Collie: Misses S & M, & Mr L Clark; Dobermann: Mrs K Le Mare; Eskimo Dog: Mrs S Hull; Estrela Mountain Dog: Mrs E J Snowdon; Finnish Lapphund: Mrs T Jackson; German Shepherd Dog: Miss L Graham; Giant Schnauzer: T Jeffries, R Joy; Great Dane: Mrs K Le Mare; Hovawart: T Smith; Hungarian Kuvasz: T Koryniaka; Hungarian Puli: Mrs J Farnfield; Komondor: M P & E Froome; Lancashire Heeler: Mrs J Farnfield; Maremma Sheepdog: Mrs J Downes; Mastiff: Mr K Taylor; Neapolitan Mastiff: Ms V Roach & Mr N Davis; Newfoundland: Messrs Cutts & Galvin; Norwegian Buhund: Mr M Guidhouse; Old English Sheepdog: L Powell; Pinscher: A Handly; Polish Lowland Sheepdog: Mr & Mrs C Hastie; Portuguese Water Dog: J Johns; Pyrenean Mountain Dog: Mr Duffell; Pyrenean Sheepdog: Mrs B Judson; Rottweiler: Mrs Boas; St Bernard: Mrs L Byles; Samoyed: J I Rees; Shetland Sheepdog: Mrs R Crossley; Siberian Husky: Mrs S Hull; Swedish Lapphund: Mrs Mackie; Swedish Vallhund: Mrs J Wilton; Tibetan Mastiff: K Childs; Welsh Corgi (Cardigan): Miss Tonkyn; Welsh Corgi (Pembroke): Miss S Taylor.

THE TOY GROUP:
Affenpinscher: Mrs A J Teasdale; Australian Silky Terrier: J Sharpe, Mr & Mrs B Faulkner & Mrs K Whiteford; Bichon Frise: C Wyatt; Bolognese: S & C McCarthy; Cavalier King Charles Spaniel: Mrs J Read; Chihuahua: Mrs K Le Mare; Chinese Crested Dog: R Tillman; English Toy Terrier: Mrs Bonifas; Griffon Bruxellois: Miss M Downey, Miss John; Italian Greyhound: Mrs M Sprague-White; Japanese Chin: M Moss; King Charles Spaniel: M Moss; Lowchen: J Creffield; Maltese: Mrs C Memsley; Miniature Pinscher: Mrs S Colborne Baber; Papillon: A Broughton; Pekingese: Misses A Summers & V Williams; Pomeranian: Mrs C McCutchon-Clarke; Pug: Mr I Herold; Yorkshire Terrier: O A Sameja.

PHOTOGRAPHER'S ACKNOWLEDGEMENTS
I would like to express my thanks to the breeders and to: C Fry, L Graham, M Peacock, S Bradley, A Wells, P Beaven, J & P Canning, L & A Piatneuer, V Dyer, B Stnet and J Hay. Thanks also to Pampered Pets of Godalming, Colin Clarke Veterinary Practice, Celia Cross Greyhound Rescue, Canine Partners for Indpendence and Weycolour Limited. Last but not least thanks to my partner Alison Hay for her administration and assistance.